GLOBAL ENVIRONMENTAL MACROECONOMICS

GLOBAL ENVIRONMENTAL MACROECONOMICS

Harland Wm. Whitmore, Jr.

M.E. Sharpe
Armonk, New York
London, England

Library of Congress Cataloging-in-Publication Data

Whitmore, Harland Wm., 1939–
Global environmental macroeconomics / Harland Wm. Whitmore, Jr.
p. cm.
Includes bibliographical references and index.
ISBN 0-7656-0498-1 (alk. paper)
1. Environmental economics. 2. Macroeconomics. I. Title.
HD75.6.W49 1999
333.7—dc21 99-26040
CIP

Printed in the United States of America

The paper used in this publication meets the minimum requirements of American National Standard for Information Sciences—Permanence of Paper for Printed Library Materials, ANSI Z 39.48-1984.

∞

BM (c) 10 9 8 7 6 5 4 3 2 1

To my wife, Jan, and to my daughters
Christine, Beth, Megan, and Leighann.

Contents

List of Figures

CHAPTER ONE

Introduction

Pollution created by the extraction and use of non-renewable resources together with the harvesting of renewable resources adversely affect the maintainability of the global ecosystem. According to recent reports, the 1990s have been the warmest years on record, continuing an extended world-wide warming trend, due at least in part to greenhouse gases. In the Western Pacific, rising ocean temperatures are killing the coral reefs, thereby disrupting the food chain in that part of the world. Climatologists worry that were Alaska's permafrost start to thaw significant amounts of harmful carbon would be released into the atmosphere. A number of countries have become so concerned with the adverse effects of pollution upon the environment that in 1997 the Parties to the UN Framework Convention on Climate Change agreed to what has become known as the Kyoto Protocol, which sets emissions targets on six major greenhouse gases for the developed nations and institutes a mechanism for trading emission permits. The obvious concern is that failure to control greenhouse gas emissions increases the likelihood that the physical environment will impose significant binding constraints not only upon ecosystem maintainability, but also upon global economic activity.

Surely, technological progress may eventually relax these potential constraints. But, for technology to come to the rescue, the anticipated value of the marginal product of technical progress must be large enough to justify the anticipated explicit and implicit costs associated with the research and development of that progress. Whether we achieve the appropriate rates and types of technical progress will depend in part upon whether we reckon with the current and future costs incurred because of pollution and because of depletion of our global natural resources and, therefore, whether we explicitly recognize the potential for technical progress to mitigate these costs. Unfettered access to natural resources simply will not internalize these costs. Standard macroeconomic models do not explicitly recognize the existence of actual or potential natural resource restrictions upon ecosystem maintainability or global economic activity. Consequently, conventional macro models fail to reveal either the relevant natural resource costs resulting from aggregate economic activity or the potential economic returns to technical progress.

The purpose of this study is to build a complete macroeconomic model that explicitly views the world economy as a subsystem of the earth's ecosystem. In particular, our model explicitly recognizes that the world economy not only withdraws renewable and non-renewable resources from the global ecosystem, but also emits pollutants that diminish the ecosystem's ability to regenerate renewable resources. We confront the world economy with certain overriding environmental restrictions imposed to ensure global ecosystem resilience and protect the "global natural commons" (see Goodwin 1991).

Environmental Constraints

Specifically, we posit, first, a global target level of pollution agreed to by international treaty and monitored by an international agent. The international agent determines the amount of pollution the biosphere can assimilate during the current period. It then sells pollution rights equal to that amount to the sectors that create pollution in the course of extracting and using their country-specific non-renewable resources. These sectors also have the option of devoting some resources to pollution abatement in order to reduce the number of pollution rights they purchase.

Given the target level of pollution, which adversely affects the growth in the global renewable resource, the international agent then also determines the optimal amount of growth in the global renewable resource for the current period. This optimal growth is presumed to be greater than zero, but less than the amount by which the resource would grow naturally, given the current level of pollution, if no harvesting were permitted. It then sells harvesting permits equal to the difference between the natural growth and the optimal growth.

Finally, the international agent arbitrarily imposes minimum stocks for the non-renewable resources. As they formulate their plans for the current and future periods, the sectors that extract and use these resources may not permit their stocks to fall below prescribed levels.

After determining the levels of pollution and harvesting of the renewable resource consistent with maintaining the global commons, the international agent makes markets for both pollution rights and harvesting rights. For simplicity, we assume that both the price of pollution rights and the price of harvesting rights for the renewable resource are competitively determined. In addition, we assume that the revenue which the international agent collects from the sales of pollution rights and harvesting rights to the non-financial business sector located in a particular country is returned during the current period to the government sector located in that country.

Thus, we develop a dynamic two-country model of the world economy incorporating restrictions with respect to: the availability of non-renewable resources, the ability of the global environment to assimilate pollutants, the ability of the environment to replenish renewable resources, and the productivity of real resources (labor) in pollution abatement.[1] Ecological imperatives, which the international community recognizes and respects, impose limits upon all economic activity.

Other Features of the Macroeconomic Model

The macroeconomic model developed in this study represents an extension of the author's companion work, Whitmore (1997). In particular, the present model features decision making under genuine pervasive uncertainty (limited, asymmetric, partial knowledge with no known probability distribution), price- and wage-setting by optimizing economic agents, product and labor markets that generally fail to clear, and endogenously determined money stocks. Consequently, both involuntary unemployment and unanticipated changes in inventories may occur in the present model. This differs from (i) classical models, in which interest rates adjust to ensure that supply creates its own demand, (ii) Keynesian models, in which output adjusts to ensure that demand creates its own supply,[2] (iii) and real business cycle and economic growth models, in which demand identically equals supply in both the labor and product markets because the agents that decide supply in those markets are precisely the ones simultaneously deciding demand as well.

The present model does adopt several desirable features of real business cycle models, however, including an emphasis on microfoundations and an explicit recognition that current real investment alters the end-of-period stock of physical capital and future production opportunities. We model a global economy following a unique non-repetitive path over time.

Besides the international agent, our model contains two countries with their own government, central bank, non-financial business, private banking and household sectors. At each stage in the construction of the model, we fully develop the first principles underlying the decisions of every relevant sector in every relevant market. Besides the markets for pollution and harvesting rights, the model includes explicit markets for real output, labor, bonds, checkable deposits and non-interest-bearing money in each country as well as global spot and forward markets for the countries' units of account. Bond rates and spot and forward exchange rates are mutually determined.[3]

A central feature of the present model is that we explore the interdependencies among the world's resource, product, and financial markets, paying particular attention to the implications for these markets of environmental policies concerning the maximum amount of pollution and the minimum amounts of renewable and non-renewable resources consistent with ecosystem maintainability. Our model reveals how the endogenously-determined current levels of extraction and utilization of the non-renewable resources in the two countries—together with the endogenously determined current prices of pollution rights and harvesting rights for the global renewable resource—impact not only current production of private and public goods and spending, but also current product prices, wages and interest rates as well as spot and forward exchange rates. These current production, spending and financial variables (including the endogenous money stocks), in turn, help to establish relative factor prices relevant to future production and resource allocation among labor, physical capital, the non-renewable resource, the renewable resource and the imported factor of production in each country.

Construction of the Model

To enhance the model's tractability, we posit a sequential decision-making process. The model is constructed in three stages. In the first stage, each government sector not only decides the efficient combination of resources with which to produce the predetermined level of public goods in the current period, but also prepares a menu of alternative levels of public good production for next period together with the corresponding levels of future tax liability. The tax liability is diminished by revenue the government anticipates receiving from the international agent in association with sales of pollution and harvesting rights to that country's non-financial business sector. The household sector in each country then decides the level of public goods (and the corresponding tax liability) it wants its government sector to provide next period. Government policy is both time consistent and optimal.

In the second stage, before current period interest rates and exchange rates are determined, both optimizing non-financial business sectors set current product prices (the private goods produced in one country are imperfect substitutes for those produced in the other country) and decide current production and current resource use (including renewable and non-renewable resources) based upon their forecasts of the market demand curves for their respective products. (Each sector also announces the wage rate at which it is willing to employ people next period, based upon its forecast of the net labor supply function facing it.) Simultaneously, the interaction of the non-financial business sectors' demands for pollution rights and harvesting rights coupled with the number of these rights the international agent makes available, determine the current market prices of pollution rights and harvesting rights.

In the third stage, world interest rates and the spot and forward exchange rates between the units of account of the two countries are jointly determined together with end-of-period stocks of real and financial variables, including the amounts of physical capital held by the two non-financial business sectors at the end of the current period as well as how many people they employ by the end of the period, the end-of-period stocks of their respective non-renewable resources, their ending inventories of final goods, and the amounts of the imported factors they currently order from each other for delivery and use next period.

Social Accounting

Each country's measure of net domestic (national) product should reflect the depletion and degradation of global natural capital resulting from current production. El Serafy and Lutz (1989) advocate deducting both "defensive expenditures" associated with cleaning up pollution and the "depletion and degradation of natural capital" from the conventional measure of a country's net national product to obtain a measure of "sustainable net national product".

In the process of constructing our model, a simplified set of social accounts emerges that measures the value added by every sector of the world economy. Accordingly, in this model a country's net national (domestic) product is reduced not only by the amount that its non-financial business sector spends on pollution and harvesting rights, but also by the value of the reduction in the inventory of its non-renewable resource. Also, the growth in the world's renewable resource contributes to the value added not by a particular nation, but by the international agent. This value added also corresponds to the value of the sales of pollution and harvesting rights to other sectors plus the net change in its inventories, where the last item is calculated by subtracting the value of environmental degradation resulting from the sale of pollution rights (sales from the initial inventory of environmental quality) from the value of the target growth in the renewable resource.

Valuation of Depletion in the Non-Renewable Resource

An issue closely related to the appropriate social accounting measure for national product concerns imputing a value to the stock of the non-renewable resource depleted in each country during the course of current production, since no explicit markets exist for non-renewable resources in this model (see, for instance, El Serafy 1993). Ideally, the correct valuation of depletion equals the net present value of the marginal product foregone by extracting the resource during the current period rather than saving it for future use, where the net present value is defined as the present value of the marginal product foregone by extracting the resource during the current period minus the present value of the pollution rights that would have been necessary for the user to purchase in the future if the resource had been extracted then. However, as we show below (see the discussion of expression (3.22) on page 37), for present-value maximizing firms, on the margin, this net present value corresponds exactly to the difference between the value of the marginal product of the resource applied to current production minus the market value of the right to pollute during the current period at a level dictated by the current extraction and use of this non-renewable resource. Since the value of the marginal product of the resource in current production and the market value of the right to pollute during the current period are currently observable in principle, the valuation of depletion is also readily measurable, in principle.

Environmental Policies

After constructing our model of the global economy, we conduct two sets of conceptual experiments that illustrate the interdependence among the world's resource, product and financial markets over time. In the first set, we consider actions by the international agent to increase the volume of pollution rights or the volume of harvesting rights for the renewable resource. (Ceteris paribus, a change in the beginning-of-current period stock of the world's renewable resource may be treated as a change in the volume of harvesting rights issued by the international agent equal to the current change in growth in that resource produced by the change in its initial stock.) In the second set, we consider reductions in the beginning-of-current period amounts of the non-renewable resources held by each country. In both sets of experiments, we trace the effects upon current production, real resource use, and product and factor prices. These variables affect the level of current income and spending in the economy, which then impact the financial markets, potentially affecting interest rates in both countries as well as the spot and forward exchange rates between their units of account. Coupled with the prices of real resources, these interest rates and exchange rates then determine both the allocation of resources and the level of output in next period's production of private and public goods in both countries.

An increase in either the volume of pollution rights issued by the international agent or an increase in the volume of harvesting rights for the renewable resource issued by that agent causes the non-financial business sectors in both countries to produce more during the current period and reduce the product prices they announce. If the volume of pollution rights increases, both non-financial business sectors substitute their non-renewable resource for the other inputs they use in current period production. If the international agent increases the volume of harvesting rights for the renewable resource, both non-financial business sectors substitute that resource for their other inputs, including their non-renewable resource, in the current period. In both cases, these sectors tend to reduce their current use of the labor input. Also, since output necessarily increases more than total spending in both countries, an excess supply is created in the bond market in each country, pushing interest rates higher in both markets. However, in these instances, the effects upon the current spot and forward exchange depend upon cross-country differences in the strengths of the similar responses by the two countries, which represent opposing forces in the two foreign exchange markets.

Alternatively, a reduction in the initial stock of the home country's non-renewable resource causes production to shift from the home country to the foreign country. In addition, the home country raises product price in the current period because of the increase in its production costs; ceteris paribus, the foreign country raises product price next period because of the increased orders for its product. Both home and foreign bond rates fall and the spot and forward exchange rates rise. The home country tends to substitute physical capital, labor and the foreign country's good for its non-renewable resource in future production. The foreign non-financial business sector tends to substitute physical capital for the factor it buys from the home country in its own future production.

We begin the specification of our model by considering the government sectors' preparations of their public goods menus and their respective household sectors' choices of the amounts of those goods.

Notes

1. With respect to these concepts, our notation borrows heavily from Pezzey (1989).
2. In the standard Keynesian model, real output adjusts to equate output with demand; in the classical model, interest rates adjust to equate market demand with output.
3. While all lenders in this model view the bonds issued by the government and non-financial business sectors in one country as perfect substitutes, all lenders simultaneously view these bonds as close but imperfect substitutes for those issued in the other country.

CHAPTER TWO

Selection of Public-Goods Production

In conventional macroeconomic analysis, the government sector in each country autonomously decides the levels of taxes and government spending in accordance with its attempt to stabilize the domestic economy. In contrast, the primary reason the government sector exists in the present study is not to stabilize the domestic economy but to provide the public goods and services that its household sector wants it to provide. Presumably, these government-produced goods are "non-rival in consumption" and/or their benefits are "non-excludable in payment" so that it is difficult for the private sector to produce these goods profitably. In the present model, the government sectors produce and distribute these "public" goods to their respective household sectors "free of charge" in the sense that they are not sold to the households in the marketplace. However, because the government sectors must purchase the services of various factors of production in order to provide these public goods, each government must tax its respective household sector in order to finance the production of public goods. Consequently, we distinguish the public goods that enter the household sectors' utility functions from "government spending," or outlays by the government for the purpose of acquiring the inputs necessary to the production of public goods. In the present model, the objective of each government is to produce public goods up to the point at which the marginal social benefit to its household sector equals the marginal social cost associated with that production.

As the current period opens in this model, each government sector faces two immediate tasks. The first involves producing the quantity of public goods during the current period that was selected by their respective household sectors (or their representatives) last period. The second involves preparation of a menu of alternative levels of public-goods production for next period accompanied by the corresponding minimum taxes required to finance the production of each alternative. Each government then presents the menu to its respective household sector so that it may select next period's production of public goods. Since the selection by the household sector occurs before current wage rates, interest rates and exchange rates are revealed, each government sector will be free during the current period as these rates become known, to alter the combination of inputs it intends to use next period to produce the level of public goods selected in this early step by the households. Therefore, it will be necessary to revisit the government sector later in the analysis in order to derive its effective end-of-period demands for physical capital and labor, which become jointly determined with current interest rates and exchange rates.

Home Country's Public-Goods Production

Current Production and Preparation of the Menu

Current Public-Goods Production and Labor Hours Used

The number of public goods to be produced this period, g_t, was determined last period. The current period production function for these goods is given by:

(2.1) $g_t = g(h^g_t \cdot N^g_t, K^g_t)$ with $g_i > 0$, $i = 1,2$ and $g_{11} < 0$

where:

g_t = the number of public goods and services to be produced by the home government sector during the current period.

g_i = the partial derivatives with respect to labor and capital

g_{11} = the second derivative of $g(\bullet)$ with respect to current labor hours

h^g_t = the average number of hours the home government sector decides to use its employees during the current period.

N^g_t = the (predetermined) number of workers employed by the home government sector at the beginning of the current period.

K^g_t = the (predetermined) amount of physical capital held by the home government sector at the beginning of the current period.

Therefore, the average number of hours the home government requires its current employees to work is given by:

(2.2) $h^g_t = h^g(g_t, N^g_t, K^g_t)$ where $h^g_1 > 0$; $h^g_2, h^g_3 < 0$.

According to (2.2), the average number of hours, h^g_t, that the home government uses its current employees, N^g_t, to produce the predetermined amount of public goods, g_t, increases with the volume of public goods to be produced, but decreases with both the number of people employed at the beginning of the period and the amount of physical capital, K^g_t, the sector holds at the beginning of the period.

Preparation of Next Period's Menu of Public Goods

Next period's production function, depicted in Figure 2.1, is given by:

(2.3) $g_{t+1} = g^{+}(h \cdot N^{gde}_{t+1}, K^{gde}_{t+1})$ with $g^{+}_{i} > 0$, $g^{+}_{11} < 0$

where:

g_{t+1} = the number of public goods and services to be produced by the home government sector next period.

h = the "standard" average number of hours, which the home government expects this period that its employees will work next period. In fact we assume that every sector expects that all employees will work the standard number of hours next period.

N^{gde}_{t+1} = the number of workers the home government expects at the beginning of the current period (before it learns current product prices, wage rates, interest rates or exchange rates) that it will employ by the beginning of next period. The government will be free during the current period to alter its demand for workers for next period as current product prices, wage rates and interest rates become established.

K^{gde}_{t+1} = the amount of physical capital the home government sector expects at the beginning of the current period (before it learns current product prices, wage rates or interest rates) that it will hold by the beginning of next period.

Figure 2.1 **Current Period Use of Labor in Public-Goods Production**

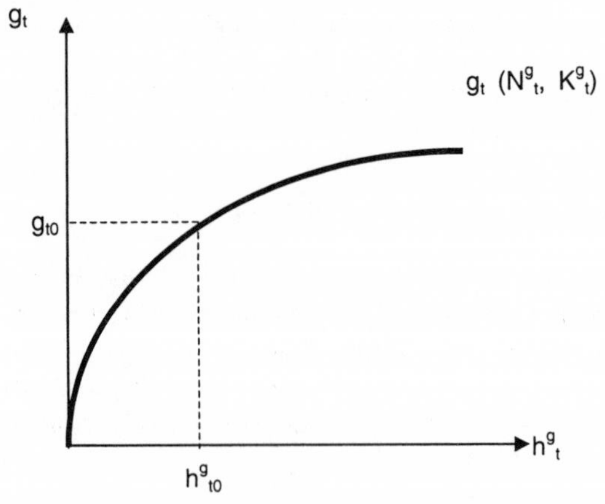

The government will be free during the current period to alter its demand for physical capital for next period as current product prices, wage rates and interest rates become established.

The home government sector's current period budget constraint is given by:

$$(2.4)\ p^{bg}_t(B^{gse}_{t+1} - B^g_t) = W_{t-1}h^g_t N^g_t + p^g_t(K^{gde}_{t+1} - K^g_t) + B^g_t - T_t - \Pi^c_t - p^{xg}_t R^{xdg}_t$$

$$- p^{pg}_t\ \bar{P}^{pdg}_t$$

where:

p^{bg}_t = the current period price of home country bonds anticipated by the home government sector at the beginning of the current period before current product prices, wages and interest rates are established.

B^{gse}_{t+1} = the number of home country bonds the home government sector plans at the beginning of the current period (before current product prices, wages and interest rates are established) to have outstanding by the end of the current period. The government will be free during the current period to alter its end-of-period supply of home country bonds as these prices and interest rates become known.

B^g_t = the (predetermined) number of home country bonds the home government sector has outstanding at the beginning of the current period.

W_{t-1} = the money wage rate announced last period by the home country's private non-financial business sector. This wage rate is paid during the current period to all workers employed during the current period in the home country.

p^g_t = the current period price of privately-produced home country goods anticipated by the home government sector at the beginning of the current period, before that price is announced by the home private non-financial business sector.

T_t = the (predetermined) tax revenue the home country's government sector collects during the current period.

Π^c_t = the (predetermined) revenue the home central bank collects and distributes to the home government sector during the current period.

p^{xg}_t = the current period price (expressed in terms of the home country's unit of account) of a unit of harvesting rights for the renewable resource anticipated by the home government sector at the beginning of the period before that price is established.

R^{xdg}_t = the amount of the renewable resource the home government sector anticipates its non-financial business sector will harvest during the current period.

p^{pg}_t = the current period price (expressed in terms of the home country's unit of account) of the right to emit a unit of pollution anticipated by the home government sector at the beginning of the current period before that price is determined.

$\bar{P}^{pdg}_t$ = the amount of pollution rights the home government anticipates its non-financial business sector will buy during the current period.

According to (2.4), the home government must plan to borrow in the home bond market during the current period the amount by which the sum of its current wage bill, purchases of physical capital during the current period and its current interest expense exceeds the sum of its current tax revenue, its revenue from the home central bank and the revenue it anticipates receiving from the international agent associated with the pollution and harvesting rights to be purchased by its non-financial business sector during the current period.

The home government sector's anticipated tax revenue next period is given by:

$$(2.5)\ T_{t+1} = W^g_t h N^{gde}_{t+1} + (1 + p^{bg}_t) B^{gse}_{t+1} - p^g_{t+1} K^{gde}_{t+1} - \Pi^{cg}_{t+1} - p^{xg}_{t+1} R^{xdg}_{t+1}$$

$$- p^{pg}_{t+1}\ \bar{P}^{pdg}_{t+1}$$

where:

T_{t+1} = the level of taxes to be collected by the home government sector next period.

W^g_t = the money wage rate the home government sector anticipates its non-financial business sector will announce this period. The wage rate set by that sector will be paid next period to all workers employed next period in the home country.

p^g_{t+1} = the average price of privately-produced home country goods which the home country's government sector anticipates at the beginning of the current period will prevail next period.

Π^{cg}_{t+1} = the revenue that the home country's government sector anticipates this period that it will receive from the home central bank next period.

p^{xg}_{t+1} = the price (expressed in terms of the home country's unit of account) of a unit of harvesting rights which the home government sector anticipates at the beginning of the current period will prevail next period.

R^{xdg}_{t+1} = the amount of the renewable resource the home government sector anticipates at the beginning of the current period that its private non-financial business sector will harvest next period.

p^{pg}_{t+1} = the price (expressed in terms of the home country's unit of account) of the right to emit a unit of pollution which the home government sector anticipates at the beginning of the current period will prevail next period.

$\bar{P}^{pdg}_{t+1}$ = the amount of pollution rights the home government sector anticipates at the beginning of the current period that its private non-financial business sector will buy next period.

According to (2.5), the home government plans during the current period that the level of taxes it collects next period is sufficient to pay next period's anticipated wage bill and the principal and interest on any debt it plans to have outstanding by the end of the current period over and above the revenue it anticipates it will collect next period from the sale of its physical capital held at the beginning of that period, the revenue it anticipates receiving next period from the home central bank, and the revenue it anticipates receiving next period from the international agent associated with the pollution and harvesting rights the home government anticipates its non-financial business sector will buy next period.

The objective of the home government sector at this point is to derive a menu for its household sector that minimizes the level of next period's taxes associated with each alternative level of public goods production for next period. See Figure 2.2. Therefore, to derive this menu, the sector minimizes (2.5) with respect to its end-of-period demand for employees and physical capital for each alternative level of g_{t+1} subject to constraints (2.3) and (2.4). Substituting these demand functions back into (2.5) yields the necessary menu, expression (2.6), showing the minimum level of taxes the government must collect next period from the household sector to provide each alternative level of public goods.

Figure 2.2 **Next Period's Public-Goods Menu**

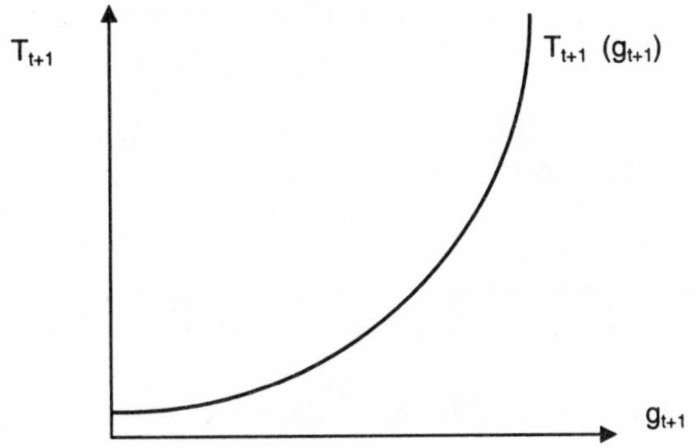

Clearly the greater the revenue the home government anticipates receiving from the sale of either pollution or harvesting rights during either the current or next periods, the less the sector must collect as taxes from the households next period in providing a given amount of public goods.

$$(2.6)\ T_{t+1} = T(\underset{+}{g_{t+1}}, \underset{+}{\Gamma}, \underset{-}{p^{xg}{}_{t}R^{xdg}{}_{t} + p^{pg}{}_{t}\ \overline{P}^{pdg}{}_{t}})$$

where:

Γ = the vector of parameters other than g_{t+1} and current revenue from the sale of pollution and harvesting rights that influence the level of taxes the government must collect next period. An increase in Γ represents a parametric change, such as an increase in current wage rates, that results, ceteris paribus, in an increase in next period's taxes.

Home Household Sector's Demand for (Selection of) Home Public Goods

The home country's household sector now chooses at the beginning of the current period, the optimal combination of g_{t+1} (and T_{t+1}) given its intertemporal preferences with respect to leisure and public- and private-goods consumption, its current disposable income, and its beginning-of-period wealth. Because the amount of public goods to be produced next period must be selected before the households learn current wages, the prices of privately-produced goods and interest rates, the other choices the household sector makes in conjunction with its choice of public goods in the present step must be viewed as purely "notional"; they will be revised later as wages, prices and exchange rates become known.

Preliminary Budget Constraint for the Home Household Sector

Let:

$c^{he}{}_{t}$ = the home household sector's notional demand at the beginning of the current period for privately-produced home country goods during the current period, before the sector learns current period prices, wages, or interest rates.

Cu_t = the volume of home country currency the home household sector holds at the beginning of the current period.

$Cu^{he}{}_{t+1}$ = the home household sector's notional demand at the beginning of the current period for currency issued by the home central bank (denominated in the home country's unit of account) to be held by the end of the current period.

$D^{h}{}_{t}$ = the volume of home country checkable deposits held by the home household sector at the beginning of the current period.

D^{he}_{t+1} = the home household sector's notional demand at the beginning of the current period for checkable deposits issued by the home private financial sector (denominated in the home country's unit of account) to be held by the end of the current period.

$h^h_t N_t$ = the total number of hours the home country's household sector anticipates at the beginning of the current period that it will work during the current period for all three of its employers.

p^h_t = the current period price of privately-produced goods in the home country (expressed in terms of the home country's unit or account) anticipated by the home household sector at the beginning of the current period.

r^d_{t-1} = the interest rate on checkable deposits issued by the home country's private financial sector announced by that sector last period and payable during the current period on each unit of those checkable deposits outstanding at the beginning of the current period.

$\bar{Y}^h_t$ = the home household sector's beginning-of-current period estimate of its current disposable income ($= W_{t-1}h^h_t N_t + \Pi^{nh}_t + \Pi^{fh}_t + r^d_{t-1}D_t - T_t$).

Π^{nh}_t = the dividends the home country's household sector anticipates at the beginning of the current period that it will receive from the home non-financial business sector during the current period.

Π^{fh}_t = the dividends the home country's household sector anticipates at the beginning of the current period that it will receive from the home private financial sector during the current period.

Then at the beginning of the current period, before it learns current period wages, prices and interest rates, the home household sector's current period budget constraint is given by:

$$(2.7) \quad \bar{Y}^h_t = p^h_t c^{he}_t + (D^{he}_{t+1} - D^h_t) + (Cu^{he}_{t+1} - Cu_t).$$

According to this restriction, at the beginning of the current period, the home household sector plans to apply its anticipated current disposable income to current consumption of privately-produced home country goods, to the accumulation of home country checkable deposits, and to the accumulation of home country currency.

Let:

c^{he}_{t+1} = the home household sector's notional demand at the beginning of the current period for privately-produced home country goods next period, before the sector learns current period prices, wages, or interest rates.

N^{he}_{t+1} = the number of people the home household sector would like to have working by the end of the current period before the sector learns current wages, product prices and interest rates; i.e., the sector's notional supply of labor at the beginning of the current period for next period.

p^{he}_{t+1} = the price of home country goods (expressed in units of the home country's unit of account) that the home household sector anticipates at the beginning of the current period will prevail next period (before the sector learns current wages, product prices and interest rates).

r^{de}_{t} = the interest rate the home household sector anticipates at the beginning of the current period (before it learns current wages, product prices and interest rates) will prevail during the current period on checkable deposits issued by the home private financial sector. (The interest rate established during the current period will be paid next period on each unit of checkable deposits held at the beginning of next period.)

W^{h}_{t} = the wage rate (in the home unit of account) that the home household sector anticipates at the beginning of the current period the home non-financial business sector will announce in the current period and that will be paid next period to everyone employed by the end of the current period in the home country.

Π^{h}_{t+1} = the total dividends the home household sector anticipates at the beginning of the current period that it will receive next period from the home non-financial business and home private financial sectors (denominated in the home country's unit of account).

Given the menu—expression (2.6)—prepared for it by the home government sector, the home household sector's anticipated budget constraint for next period, as viewed at the beginning of the current period before current wages, product prices and interest rates are known, may be represented by:

$$(2.8)\quad W^{h}_{t}hN^{he}_{t+1} + \Pi^{h}_{t+1} + (1+r^{de}_{t})D^{he}_{t+1} + Cu^{he}_{t+1} - T(g_{t+1}, \Gamma, p^{xg}_{t}R^{xdg}_{t} + p^{pg}_{t}\ \bar{P}^{dg}_{t}) = p^{he}_{t+1}c^{he}_{t+1}.$$

According to this constraint, the sector plans at the beginning of the current period to spend an amount on privately-produced home country goods next period equal to next period's disposable income plus the wealth the sector plans to hold at the beginning of that period.

Preliminary Transactions-Time Functions

Since the households may accumulate both checkable deposits and currency during the current period, and since checkable deposits yield a market return while currency does not, currency must yield a non-market return for the households to be willing to hold it. In fact, whether it be in the form of currency or checkable deposits, by holding money an individual holds an asset that virtually everyone else accepts as payment for her purchases. In general, to the extent that the individual holds money at the beginning of the period, she conserves time because she reduces the number of times she must sell another asset or borrow the necessary funds before making a purchase. In the real world, this time-saving characteristic of money distinguishes it from other storable assets whose prices are fixed in terms of the unit of account. It is this characteristic which explains why economic agents are willing to hold money even though equally safe alternatives exist which yield higher market returns. Similarly, agents are also willing to hold some currency even though an equally safe alternative, checkable deposits, exists which yields a market return, while currency yields no such return. Currency is more convenient than checkable deposits for undertaking certain transactions; currency and checkable deposits are imperfect substitutes as a medium of exchange.

In the present model, we assume that the amount of time the home country's household sector spends undertaking transactions during a given period is directly related to the number of privately-produced home country goods that sector purchases that period, but negatively related to the real amounts of currency and checkable deposits it holds at the beginning of that period. Therefore, for the current period we specify the following transactions-time function faced by the home country's household sector:

$$(2.9)\quad \bar{\tau} = \bar{\tau}(c^{he}_t, D_t/p^h_t, Cu_t/p^h_t) \text{ where } \bar{\tau}_1 > 0,\ \bar{\tau}_2 < 0, \text{ and } \bar{\tau}_3 < 0$$

and where $\bar{\tau}$ = current period transactions time for the home country's household sector. See Figure 2.3.

By the same token, next period's transactions time for the home country's household sector may be represented by:

$$(2.10)\ \tau = \tau(c^{he}_{t+1}, D^{he}_{t+1}/p^{he}_{t+1}, Cu^{he}_{t+1}/p^{he}_{t+1})$$

where $\tau_1 > 0$, $\tau_2 < 0$, $\tau_3 < 0$, $\tau_{11} = 0$, $\tau_{12} < 0$, $\tau_{13} < 0$, $\tau_{22} > 0$, $\tau_{23} > 0$, $\tau_{33} > 0$ and where τ denotes the home household sector's transactions time next period. According to expression (2.10), ceteris paribus, an increase in the amount consumed next period increases next period's transactions time at a constant rate.

Figure 2.3 **Current Period Transactions Time as a Function of Current Consumption, Initial Real Holdings of Currency (a), and Initial Real Holdings of Checkable Deposits (b)**

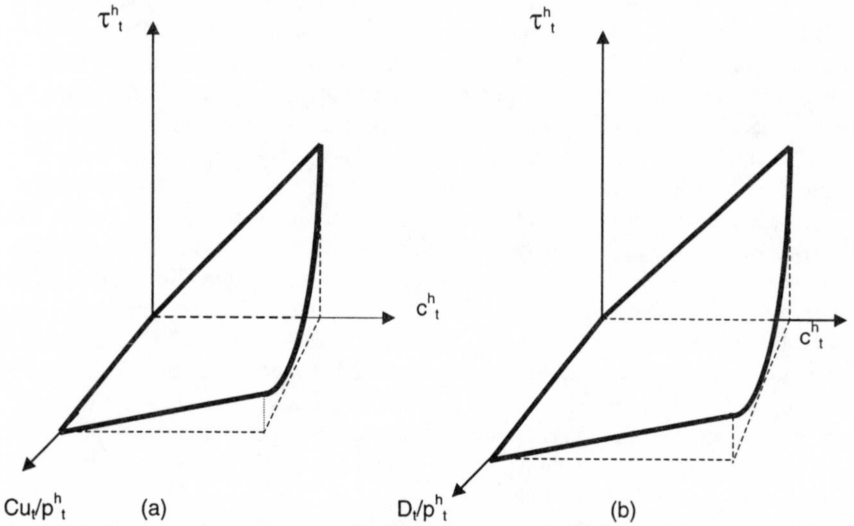

But this rate is reduced, at a decreasing rate, to the extent that the sector holds (real) balances of currency and checkable deposits by the beginning of that period. Furthermore, the larger the real balances of one type of money held at the beginning of next period, the smaller the transactions time saved by an additional unit of the other type of money.

Present-Utility Maximization

At this point in the analysis, the objective of the home country's households or their representatives is to decide at the beginning of the current period—before current period wages, product prices or interest rates have been established—upon the optimal level of public goods production next period consistent with the sector's desire to maximize its present utility. We assume that the sector's present utility is a positive increasing function of current and future consumption of home country goods, both public and private. In addition, we assume that present utility is negatively related to current and future transactions time, but positively related to current and future leisure. Specifically, we posit the following additive utility function:

$$(2.11)\ U = U_1(c^{he}_t) + U_2(g_t) + U_3(\bar{h}N - h^h_t N_t) + U_4[\ \bar{\tau}(c^{he}_t, D_t/p^h_t, Cu_t/p^h_t)]$$

$$+U_5(c^{he}_{t+1}) + U_6(g_{t+1}) + U_7(\hat{h}N - hN^{he}_{t+1}) + U_8[\tau(c^{he}_{t+1}, D^{he}_{t+1}/p^{he}_{t+1}, Cu^{he}_{t+1}/p^{he}_{t+1})]$$

where $U_i(\bullet) > 0$ and $U'_i > 0$ for $i \neq 4$ or 8 (all goods and leisure yield positive utility and positive, but diminishing marginal utility) and where, for $i = 4$ or 8, $U'_i < 0$ (current and future transactions time yield negative utility (disutility) and negative and decreasing marginal utility in algebraic terms). Also, we let $U''_i < 0$ for all i. In addition, let $\bar{h}$ = the total number of hours in the current period, $h^{\wedge}$ = the total number of hours in the next period and N = the total adult population in the home country. Given the menu prepared by the government, the objective of the home country's household sector is to select the optimal level of public-goods production for next period conditional upon its limited information at the beginning of the period. In particular, the sector attempts to select the level of public goods for next period consistent with maximizing (2.11) subject to budget restrictions (2.7) and (2.8) and to transactions-time constraints (2.9) and (2.10). Solving (2.7) for the sector's notional end-of-period demand for currency and substituting this expression into (2.8)–(2.11), then at this stage, we view the home household sector as maximizing (2.12) with respect to its notional demands for current and future privately-produced goods, its notional end-of-period demand for checkable deposits, its notional supply of employees for next period, and its effective demand for public goods next period:

$$(2.12)\ U = U_1(c^{he}_t) + U_2(g_t) + U_3(\bar{h}N - h^h_t N_t) + U_4[\bar{\tau}(c^{he}_t, D_t/p^h_t, Cu_t/p^h_t)]$$
$$+U_5(c^{he}_{t+1}) + U_6(g_{t+1}) + U_7(h^{\wedge}N - hN^{he}_{t+1})$$
$$+U_8\{\tau[c^{he}_{t+1}, D^{he}_{t+1}/p^{he}_{t+1}, (\bar{Y}^h_t - p^h_t c^{he}_t - D^{he}_{t+1} + D^h_t + Cu_t)/p^{he}_{t+1}]\}$$
$$+\lambda[W^h_t hN^{he}_{t+1} + \Pi^h_{t+1} + (1+r^{de}_t)D^{he}_{t+1} + \bar{Y}^h_t - p^h_t c^{he}_t - D^{he}_{t+1}$$
$$+D^h_t + Cu_t - T(g_{t+1}, \Gamma, p^{xg}_t R^{xdg}_t + p^{pg}_t \bar{P}^{dg}_t) - p^{he}_{t+1} c^{he}_{t+1}].$$

At this stage, the first-order necessary conditions for utility maximization are given by (2.13)–(2.18).

$$(2.13)\ [U'_1 + U'_4 \cdot \bar{\tau}_1 - U'_8 \tau_3 (p^h_t/p^h_{t+1})] - \lambda p^h_t = 0$$

$$(2.14)\ [U'_5 + U'_8 \tau_1] - \lambda p^h_{t+1} = 0$$

$$(2.15)\ U'_6 - \lambda T_1 = 0$$

$$(2.16)\ U'_8 \cdot (\tau_2 - \tau_3)/p^h_{t+1} + \lambda r^{de}_t = 0$$

$$(2.17)\ U'_7 \cdot (-h) + \lambda W^h_t h = 0$$

$$(2.18)\ W^h_t hN^{he}_{t+1} + \Pi^h_{t+1} + (1+r^{de}_t)D^{he}_{t+1} + \bar{Y}^h_t - p^h_t c^{he}_t - D^{he}_{t+1} + D^h_t + Cu_t$$

$$-T(g_{t+1}, \Gamma, p^{xg}_t R^{xdg}_t + p^{pg}_t \bar{P}^{dg}_t) - p^{he}_{t+1} c^{he}_{t+1} = 0.$$

Although all of the above first-order conditions are important to the home household sector's demand for public goods for next period, condition (2.15) explicitly states the principle upon which the provision of public goods is based in this model. The marginal cost to the home household sector of an extra unit of public goods next period is the loss in utility due to the reduction in next period's disposable income, λT_1, where λ denotes the marginal utility of income and where T_1 represents the marginal tax the home government sector must levy next period to provide an extra unit of public goods. The term U'_6 denotes the marginal utility the home household sector receives from an extra unit of public goods. Therefore, (2.15) stipulates that the home household sector or its representatives should instruct the home government to produce public goods up to the point at which the marginal social benefit, U'_6, equals the marginal social cost, λT_1.

Subjective and Market Rates of Substitution between Public and Private Goods and between Public Goods and Financial Assets

From conditions (2.13) and (2.15) we obtain the following condition relating the subjective rate of substitution of next period's public goods for current privately-produced goods:

$$(2.19)\ U'_6 / [U'_1 + U'_4 \cdot \bar{\tau}_1 - U'_8 \tau_3 (p^h_t / p^h_{t+1})] = T_1 / p^h_t.$$

The left-hand side of (2.19) denotes the number of privately-produced goods the home household sector is willing to give up during the current period to obtain an extra unit of publicly-produced goods next period. The denominator of this subjective rate of substitution denotes the net marginal utility to the home household sector from an added unit of current period consumption of privately-produced goods. Although an extra unit of current period consumption of privately-produced goods adds directly to present utility, $U'_1 > 0$, an extra unit of current consumption not only increases current transactions time, thereby diminishing present utility, $U'_4 \cdot \bar{\tau}_1 < 0$, but also reduces, ceteris paribus, the volume of real currency the sector may hold by the beginning of next period, thereby raising next period's transactions time and reducing present utility as well, $-U'_8 \tau_3 (p^h_t / p^h_{t+1}) < 0$. The ratio on the right-hand side of (2.19) denotes the market rate of substitution of a unit of public goods next period for privately-produced goods this period, i.e., the number of privately-produced goods the sector must give up this period to obtain an extra unit of public goods next period (the marginal financing cost of which is T_1). From this condition, the higher the marginal financing cost, the greater the tendency for the home household sector to substitute current privately-produced goods for next period's public goods. See Figure 2.4.

From conditions (2.14) and (2.15), we find:

$$(2.20)\ U'_6 / [U'_5 + U'_8 \tau_1] = T_1 / p^h_{t+1}$$

where the left-hand side of (2.20) denotes the subjective rate of substitution of public goods next period for privately-produced goods next period and the right-hand side represents the anticipated market rate of substitution of public for private goods next period. The sum in brackets in the denominator of (2.20) depicts the net marginal present utility from an extra unit of private-goods consumption next period, allowing for the marginal disutility from the extra transactions time associated with that consumption. From this condition, as the marginal financing cost of a unit of public goods rises, the home household sector elects on the margin to substitute privately-produced goods for public goods next period.

Figure 2.4 **Subjective vs. Technical Rates of Substitution of Next Period's Public Goods for Current Private Goods**

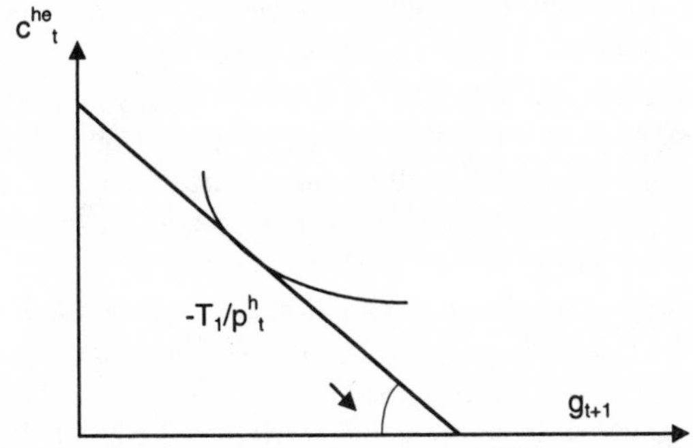

Condition (2.16) denotes the first-order condition with respect to the home household sector's end-of-period demand for checkable deposits issued by the home private financial sector. Because both home checkable deposits and home currency held at the end of the current period are useful to the home household sector in reducing that sector's transactions time next period, both τ_2 and τ_3 are negative. Because we take the marginal utility of income to be positive, $\lambda > 0$, because transactions time reduces present utility, $U'_8 < 0$, and because the anticipated nominal interest rate on home checkable deposits is positive, $r^{de}_t > 0$, condition (2.16) states that when the home household sector demands a positive end-of-period balance of checkable deposits, the marginal product of home currency, $|\tau_3|$, necessarily exceeds the marginal product of checkable deposits, $|\tau_2|$. The sector continues to add to its holdings of checkable deposits until the value of the marginal product of home checkable deposits (in terms of the reduction in disutility associated with undertaking transactions), $U'_8 \cdot \tau_2$, is sufficiently below the value of the marginal product of home currency, $U'_8 \cdot \tau_3$, so that the sum of the value of the marginal product of checkable deposits (its non-market return) plus the value of its market return (in terms of present utility), λr^{de}_t, equals the value of the marginal product of home currency. Therefore the term $U'_8 \cdot (\tau_2 - \tau_3)/p^h_{t+1}$ in (2.16) denotes the marginal reduction in present utility from adding a unit to the sector's end-of-period balances of home checkable deposits at the expense of its end-of-period holdings of home currency.

From this interpretation of (2.16), when we combine conditions (2.15) and (2.16) to form the following expression:

$$(2.21)\ U'_6 /[U'_8 \cdot (\tau_2 - \tau_3)/p^h_{t+1}] = -T_1 /r^{de}_t$$

the left-hand side of (2.21) represents the subjective rate of substitution of a unit of public goods next period for home checkable deposits held at the end of the current period, with the denominator in that ratio denoting the marginal disutility of adding a unit of home checkable deposits to the sector's end-of-period balances of that asset (at the expense of the sector's end-of-period holdings of home checkable deposits). This subjective rate of substitution is negative because to the extent that the home household sector opts for an extra unit of public goods for next period so that present utility increases, it must (reduce its end-of-period holdings of currency and) increase its end-of-period holdings of home checkable deposits if the sector is to remain at the same level of present utility as originally. The right-hand side of (2.21) represents the market rate of substitution of public goods for home checkable deposits, which is also negative. That is if the sector decides to spend an extra T_1 dollars next period on public goods, then, ceteris paribus, it must increase its end-of-period holdings of home checkable deposits (and reduce end-of-period holdings of home currency) to finance the extra public goods. See Figure 2.5. Clearly, the higher T_1 happens to be the smaller the sector's demands for both public goods and checkable deposits, provided the substitution effect dominates.

From (2.15) and (2.17), we obtain the following equality between the subjective rate of substitution of next period's public goods and next period's employment and the market rate of substitution between these items:

$$(2.22)\ U'_6 /U'_7(-h) = -T_1 /(W^h_t \cdot h).$$

Since whenever the home household sector adds one person to the number employed next period, it sacrifices "h" hours of leisure, the denominator on the left-hand side of (2.22) represents the reduction in present utility from the loss of those hours of leisure. Therefore, next period's subjective rate of substitution

Figure 2.5 **Subjective vs. Market Rates of Substitution of Next Period's Public Goods for End-of-Period Holdings of Home Checkable Deposits**

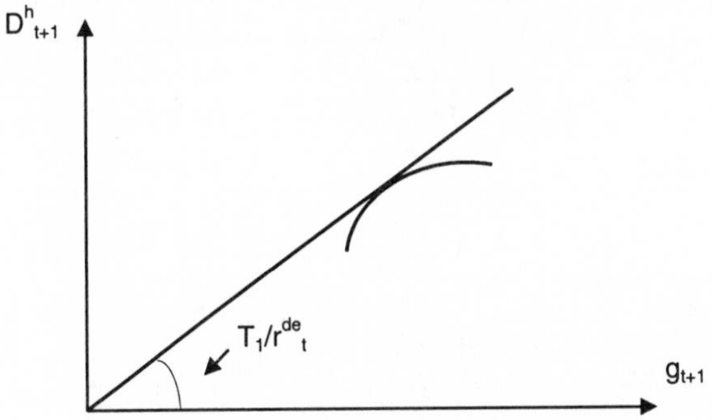

of public goods for employment is negative; if the home households decide to add a unit to their enjoyment of public goods next period thereby increasing present utility, ceteris paribus, they must also elect to have more people employed next period if present utility is to remain unchanged.

The right-hand side of (2.22) denotes the negative market rate of substitution of future public goods for future employment. If the home households elect to enjoy an extra unit of public goods next period, thereby incurring a marginal outlay of T_1, they must increase the number of people employed next period by $T_1/W^h_t \cdot h$ in order to finance the extra unit of public goods. See Figure 2.6. Clearly, as T_1 increases, the substitution effect causes the sector to reduce both its demand for public goods and its supply of workers.

Figure 2.6 **Subjective vs. Market Rates of Substitution of Next Period's Public Goods for Next Period's Employment**

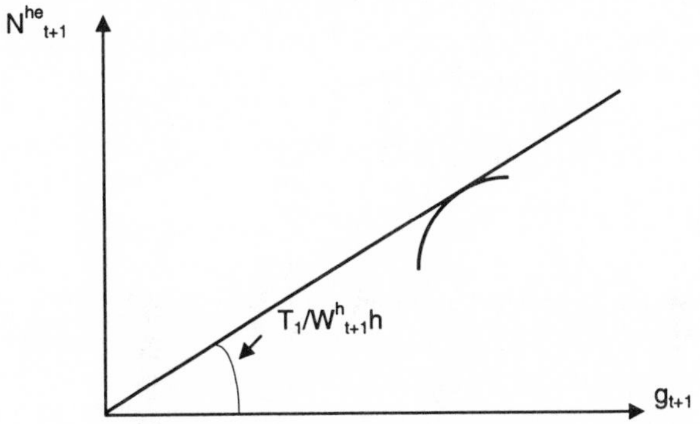

Home Household Sector's Selection of Next Period's Public Goods

Totally differentiating expressions (2.13)–(2.18) we may solve for the home household sector's effective demand for public goods for next period. Assuming that next period's public goods are normal goods, the home households will demand more of these goods, the greater the sector's current disposable income and/or financial wealth at the beginning of the current period.

$$(2.23)\ g^{d}_{t+1} = g^{d}_{t+1}(\underset{+}{\bar{Y}^{h}_{t}},\ \underset{+}{D_t + Cu_t},\ \underset{-}{T_1},\ \underset{-}{\Gamma}).$$

From (2.18) it appears that the greater the home government sector's current revenue from the sale of pollution and harvesting rights, the less the sector must collect as taxes from the home household sector next period in order to provide a given amount of public goods that period. By itself, this increase in current disposable income would induce the home household sector to increase its demands for all goods, including next period's public goods. However, the extra revenue that the government receives from the sale of these rights ultimately derives from payments for these rights by the country's non-financial business sector. As the ultimate owners of these firms, the households therefore experience a corresponding reduction in the income they receive as dividends from the non-financial businesses equal to the reduction in their tax payments to the government. Therefore, an increase in the payments by the home non-financial businesses to the home government via the international agent for pollution and harvesting rights produces no direct net effect upon the home household sector's anticipated disposable income. Therefore, by itself, the increase in the home government sector's current revenue from the current sale of pollution and harvesting rights produces no direct effect upon the home household sector's demand for public goods for next period.

Selection of Public-Goods Production in the Foreign Country

In a similar fashion, the foreign government sector's menu of goods and services it provides its households may be derived as:

$$(2.24)\ T^{*}_{t+1} = T^{*}(\underset{+}{g^{*}_{t+1}},\ \underset{+}{\Gamma^{*}},\ \underset{-}{(p^{xg^*}{}_{t}R^{x^*dg^*}{}_{t} + p^{pg^*}{}_{t}\ \bar{P}^{p^*dg^*}{}_{t})/\varepsilon^{g^*}{}_{t}})$$

where:

$p^{xg^*}{}_{t}$ = the current period price (expressed in terms of the home country's unit of account) of a unit of harvesting rights for the renewable resource anticipated by the foreign government sector.

R^{x*dg*}_t = the amount of the renewable resource the foreign government sector anticipates its non-financial business sector will harvest during the current period.

p^{pg*}_t = the current period price (expressed in terms of the home country's unit of account) of the right to emit a unit of pollution anticipated by the foreign government sector at the beginning of the current period.

$\bar{P}^{p*dg*}_t$ = the amount of pollution rights the foreign government anticipates its non-financial business sector will buy during the current period.

Γ^* = the vector of parameters, other than the level of next period's production of public goods and the current revenue from the sale of pollution and harvesting rights, affecting next period's taxes.

ε^{g*}_t = the current spot value of the foreign country's unit of account in terms of the home country's unit of account anticipated by the foreign country's government sector before that spot rate is established.

The household sector in the foreign country then chooses the optimal combination of g^*_{t+1} (and T^*_{t+1}) given its intertemporal preferences among private and public goods and leisure, its current disposable income, and its beginning-of-period wealth. The relevant first-order conditions are directly analogous to (2.13)–(2.18). Therefore, the foreign household sector's demand for public goods for next period may be given by:

$$(2.25)\ g^{d*}_{t+1} = g^{d*}_{t+1}(\underset{+}{\bar{Y}^{*h*}_t},\ \underset{+}{D^*_t + Cu^*_t},\ \underset{-}{T^*_1},\ \underset{-}{\Gamma^*}).$$

According to our model, the foreign government sector will produce public goods next period consistent with condition (2.24) and will collect taxes next period consistent with condition (2.25). Just as the home government, the foreign government plans to reduce taxes paid by its household sector by the same amount that it anticipates receiving from the international agent next period.

Now that the households in both countries have chosen the amounts of public goods they want produced next period, the non-financial business sectors in each country decide their current production and employment and set current period wages and prices. In the present model, they make these decisions before current aggregate demand is revealed and before current interest rates and exchange rates are known. Aggregate demand, interest rates and exchange rates will become jointly determined after product prices and wage rates are announced.

CHAPTER THREE

Pollution Rights, Harvesting Rights, and National Product

International Agent

Pollution Rights

The international agent issues pollution rights at the beginning of the current period equivalent to the volume of pollution it determines the biosphere is capable of assimilating during the current period at the pre-existing target level. In this fashion, the volume of pollution at the end of the current period will once again equal the target amount. Both non-financial business sectors purchase these pollution rights. The market price for pollution rights is established at the point at which the sum of the (net) demands for pollution rights by the two non-financial business sectors is equal to the target volume issued by the international agent. The demand for pollution rights by an individual sector is equal to the amount of pollution it wants to create in extracting and using its own non-renewable resource minus the amount of pollution abatement it wishes to produce at the current price of pollution rights. The demand for pollution rights by an individual country's non-financial business sector may be negative, in which case that sector decides to clean up more pollution than it creates, thereby earning an income from that operation. (We may view the international agent as paying that sector the market price of a unit of emissions rights for every unit by which that sector reduces the level of pollution. The international agent would then sell emissions rights to the other country's non-financial business sector equal to the assimilation level plus the amount of pollution abatement bϕy the first country.)

Let:

$\bar{P}$ = the target level of pollution decided by the international agent; for simplicity, we assume this is also the amount of pollution in existence at the beginning of the current period.

$\phi \cdot \bar{P}$ = the amount of pollution the biosphere can assimilate at the target level of pollution, where $\phi \leq 1$. The international body issues pollution rights during the current period equal to $\phi \cdot \bar{P}$.

$q^{\wedge d}_t$ = the amount of the home country's non-renewable resource that the home country's non-financial business sector desires to extract and use during the current period.

$q^{\wedge *d}_t$ = the amount of the foreign country's non-renewable resource that the foreign country's non-financial business sector desires to extract and use during the current period.

κ = the amount of pollution created per unit of the home country's non-renewable resources extracted during the current period.

κ^* = the amount of pollution created per unit of the foreign country's non-renewable resources extracted during the current period.
Then the total amount of pollution the two non-financial business sectors plan to generate this period is given by the sum: $\kappa\, q^{\wedge d}_t + \kappa^*\, q^{\wedge *d}_t$.
Let:
μ = the level of pollution abatement by the home country's non-financial business sector.

μ^* = the level of pollution abatement by the foreign country's non-financial business sector.
We suppose that within each country pollution abatement is a positive increasing function of the amount of labor services the respective non-financial business sector devotes to pollution abatement. The home country's pollution abatement function will be specified in the next section, where we discuss the non-financial business sector's decision-making in detail.
Let:
$\bar{P}^{pd}_t$ = the amount of pollution rights the home country's non-financial business sector demands during the current period.

$\bar{P}^{p*d}_t$ = the amount of pollution rights the foreign country's non-financial business sector demands during the current period.

p^P_t = the current equilibrium price of pollution rights (expressed in terms of the home country's currency).
Then, from the above discussion, the equilibrium price of pollution rights (expressed in terms of the home country's currency), p^P_t, is the one for which:

$$(3.1)\ \phi\cdot\ \bar{P} = (\kappa\, q^{\wedge d}_t - \mu) + (\kappa^*\, q^{\wedge *d}_t - \mu^*) = \bar{P}^{pd}_t + \bar{P}^{p*d}_t.$$

Harvesting Rights

Given the target level of pollution, the international body determines the optimal increase in the renewable resource for the current period. The optimal growth in the resource for the current period is presumed to be between zero and the amount by which the resource would grow given the beginning-of-period stock of the resource and the target level of pollution.

Let:

S_t = the beginning-of-period world stock of the renewable resource.

$G(S_t, \bar{P})$ = the natural amount of growth in the renewable resource, where $G(\bullet)$ is positively related to S_t, but negatively related to $\bar{P}$.

Ω = the international agent's target increase in the stock of the renewable resource.

Then the international body issues extraction permits during the current period equal to $G(S_t, \bar{P}) - \Omega$. Under these assumptions, the stock of the renewable resource at the end of the current period, S_{t+1}, will be equal to $S_t + \Omega$.

Let:

R^{xd}_t = the amount of the shared renewable resource that the home country's non-financial business sector demands for harvesting and use this period.

R^{x*d}_t = the amount of the shared renewable resource that the foreign country's non-financial business sector demands for harvesting and use this period.

p^x_t = the current market price of harvesting rights for the renewable resource (expressed in units of the home country's currency).

Then p^x_t is established where:

$$(3.2)\ G(S_t, \bar{P}) - \Omega = R^{xd}_t + R^{x*d}_t.$$

In the next section we derive the home country's non-financial business sector's demand functions for the non-renewable and renewable resources.

Home Country's Non-Financial Business Sector

Objective Function

The home country's non-financial business sector attempts to maximize its present value. This sector's current period production function may be given by:

$$(3.3)\ q_t = \bar{q}(h^q_t, N^n_t, q^{*n}_t, K^n_t, R^x_t, \hat{q}_t)$$

with $\bar{q}_i > 0$, $\bar{q}_{ii} < 0$ and, for simplicity, $\bar{q}_{ij} = 0$, where:

q_t = the number of goods produced by the home country's non-financial business sector during the current period.

h^q_t = the average number of hours the home country's non-financial business sector uses their current employees during the current period for the purpose of producing private goods.

N^n_t = the number of people employed by the home country's non-financial business sector at the beginning of the current period.

q^{*n}_t = the number of intermediate goods the home country's non-financial business sector decided last period to import during the current period; i.e., its order placed last period for delivery and use this period.

K^n_t = the home country's non-financial business sector's stock of physical capital at the beginning of the current period.

R^x_t = the amount of the renewable resource the home country's non-financial business sector extracts and uses during the current period.

$\hat{q}_t$ = the amount of its non-renewable resource the home country's non-financial business sector extracts and uses during the current period.

We assume that current production by the home non-financial business sector is a positive increasing function of current labor hours, the amount of the imported factor, the beginning-of-period stock of capital and the amounts of the renewable resource and the non-renewable resource extracted and used during the current period. Each factor presumably displays diminishing marginal returns that are independent of all other factors.

The home country's non-financial business sector's current period dividends may be represented by:

$$(3.4)\quad \Pi^n_t = p_t[\,\bar{q}(h^q_t N^n_t, q^{*n}_t, K^n_t, R^x_t, \hat{q}_t)] - W_{t-1}h^n_t N^n_t - \hat{\varepsilon}_{t-1}p^*_{t-1}q^{*n}_t - B^n_t$$

$$-p^x_t R^x_t - p^p_t[\kappa\,\hat{q}_t - \mu(h^n_t N^n_t - h^q_t N^n_t)]$$

with $\mu' > 0$ and $\mu'' < 0$ and where:

Π^n_t = the dividends that the home country's non-financial business sector announces at the beginning of the current period that it will distribute to its shareholders (i.e., to the home household sector) during the current period.

p_t = the price (in terms of the home country's unit of account) announced by the home country's non-financial business sector at the beginning of the current period for the goods it sells during the current period.

h^n_t = the overall average number of hours the home country's non-financial business sector uses its current employees.

$\varepsilon^{\wedge}_{t-1}$ = last period's forward exchange rate; the value of the foreign country's unit of account in terms of the home country's unit of account contracted last period for exchanges during the current period involving items denominated in different units of account.

p^*_{t-1} = the price (in terms of the foreign unit of account) of the foreign (intermediate) good ordered by the home country's non-financial business sector last period and which the sector agreed to pay upon delivery of the foreign good this period.

B^n_t = the number of bonds (issued in the home country's bond market) the home country's non-financial business sector has outstanding at the beginning of the current period.

$h^n_t N^n_t - h^q_t N^n_t$ = the amount of labor the home country's non-financial business sector devotes to pollution abatement during the current period.
We have assumed that the sector distributes all current period net income to its household sector.

The function $\mu(h^n_t N^n_t - h^q_t N^n_t)$ denotes the level of pollution abatement produced by the home non-financial business sector. This function is a positive increasing function of the amount of labor devoted to pollution abatement; as the sector increases its use of that labor, its marginal product diminishes.

The home non-financial business sector's current period budget constraint is given by:

$$(3.5) \quad p_t [(K^{nde}_{t+1} - K^n_t) - Q_t] - p^{bn}_t (B^{nse}_{t+1} - B^n_t) = 0$$

where:

K^{nde}_{t+1} = the amount of physical capital the home non-financial business sector expects at the beginning of the current period (as it announces its current product price and the wage rate and decides current production, but before it learns current interest rates or exchange rates) that it will hold by the beginning of next period. The sector will be free during the current period to alter its demand for physical capital for the beginning of next period as current interest rates and exchange rates become established.

Q_t = the home non-financial business sector's inventory of unsold goods at the beginning of the current period. The sector presumably sets product price during the current period at a level that it plans will yield no unsold inventory by the end of the period.

p^{bn}_t = the current period average price of home country bonds (in terms of the home country's unit of account) that the home non-financial business sector anticipates at the beginning of the current period before this price is determined.

B^{nse}_{t+1} = the number of home country bonds the home non-financial business sector plans at the beginning of the current period (as it announces its current product price and the wage rate and decides current production, but before current interest rates and exchange rates are established) to have outstanding by the end of the current period. The sector will be free during the current period to alter its end-of-period supply of home country bonds as these interest rates and exchange rates become known.

Next period's production function may be represented by:

$$(3.6)\ q^{ne}_{t+1} = q^{ne}(\ hN^{nde}_{t+1}, q^{*ne}_{t+1}, K^{nde}_{t+1}, R^{xdn}_{t+1}, \hat{Q}_t - \hat{q}_t)$$

where:

q^{ne}_{t+1} = the number of goods the home non-financial business sector plans in the current period to produce next period.

h = the standard number of hours that every sector anticipates at the beginning of the current period that employees will work next period.

N^{nde}_{t+1} = the number of people the home non-financial business sector expects at the beginning of the current period (as it announces its current product price and the wage rate and decides current production, but before it learns current interest rates or exchange rates) that it will employ by the beginning of next period. The sector will be free during the current period to alter its demand for workers for the beginning of next period as current interest rates and exchange rates become established.

q^{*ne}_{t+1} = the number of intermediate goods the home country's non-financial business sector plans at the beginning of the current period (as it announces its current product price and the wage rate and decides current production, but before it learns current interest rates or exchange rates) to buy from the foreign country next period. The sector will be free during the current period to alter its demand (orders) for the intermediate good during the current period as interest rates and the exchange rate become known. The orders the sector places by the end of the current period will be delivered and paid for next period.

R^{xdn}_{t+1} = the amount of the world's renewable resource that the home country's non-financial business sector anticipates this period that it will extract and use next period. The sector will be free next period to demand a different amount in light of changing market conditions.

$Q^{\wedge}_t - q^{\wedge}_t$ = the amount of the non-renewable resource that the home non-financial business sector will have available at the beginning of next period, where $Q^{\wedge}_t$ denotes the stock of the non-renewable resource available at the beginning of the current period after deducting the minimum amount of that resource which the international agent has identified as necessary for maintainability.

We assume that the marginal products of the factors appearing in (3.6) are positive and decreasing. We ignore cross partials. In addition, the production sector's anticipated dividends next period is represented by:

$$(3.7)\ \Pi^{ne}_{t+1} = p^{n}_{t+1} q^{ne}_{t+1} - W_t hN^{nde}_{t+1} - B^{nse}_{t+1} - \varepsilon^{\wedge n}_t p^{*n}_t q^{*ne}_{t+1}$$

$$- p^{xn}_{t+1} R^{xdn}_{t+1} - p^{pn}_{t+1}[\kappa^{e}(Q^{\wedge}_t - q^{\wedge}_t) - \mu^{e}(hN^{nde}_{t+1} - hN^{qde}_{t+1})] - S^{ne}_{t+1}$$

where:

Π^{ne}_{t+1} = the dividends that the home non-financial business sector plans this period to distribute next period.

p^{n}_{t+1} = the product price (in terms of the home country's unit of account) which the home non-financial business sector plans at the beginning of the current period to announce next period.

W_t = the wage rate (in the home unit of account) that the home non-financial business sector announces at the beginning of the current period. All people employed by the beginning of next period by a sector in the home country will receive that wage rate next period.

$\varepsilon^{\wedge n}_t$ = the current period forward exchange rate that the home non-financial business sector anticipates at the beginning of the current period (as it announces its current product price and the wage and as it decides current production, but before it learns current interest rates or exchange rates) will prevail during the current period.

p^{*n}_t = the price (in terms of the foreign unit of account) of the foreign (intermediate) good that the home non-financial business sector anticipates that the foreign business sector will announce this period.

p^{xn}_{t+1} = the price (expressed in terms of the home country's unit of account) of a unit of harvesting rights which the home non-financial business sector anticipates at the beginning of the current period will prevail next period.

p^{pn}_{t+1} = the price (expressed in terms of the home country's unit of account) of the right to emit a unit of pollution which the home non-financial business sector anticipates at the beginning of the current period will prevail next period.

$\bar{p}^{pdn}_{t+1} = \kappa^e (Q^\wedge_t - q^\wedge_t) - \mu^e(hN^{nde}_{t+1} - hN^{qde}_{t+1})$ = the amount of pollution rights the home non-financial business sector anticipates at the beginning of the current period that it will buy next period.

S^{ne}_{t+1} = the amount that the home non-financial business sector anticipates this period that it will save next period.

The amount the sector plans this period to save next period corresponds to the right-hand side of (3.8):

$$(3.8)\ S^{ne}_{t+1} = -p^n_{t+1}K^{nde}_{t+1} + p^{bn}_{t+1}B^{nse}_{t+1}.$$

Next, substitute the right-hand side of (3.8) for S^{nde}_{t+1} into (3.7); solve (3.5) for B^{nse}_{t+1} and substitute the expression for B^{nse}_{t+1} into (3.7); then, substitute the right-hand side of (3.6) for q^{ne}_{t+1} into (3.7) to obtain the following expression for the home non-financial business sector's anticipated future dividends.

$$(3.9)\ \Pi^{ne}_{t+1} = p^n_{t+1}\,[q^{ne}(hN^{nde}_{t+1}, q^{*ne}_{t+1}, K^{nde}_{t+1}, R^{xdn}_{t+1}, Q^\wedge_t - q^\wedge_t)] - W_t hN^{nde}_{t+1}$$

$$-\varepsilon^{\wedge n}_t p^{*n}_t q^{*ne}_{t+1} - p^{xe}_{t+1}R^{xdn}_{t+1}$$

$$-p^{pe}_{t+1}[\kappa^e (Q^\wedge_t - q^\wedge_t) - \mu^e(hN^{nde}_{t+1} - hN^{qde}_{t+1})] + p^n_{t+1}K^{nde}_{t+1}$$

$$-(1 + p^{bn}_{t+1})\{p_t[(K^{nde}_{t+1} - K^n_t) - Q_t]/p^{bn}_t + B^n_t\}.$$

Assuming that the objective of the home country's production sector is to maximize its present value, the production sector attempts to maximize $\Pi^n_t + \Pi^{ne}_{t+1}/(1 + r^{dn}_t)$, where r^{dn}_t denotes the rate of return the home non-financial business sector expects that the home country's household sector can earn in its next best market alternative, checkable deposits held at the home country's private financial sector, before that interest rate is established. Therefore we view the home non-financial business sector as maximizing:

$$(3.10)\ \Pi^n_t + \Pi^{ne}_{t+1}/(1 + r^d_t) = p_t[\ \bar{q}(h^q_t N^n_t, q^{*n}_t, K^n_t, R^x_t, q^\wedge_t)]$$

$$-W_{t-1}h^n_t N^n_t - \varepsilon^\wedge_{t-1}p^*_{t-1}q^{*n}_t - B^n_t - p^x_t R^x_t - p^p_t[\kappa q^\wedge_t - \mu(h^n_t N^n_t - h^q_t N^n_t)]$$

$$+\{p^n_{t+1}[q^{ne}(hN^{qde}_{t+1}, q^{*ne}_{t+1}, K^{nde}_{t+1}, R^{xdn}_{t+1}, Q^\wedge_t - q^\wedge_t)]$$

$$-W_t hN^{nde}_{t+1} - \varepsilon^{\wedge n}_t p^{*n}_t q^{*ne}_{t+1} - p^{xe}_{t+1}R^{xdn}_{t+1}$$

$$-p^{pe}_{t+1}[\kappa^e (Q^\wedge_t - q^\wedge_t) - \mu^e(hN^{nde}_{t+1} - hN^{qde}_{t+1})] + p^n_{t+1}K^{nde}_{t+1}$$

$$-(1+p^{bn}_{t+1})\{p_t[(K^{nde}_{t+1} - K^n_t) - Q_t]/p^{bn}_t + B^n_t\}\}/(1 + r^{dn}_t).$$

In this second step, the sector sets current period wages and prices dependent upon the current market prices for pollution and harvesting rights. As the price setter in the product market, the sector forecasts the market demand for its product in both the current period and the next. As the price leader in the labor market, the sector sets the wage rate it will pay its employees next period in light of its forecast of the net market supply of labor for the beginning of next period (i.e., the number of people it expects will be willing to work next period at the wage rate it sets minus the number of people it expects the home private financial sector and the home government will want to employ at that wage rate next period). Let the sector's forecast of the current market demand for its product be given by:

$$(3.11)\ q^{de}_t = q^{de}(\, p_t\,,\, \alpha\,),$$

where $q^{de}_1 < 0$ and α denotes a vector of shift parameters. Solving the inverse function for p_t yields:

$$(3.12)\ p_t = p(q^{de}_t, \alpha\,), \text{ where } \partial p/\partial q^{de}_t < 0,$$

which represents the maximum uniform price the sector expects it can value each alternative quantity of goods it produces during the current period. Consequently, the sector's anticipated current revenue function is then given by:

$$(3.13)\ R^e_t = p_t q^{de}_t = p(q^{de}_t, \alpha\,)\cdot q^{de}_t = \bar{R}\,(q^{de}_t, \alpha\,).$$

Because the sector must value all current production and real investment in a manner consistent with its forecasted demand curve, that is, since $q^{de}_t = q_t - [(K^{nde}_{t+1} - K_t) - Q_t]$, we combine all terms in expression (3.10) that involve p_t and value these terms within the appropriate revenue function $\bar{R}\,(\bullet, \alpha\,)$.

In a similar fashion, the sector must obtain a preliminary forecast of next period's demand for its product, q^{de}_{t+1}, from which we may derive the anticipated revenue function associated with next period's demand:

$$(3.14)\ R^e_{t+1} = p^n_{t+1} q^{de}_{t+1} = p^n(q^{de}_{t+1}, \beta)\cdot q^{de}_{t+1} = \bar{R}\,(q^{de}_{t+1}, \beta\,),$$

where $q^{de}_{t+1} = q^{ne}_{t+1} + K^{nde}_{t+1}$, that is, the sector plans that next period it will sell all that it produces next period plus the physical capital it holds at the beginning of that period.

Besides the forecasted demand curves for its product in the current and next periods, the sector also forecasts the market supply of labor. This market supply represents the number of people the sector anticipates it will be able to hire next period at the wage rate it sets taking into account both the number of people who would be willing to become employed at that wage and the number of people the home private financial and government sectors would be willing to employ at that wage. We assume that the sector forecasts that the net labor supply is positively related to the money wage it announces:

$$(3.15)\quad N^{se}_{t+1} = N^{se}(\, W_t \,, \gamma \,)$$

where γ denotes a vector of shift parameters. Taking the inverse function, we find:

$$(3.16)\quad W_t = W(\, N^{se}_{t+1} \,, \gamma \,) \text{ where } W_1 > 0 \text{ and } W_2 < 0$$

so that next period's forecasted labor cost function is given by:

$$(3.17)\quad C_{t+1} = W_t(\, N^{nde}_{t+1} \,, \gamma \,)\cdot N^{nde}_{t+1} = \bar{C}\,(\, N^{nde}_{t+1}, \gamma \,)$$

where $\bar{C}_1 = W_t + \partial W_t/\partial N^{nde}_{t+1}$ denotes the marginal factor (labor) cost and where we have taken into account the fact that the sector intends to set the wage rate so that it generates the number of employees that the sector wants to employ next period. The right-hand side of (3.17) must be substituted for $W_t\, N^{nde}_{t+1}$ in expression (3.10).

In light of the above discussion, the relevant expression for the maximization of the present value of the sector is given by:

$$(3.18)\quad \Pi^n_t + \Pi^{ne}_{t+1}/(\, 1 + r^d_t \,) =$$

$$\bar{R}\{\, \bar{q}(\, h^q_t\, N^n_t,\, q^{*n}_t,\, K^n_t,\, R^x_t,\, \hat{q}_t)$$

$$-[(1+p^{bn}_{t+1})/p^{bn}_t(\, 1 + r^d_t)]\cdot[(K^{nde}_{t+1} - K^n_t) - Q_t],\, \alpha\}$$

$$-W_{t-1}h^n_t N^n_t - \hat{\varepsilon}_{t-1} p^*_{t-1} q^{*n}_t - B^n_t - p^x_t R^x_t$$

$$-p^p_t[\kappa\, \hat{q}_t - \mu(\, h^n_t\, N^n_t - h^q_t\, N^n_t)]$$

$$+\{\, R^e[q^{ne}(hN^{qde}_{t+1},\, q^{*ne}_{t+1},\, K^{nde}_{t+1},\, R^{xdn}_{t+1},\, \hat{Q}_t - \hat{q}_t) + K^{nde}_{t+1} \,,\, \beta]$$

$$-h\cdot\, \bar{C}\,(N^{nde}_{t+1},\gamma) - \hat{\varepsilon}^n_t p^{*n}_t q^{*ne}_{t+1} - p^{xe}_{t+1} R^{xdn}_{t+1} \;\; -(1 + p^{bn}_{t+1}\,)B^n_t$$

$$-p^{pe}_{t+1}[\, \kappa^e\, (\hat{Q}_t - \hat{q}_t\,) - \mu^e(\, hN^{nde}_{t+1} - hN^{qde}_{t+1})]\,\}/(\, 1 + r^{dn}_t).$$

During the first phase of the non-financial business sector's decision-making in the current period (occurring in the second stage of the broader decision-making sequence and simultaneously with the determination of the prices of pollution and harvesting rights), the sector announces current period product price and the current period wage rate (labor is immobile across countries); it also decides the volume of its current period output, the number of hours it will use its current employees and the amounts of the renewable and non-renewable resources it will extract and use during the current period. These decisions must be made jointly with the sector's notional decisions as to how much of the imported factor to order this period, how much physical capital to accumulate during the period and how many people to employ by the beginning of next period. All of these announcements and notional decisions are made at the beginning of the current period before current interest rates and exchange rates are known. As the current period progresses, however, current period interest rates and exchange rates become jointly determined with the spending and portfolio and factor market decisions of the various sectors. Therefore, during the current period, after wages and prices and production have been decided, the non-financial businesses are free to alter the number of goods they order from foreign firms during the period, the amount of physical capital they accumulate this period and the number of people they want to employ by the beginning of next period. That is, they will be free to adjust these notional demands for inputs in light of current interest rates and exchange rates. In the present section, our interest focuses upon the first phase of this two-part decision-making process. The second phase of the non-financial business sector's decision-making occurs in stage three of the overall decision-making sequence, when current interest rates and exchange rates are revealed.

First-Order Conditions

Partially differentiating (3.18) with respect to each of the nine decision variables h^n_t, h^q_t, R^x_t, $\hat{q}_t$, K^{nde}_{t+1}, N^{nde}_{t+1}, N^{qde}_{t+1}, R^{xdn}_{t+1} and q^{*ne}_t and setting these partial derivatives equal to zero, yields an equal number of first-order conditions which are necessary for the maximization of (3.18).

Average Total Current Labor Hours

The first-order optimizing condition with respect to the average total number of hours the firms employ their current workers, h^{ne}_t, is presented by:

$$(3.19)\ p^p_t \mu' N^n_t = W_{t-1} \cdot N^n_t.$$

According to this condition, the sector will employ labor during the current period up to the point at which the value of the marginal product of labor in current pollution abatement, depicted by the left-hand side of (3.19), is equal to the marginal cost of adding an extra hour to the average number of hours worked by its current employees.

Average Current Labor Hours Spent on Home Goods Production

The first-order optimizing condition with respect to the average number of hours the firms employ their current workers for the purpose of producing home country goods (as opposed to pollution abatement), h^{qe}_t, is presented by:

(3.20) $\bar{R}_1 \cdot \bar{q}_1 \cdot N^n_t = p^p_t \mu' N^n_t$.

According to this condition, the sector will employ labor during the current period up to the point at which the marginal revenue product of labor in the production of home country goods, depicted on the left-hand side of (3.20), is equal to the value of the marginal product of labor in pollution abatement, which, from (3.19) must also equal the marginal cost of adding an extra hour of labor. Given the positive marginal product of labor in home-goods production, firms necessarily decide to sell an amount of privately-produced goods during the current period for which marginal revenue is positive. In other words, the firms necessarily set product price somewhere in the elastic portion of the forecast of the market demand curve for their product. This is the standard result for price-setters.

Demand for Current Use of the Renewable Resource

The first-order condition with respect to the amount of the renewable resource the sector demands during the current period is given by:

(3.21) $\bar{R}_1 \cdot \bar{q}_4 = p^x_t$.

The sector simply demands the renewable resource up to the point at which the marginal revenue product of that resource is equal to the "competitive" price of the right to extract a unit of the resource.

Demand for Current Use of the Non-Renewable Resource

The first-order condition with respect to the amount of the non-renewable resource the sector demands during the current period is given by:

(3.22) $(\bar{R}_1 \cdot \bar{q}_5 - p^p_t \kappa) - (R^e_1 q^{ne}_5 - p^{pe}_{t+1} \kappa^e)/(1 + r^{dn}_t) = 0$.

According to this condition, the home non-financial business sector should continue to extract and use the non-renewable resource during the current period as long as the marginal revenue product from this resource—net of the marginal cost of the right to add a unit to pollution during the period—is at least as great as the present value of the marginal revenue product (net of future pollution-right costs) the sector forgoes by using the non-renewable resource during the current period rather than in the future.

Notional Demand for the End-of-Period Stock of Physical Capital

The first-order condition with respect to the sector's demand for physical capital to be held at the beginning of next period is given by:

$$(3.23)\ [1/(1 + r^{dn}_t)]\cdot[-(1 + r^{bn}_t)\cdot \bar{R}_1 + R^e_1\cdot(q^{ne}_3 + 1)] = 0.$$

The first term inside the second set of brackets, $-(1 + r^{bn}_t)\cdot \bar{R}_1$, represents the marginal cost to the sector of adding one unit to its end-of-period stock of physical capital. In particular, as the sector adds one unit to K^{nde}_{t+1}, it sacrifices $\bar{R}_1$ in current sales revenue which it could have received if it had sold the unit rather than accumulating it. Since we are stipulating that the sector pays out as income to the owners of the factors of production during the current period an amount equal to the value of the sector's current production no matter whether it receives sales revenue of that amount, the $\bar{R}_1$ reduction in sales revenue in this case must be borrowed during the current period and repaid with interest next period. The present value of this marginal cost does not equal $\bar{R}_1$, in general, simply because the interest rate at which the sector anticipates the owners of the firm will be able to lend, r^{dn}_t, differs, in general, from the interest rate at which the non-financial business sector anticipates it will be able to borrow, r^{bn}_t.

The term $R^e_1(q^{ne}_3+1)$ in expression (3.23) denotes the marginal revenue the sector anticipates receiving next period as it sells not only the extra output that the extra unit of capital will enable it to produce next period, q^{ne}_3, but also the extra unit of capital itself. According to (3.21), the sector will add to its end-of-period stock of physical capital as long as the present value of the marginal revenue product of capital is at least as great as the present value of its marginal cost.

Notional Total Demand for Employees for Next Period

The first-order condition with respect to the total number of people the home non-financial business sector plans to employ next period is given by:

$$(3.24)\ \ [1/(1 + r^{dn}_t)]\cdot[p^{pe}_{t+1}\mu^{e'} - h\ \bar{C}_1] = 0.$$

The present-value maximizing production sector will add employees (by raising the wage rate it announces) until the value of the marginal product of an employee in pollution abatement falls to the level equal to the marginal factor cost of an extra employee.

Notional Demand for Home-Goods Employees for Next Period

The first-order condition with respect to the number of people the sector plans to employ next period for the purpose of producing home country goods is given by:

$$(3.25)\quad [1/(1 + r^{dn}{}_t)]\cdot[hR^e{}_1\cdot q^{ne}{}_1 - p^{pe}{}_{t+1}\mu^{e'}] = 0.$$

The present-value maximizing production sector will add employees for the purpose of producing home country goods until the marginal revenue product of an employee in that activity equals the value of the marginal product of labor in pollution abatement, which, from (3.25), must equal the marginal factor cost associated with another employee.

Notional Demand for the Imported Factor for Use Next Period

The first-order necessary condition with respect to the amount of the imported factor the home non-financial business sector plans to order from the foreign non-financial business sector this period (and pay for and use next period) is given by:

$$(3.26)\ [1/(1 + r^{dn}{}_t)]\cdot[R^e{}_1\cdot q^{ne}{}_2 - \varepsilon^{\wedge n}{}_t\cdot p^{*n}{}_t] = 0.$$

This condition states that in order to maximize its present value, the sector will add to its current period order for the imported factor as long as the (present value of the) marginal revenue product of that factor, $R^e{}_1\cdot q^{ne}{}_2$, is at least as great as the (present value of the) marginal cost of adding to that factor, where $\varepsilon^{\wedge n}{}_t\cdot p^{*n}{}_t$ denotes the price of a unit of the imported factor expressed in terms of the home country's unit of account.

Notional Demand for Next Period's Use of the Renewable Resource

The first-order condition associated with the amount of the renewable resource the sector plans this period to extract and use next period is given by:

$$(3.27)\quad [R^e{}_1 q^{ne}{}_4 - p^{xe}{}_{t+1}]/(1 + r^{dn}{}_t) = 0.$$

According to (3.27), the sector plans this period to use the renewable resource next period up to the point at which the present value of the marginal revenue product of that resource equals the present value of the anticipated future price of the right to extract and use a unit of the resource.

Current Period Wages, Prices, and Production

We are now prepared to discuss the effects of various parameters upon the home non-financial business sector's product-pricing, wage-setting, production and input decisions at the beginning of the current period before the sector learns current interest rates and exchange rates.

Number of Current Employees

The larger N^n_t happens to be at the beginning of the period, ceteris paribus, the sector reduces proportionately the average number of hours it intends to use these employees, keeping total labor hours unchanged. No other decision variable is affected because, in this model, total labor hours matters, but not the composition of those hours between number of workers and average hours worked.

Wage Rate Announced Last Period

The higher the wage rate, W_{t-1}, that the home non-financial business sector announced last period, the higher the current marginal cost of using current labor services. Therefore, ceteris paribus, from (3.19), the sector will tend to cut back on the total average number of hours it uses its current employees. As it does so, the value of the marginal product of labor in current pollution abatement rises (holding p^P_t unchanged, the rise is due to the increase in the marginal product of labor in pollution abatement) to equal the higher W_{t-1}.

From (3.20), the sector also reduces the average number of hours it uses its employees in the production of home country goods. As a result, both the marginal product of current labor in home goods production and current marginal revenue rise as the sector produces (and anticipates selling) less while using less labor. Therefore, $\overline{R}_1 \cdot \overline{q}_1$ rises to equal the higher value of W_{t-1}. Given the downward sloping forecasted demand curve for its product, the sector announces a higher current price for its product.

From (3.21) and (3.22), the rise in $\overline{R}_1$ raises the marginal revenue products of both the renewable and non-renewable resources. Consequently, the higher the wage rate the sector pays its current employees, the more the sector tends to substitute both the renewable and non-renewable resources for labor during the current period production of privately-produced goods in the home country.

According to (3.23), the rise in $\overline{R}_1$, which in this case results from an increase in W_{t-1}, directly raises the marginal (opportunity) cost of current real investment, thereby reducing the sector's end-of-period demand for physical capital. As the sector reduces its demand for physical capital for the end of the current period, the marginal product of that capital rises. In addition, since the drop in this end-of-current period stock adversely affects the sector's future output, next period's anticipated marginal revenue, R^e_1, also rises. The rise in R^e_1 produces several effects. From (3.22), it raises the present value of the marginal revenue product of the non-renewable resource in next period's production. This tends to offset, only partially, we assume, the more direct positive effect of the rise in $\bar{R}_1$ upon the demand for the non-renewable resource in the current period. Also, from (3.25), (3.26) and (3.27) respectively, the rise in R^e_1 raises the marginal revenue product of labor, the imported factor, and the renewable resource in the production of home goods next period. Consequently, the sector's notional demands for all three of these factors in next period's production increase. Furthermore, ceteris paribus, as the sector adds to its notional demand for labor in next period's production, the marginal product of labor in pollution abatement, $\mu^{e\prime}$, increases. As it does, from (3.24), the value of the marginal product of the total amount of labor rises as well, inducing the sector to announce a higher wage rate for next period than it would have otherwise. Therefore, we obtain the following effects of a change in W_{t-1} upon the home non-financial business sector's decision variables that are observable to an outsider:

$$\partial h^n_t/\partial W_{t-1}<0, \partial h^q_t/\partial W_{t-1}<0, \partial q_t/\partial W_{t-1}<0, \partial p_t/\partial W_{t-1}>0,\ \partial R^x{}_t/\partial W_{t-1}>0,\ \partial q\hat{}_t/\partial W_{t-1}>0,$$

$$\partial W_t/\partial W_{t-1}>0, \partial K^{nde}{}_{t+1}/\partial W_{t-1}<0, \partial N^{nde}{}_{t+1}/\partial W_{t-1}>0,\ \partial R^{xdn}{}_{t+1}/\partial W_{t-1}>0, \partial q^{*ne}{}_t/\partial W_{t-1}>0.$$

Initial Inventory of the Sector's Product

Ceteris paribus, the higher the sector's initial inventory of its product the more goods the sector is capable of selling during the current period at each level of current output. Given its forecast of the demand curve for its product, in order to actually sell the extra goods, the sector must reduce current product price below what it would have been otherwise, thereby reducing current marginal revenue of privately-produced goods in the home country, $\bar{R}_1$. This reduction causes the sector to reduce its demand for current hours spent producing home country goods as well as to reduce its current period demands for both the renewable and non-renewable resources. With W_{t-1} and the current price of the right to generate a unit of pollution, $p^p{}_t$, held constant, the marginal product of labor in pollution abatement must also remain unchanged; therefore, the sector reduces its demand for total hours of labor, $h^n{}_t$, by the same amount that it reduces its demand for labor for producing home country goods, $h^q{}_t$, thereby leaving unchanged the amount of labor it devotes to pollution abatement.

On the other hand, the fall in $\bar{R}_1$ means that the opportunity cost of current real investment in physical capital falls; therefore, the sector increases its notional end-of-period demand for physical capital. Consequently, the marginal revenue associated with next period's privately-produced goods in the home country falls, reducing, among other things, the anticipated marginal revenue product of next period's labor.[1] This causes the home non-financial business sector's notional demand for labor in goods-production for next period to fall, which in turn reduces the marginal product of labor in next period's pollution abatement. The sector tends to reduce the wage rate it announces this period as a result. The fall in the anticipated marginal revenue associated with next period's production of private goods in the home country also reduces both the anticipated value of the marginal product of the imported factor and the anticipated value of the marginal product of the renewable resource in next period's production. Therefore, we obtain the following effects of a change in Q_t upon the variables observable to an outsider:

$$\partial h^n_t/\partial Q_t < 0,\ \partial h^q_t/\partial Q_t < 0,\ \partial q_t/\partial Q_t < 0,\ \partial p_t/\partial Q_t < 0,\ \partial R^x{}_t/\partial Q_t < 0,\ \partial q^{\wedge}{}_t/\partial Q_t < 0,$$

$$\partial W_t/\partial Q_t < 0,\ \partial K^{nde}_{t+1}/\partial Q_t > 0,\ \partial N^{nde}_{t+1}/\partial Q_t < 0,\ \partial R^{xdn}_{t+1}/\partial Q_t < 0,\ \partial q^{*ne}_t/\partial Q_t < 0.$$

Number of Units of the Imported Factor Ordered Last Period

The greater the number of units of the imported factor ordered last period and delivered this period, q^{*n}_t, the greater the number of privately-produced goods the home non-financial business sector can produce this period using the same amount of labor. To sell the extra output, the sector would have to reduce current product price, thereby reducing current marginal revenue. The responses in the remaining variables will be analogous to those associated with an increase in the current beginning-of-period inventory of finished goods. Therefore, we obtain the following effects of a change in q^{*n}_t upon the variables observable to an outsider:

$$\partial h^n_t/\partial q^{*n}_t < 0,\ \partial h^q_t/\partial q^{*n}_t < 0,\ \partial q_t/\partial q^{*n}_t > 0,\ \partial p_t/\partial q^{*nt} < 0,\ \partial R^x{}_t/\partial q^{*n}_t < 0, \partial q^{\wedge}{}_t/\partial q^{*n}_t < 0,$$

$$\partial W_t/\partial q^{*n}_t < 0,\ \partial K^{nde}_{t+1}/\partial q^{*n}_t > 0, \partial N^{nde}_{t+1}/\partial q^{*n}_t < 0, \partial R^{xdn}_{t+1}/\partial q^{*n}_t < 0, \partial q^{*ne}_t/\partial q^{*n}_t < 0.$$

Initial Stock of Physical Capital

The higher the initial stock of physical capital, the more the sector can produce this period using the same amount of labor. The sector will again lower product price, reduce current labor hours and increase current output. The responses in the remaining decision variables will be analogous to those associated with an increase in the beginning inventory of finished goods. Therefore, we obtain the following effects of a change in K_t upon the variables observable to an outsider:

$$\partial h^n_t/\partial K_t < 0,\ \partial h^q_t/\partial K_t < 0,\ \partial q_t/\partial K_t > 0,\ \partial p_t/\partial K_t < 0,\ \partial R^x{}_t/\partial K_t < 0,\ \partial q^{\wedge}{}_t/\partial K_t < 0,$$

$$\partial W_t/\partial K_t < 0,\ \partial K^{nde}_{t+1}/\partial K_t > 0,\ \partial N^{nde}_{t+1}/\partial K_t < 0,\ \partial R^{xdn}_{t+1}/\partial K_t < 0,\ \partial q^{*ne}_t/\partial K_t < 0.$$

Initial Stock of the Non-Renewable Resource

Barring new discoveries, the amount of the non-renewable resource cannot be augmented. Therefore, we look at the effects of a **smaller** initial stock of the resource at the beginning of the current period. Holding constant the amount the sector plans to extract and use this period, the smaller $Q^{\wedge}_t$ happens to be, the smaller the amount of the resource the sector plans will be available next period. This not only raises the anticipated marginal physical product of the non-renewable resource next period, but also reduces the amount the sector plans to produce next period, thereby increasing next period's anticipated marginal revenue. From (3.22), the rise in R^e_1 increases the opportunity cost of using the non-renewable resource during the current period. As a result, the sector reduces its current demand for the non-renewable resource, which causes current production to fall and causes the sector to raise current market price for its product; current marginal revenue, $\bar{R}_1$, increases. From (3.20) and (3.21) respectively, the rise in $\bar{R}_1$ induces the sector to increase the number of hours its current employees spend producing goods and the amount of the renewable resource devoted to that effort; the sector substitutes both labor and the renewable resource for the non-renewable resource as the initial stock of that resource diminishes. Given the current price of pollution rights and the wage rate announced last period, as the sector applies more current labor time to the production of privately-produced home goods, the marginal product of labor in pollution abatement also rises; the sector increases total labor time to restore the marginal product of labor in pollution abatement to its original level.

From (3.25), the rise in R^e_1 increases the marginal revenue product of labor next period in producing privately-produced goods in the home country. Ceteris paribus, from (3.24), as the sector plans to increase its use of labor in this activity, the marginal product of labor increases in the area of pollution abatement since fewer labor resources would be devoted to it. Therefore the sector announces a higher wage rate this period in order to increase the number of people it employees next period.

From (3.23), the rise in R^e_1 increases the anticipated marginal revenue product of the physical capital the sector holds at the beginning of next period; ceteris paribus, the sector will channel a greater portion of current production toward building more capital goods.[2] From (3.26) and (3.27), the rise in R^e_1 also directly increases the marginal revenue products of both the renewable resource and the imported factor in next period's production, so that the sector's notional demands for these two factors increase as $Q^{\wedge}_t$ falls.

Therefore, we obtain the following effects of a change in the initial stock of the non-renewable resource, $Q^{\wedge}_t$, upon the variables observable to an outsider:

$$\partial h^n_t/\partial Q^{\wedge}_t < 0,\ \partial h^q_t/\partial Q^{\wedge}_t < 0,\ \partial q_t/\partial Q^{\wedge}_t > 0,\ \partial p_t/\partial Q^{\wedge}_t < 0,\ \partial R^x{}_t/\partial Q^{\wedge}_t < 0,\ \partial q^{\wedge}{}_t/\partial Q^{\wedge}_t > 0,$$

$$\partial W_t/\partial Q^{\wedge}_t < 0, \partial K^{nde}_{t+1}/\partial Q^{\wedge}_t < 0, \partial N^{nde}_{t+1}/\partial Q^{\wedge}_t < 0,\ \partial R^{xdn}_{t+1}/\partial Q^{\wedge}_t < 0,\ \partial q^{*ne}_t/\partial Q^{\wedge}_t < 0.$$

Pollution-Right Price

From (3.22), an increase in the price of the right to discharge a unit of pollutants during the current period reduces the current net marginal revenue product of the non-renewable resource. Therefore, the home sector reduces its current extraction and use of that resource. As it does, it also reduces current production of privately-produced goods in the home country and announces a higher price for these goods. These actions, in turn, raise the marginal revenue of current sales of home country goods, $\bar{R}_1$.

From (3.20) and (3.21) respectively, as $\bar{R}_1$ rises, it causes both the marginal revenue product of labor in producing privately-produced goods in the home country and the marginal revenue product of the renewable resource to increase; the sector will substitute labor and the renewable resource for the non-renewable resource in current production. From (3.23), the rise in $\bar{R}_1$ increases the opportunity cost of engaging in real investment during the current period. Therefore, the sector reduces its end-of-period demand for physical capital, thereby reducing, ceteris paribus, the amount of goods it will produce next period. This causes the marginal revenue associated with next period's production, R^e_1, to rise. From (3.26) and (3.27), this means that the marginal revenue products of both the imported factor and the renewable resource in next period's production increase; the sector increases its end-of-period notional demand for both factors.

From (3.21), the rise in R^e_1 also means that the anticipated marginal revenue product of labor in next period's production of privately-produced goods in the home country increases; therefore, the sector increases its notional demand for labor for the purpose of undertaking this activity next period, N^{qde}_{t+1}. From (3.24), as the sector adds to N^{qde}_{t+1}, ceteris paribus, it raises the marginal product of labor in pollution abatement next period. Therefore, the sector will announce a higher wage rate this period, W_t, to attract a larger total number of workers for next period.

The effects discussed to this point center upon those associated with the decrease in the net marginal revenue product of the non-renewable resource as p^P_t rises. However, the rise in p^P_t also directly affects the value of the marginal product of labor in pollution abatement during the current period. From (3.19), a rise in p^P_t raises the value of the marginal product of labor in this activity. The sector will add to the amount of labor it devotes to pollution abatement until the marginal product of that labor, μ', falls far enough so that the product $p^P_t \cdot \mu'$ returns to its original level. Since the sector also increases current labor for the purpose of producing home country goods, total labor hours are increasing in the current period equal to the sum of the increases in labor hours in these two activities. Therefore, we obtain the following effects of a change in p^P_t upon the sector's decision variables that are observable to an outsider:

$\partial h^n_t/\partial p^P_t > 0$, $\partial h^q_t/\partial p^P_t > 0$, $\partial q_t/\partial p^P_t < 0$, $\partial p_t/\partial p^P_t > 0$, $\partial R^x{}_t/\partial p^P_t > 0$, $\partial \hat{q}_t/\partial p^P_t < 0$,

$\partial W_t/\partial p^p_t > 0,\ \partial K^{nde}_{t+1}/\partial p^p_t < 0,\ \partial N^{nde}_{t+1}/\partial p^p_t > 0,\ \partial R^{xdn}_{t+1}/\partial p^p_t > 0,\ \partial q^{*ne}_t/\partial p^p_t > 0.$

Harvesting-Right Price of the Renewable Resource

From (3.21), as the current extraction price for the renewable resource rises, the home non-financial business sector reduces the quantity it demands of this resource. As it does so, current output of the privately-produced good in the home country falls and the current price the sector announces for the good rises. These actions raise the marginal revenue of current production, inducing the sector to substitute the non-renewable resource and labor for the renewable resource in current period production. In addition, the rise in $\bar{R}_1$ increases the marginal cost of current real investment, so that the sector reduces its end-of-period demand for physical capital. As a result, next period's marginal revenue products of the imported factor, the renewable resource and labor rise in producing privately-produced goods in the home country; therefore, the home non-financial business sector raises the wage rate it announces this period and increases its notional current demand for the imported factor, next period's demand for the renewable resource and its end-of-period demand for labor. Total labor hours during the current period rise by the same amount as the rise in current labor hours associated with the production of privately-produced goods in the home country so that the marginal product of labor in pollution abatement remains unchanged. Therefore, we obtain the following effects of a change in p^x_t upon the variables observable to an outsider:

$\partial h^n_t/\partial p^x_t > 0,\ \partial h^q_t/\partial p^x_t > 0,\ \partial q_t/\partial p^x_t < 0,\ \partial p_t/\partial p^x_t > 0,\ \partial R^x{}_t/\partial p^x_t < 0,\ \partial q^{\wedge}{}_t/\partial p^x_t > 0,$

$\partial W_t/\partial p^x_t > 0,\ \partial K^{nde}_{t+1}/\partial p^x_t < 0,\ \partial N^{nde}_{t+1}/\partial p^x_t > 0,\ \partial R^{xdn}_{t+1}/\partial p^x_t > 0,\ \partial q^{*ne}_t/\partial p^x_t > 0.$

Summary of Decisions Made by the Non-Financial Business Sectors in the Second Stage

The analysis directly above leads to the following decision functions for variables observable to an outsider for the home country's non-financial business sector. These decisions are made prior to the determination of current interest rates and exchange rates.

$$(3.28)\quad h^n_t = h^n_t(\underset{-}{N^n_t}, \underset{-}{W_{t-1}}, \underset{-}{Q_t}, \underset{-}{q^{*n}_t}, \underset{-}{K_t}, \underset{-}{Q^{\wedge}_t}, \underset{+}{p^p_t}, \underset{+}{p^x_t})$$

$$(3.29)\quad h^q_t = h^q_t(\underset{-}{W_{t-1}}, \underset{-}{Q_t}, \underset{-}{q^{*n}_t}, \underset{-}{K_t}, \underset{-}{Q^{\wedge}_t}, \underset{+}{p^p_t}, \underset{+}{p^x_t})$$

$$(3.30)\quad q_t = q_t(\underset{-}{W_{t-1}}, \underset{-}{Q_t}, \underset{+}{q^{*n}_t}, \underset{+}{K_t}, \underset{+}{Q^{\wedge}_t}, \underset{-}{p^p_t}, \underset{-}{p^x_t})$$

$$(3.31)\quad p_t = p_t(\underset{+}{W_{t-1}}, \underset{-}{Q_t}, \underset{-}{q^{*n}_t}, \underset{-}{K_t}, \underset{-}{Q^{\wedge}_t}, \underset{+}{p^P_t}, \underset{+}{p^x_t})$$

$$(3.32)\quad R^x_t = R^x_t(\underset{+}{W_{t-1}}, \underset{-}{Q_t}, \underset{-}{q^{*n}_t}, \underset{-}{K_t}, \underset{-}{Q^{\wedge}_t}, \underset{+}{p^P_t}, \underset{-}{p^x_t})$$

$$(3.33)\quad q^{\wedge}_t = q^{\wedge}_t(\underset{+}{W_{t-1}}, \underset{-}{Q_t}, \underset{-}{q^{*n}_t}, \underset{-}{K_t}, \underset{+}{Q^{\wedge}_t}, \underset{-}{p^P_t}, \underset{+}{p^x_t})$$

$$(3.34)\quad W_t = W_t(\underset{+}{W_{t-1}}, \underset{-}{Q_t}, \underset{-}{q^{*n}_t}, \underset{-}{K_t}, \underset{-}{Q^{\wedge}_t}, \underset{+}{p^P_t}, \underset{+}{p^x_t})$$

$$(3.35)\quad K^{nde}_{t+1} = K^{nde}_{t+1}(\underset{-}{W_{t-1}}, \underset{+}{Q_t}, \underset{+}{q^{*n}_t}, \underset{+}{K_t}, \underset{-}{Q^{\wedge}_t}, \underset{-}{p^P_t}, \underset{-}{p^x_t})$$

$$(3.36)\quad N^{nde}_{t+1} = N^{nde}_{t+1}(\underset{+}{W_{t-1}}, \underset{-}{Q_t}, \underset{-}{q^{*n}_t}, \underset{-}{K_t}, \underset{-}{Q^{\wedge}_t}, \underset{+}{p^P_t}, \underset{+}{p^x_t})$$

$$(3.37)\quad R^{xdn}_{t+1} = R^{xdn}_{t+1}(\underset{+}{W_{t-1}}, \underset{-}{Q_t}, \underset{-}{q^{*n}_t}, \underset{-}{K_t}, \underset{-}{Q^{\wedge}_t}, \underset{+}{p^P_t}, \underset{+}{p^x_t})$$

$$(3.38)\quad q^{*ne}_t = q^{*ne}_t(\underset{+}{W_{t-1}}, \underset{-}{Q_t}, \underset{-}{q^{*n}_t}, \underset{-}{K_t}, \underset{-}{Q^{\wedge}_t}, \underset{+}{p^P_t}, \underset{+}{p^x_t}).$$

An analogous set of functions can be derived for the foreign non-financial business sector.

$$(3.39)\quad h^{*n*}_t = h^{*n*}_t(\underset{-}{N^{*\,n*}_t}, \underset{-}{W^*_{t-1}}, \underset{-}{Q^*_t}, \underset{-}{q^{n*}_t}, \underset{-}{K^*_t}, \underset{-}{Q^{\wedge*}_t}, \underset{+}{p^P_t}, \underset{+}{p^x_t})$$

$$(3.40)\quad h^{*q*}_t = h^{*q*}_t(\underset{-}{W^*_{t-1}}, \underset{-}{Q^*_t}, \underset{-}{q^{n*}_t}, \underset{-}{K^*_t}, \underset{-}{Q^{\wedge*}_t}, \underset{+}{p^P_t}, \underset{+}{p^x_t})$$

$$(3.41)\quad q^*_t = q^*_t(\underset{-}{W^*_{t-1}}, \underset{-}{Q^*_t}, \underset{+}{q^{n*}_t}, \underset{+}{K^*_t}, \underset{+}{Q^{\wedge*}_t}, \underset{-}{p^P_t}, \underset{-}{p^x_t})$$

$$(3.42)\quad p^*_t = p^*_t(\underset{+}{W^*_{t-1}}, \underset{-}{Q^*_t}, \underset{-}{q^{n*}_t}, \underset{-}{K^*_t}, \underset{-}{Q^{\wedge*}_t}, \underset{+}{p^P_t}, \underset{+}{p^x_t})$$

$$(3.43)\quad R^{x*}_t = R^{x*}_t(\underset{+}{W^*_{t-1}}, \underset{-}{Q^*_t}, \underset{-}{q^{n*}_t}, \underset{-}{K^*_t}, \underset{-}{Q^{\wedge*}_t}, \underset{+}{p^P_t}, \underset{-}{p^x_t})$$

$$(3.44)\quad q^{\wedge*}_t = q^{\wedge*}_t(\underset{+}{W^*_{t-1}}, \underset{-}{Q^*_t}, \underset{-}{q^{n*}_t}, \underset{-}{K^*_t}, \underset{+}{Q^{\wedge*}_t}, \underset{-}{p^P_t}, \underset{+}{p^x_t})$$

(3.45) $W^*_t = W^*_t(W^*_{t-1}, Q^*_t, q^{n^*}_t, K^*_t, Q^{\wedge *}_t, p^p_t, p^x_t)$
$$\qquad\qquad + \quad - \quad - \quad - \quad - \quad + \quad +$$

(3.46) $K^{*n*de}_{t+1} = K^{*n*de}_{t+1}(W^*_{t-1}, Q^*_t, q^{n^*}_t, K^*_t, Q^{\wedge *}_t, p^p_t, p^x_t)$
$$\qquad\qquad\qquad\quad - \quad + \quad + \quad + \quad - \quad - \quad -$$

(3.47) $N^{*n*de}_{t+1} = N^{*n*de}_{t+1}(W^*_{t-1}, Q^*_t, q^{n^*}_t, K^*_t, Q^{\wedge *}_t, p^p_t, p^x_t)$
$$\qquad\qquad\qquad\quad + \quad - \quad - \quad - \quad - \quad + \quad +$$

(3.48) $R^{xdn^*}_{t+1} = R^{xdn^*}_{t+1}(W^*_{t-1}, Q^*_t, q^{n^*}_t, K^*_t, Q^{\wedge *}_t, p^p_t, p^x_t)$
$$\qquad\qquad\qquad\quad + \quad - \quad - \quad - \quad - \quad + \quad +$$

(3.49) $q^{n^*e}_t = q^{n^*e}_t(W^*_{t-1}, Q^*_t, q^{n^*}_t, K^*_t, Q^{\wedge *}_t, p^p_t, p^x_t).$
$$\qquad\qquad\quad + \quad - \quad - \quad - \quad - \quad + \quad +$$

The next step in our analysis involves solving for the equilibrium prices for pollution rights and harvesting rights.

Joint Solution for National Product and the Prices of Pollution and Harvesting Rights

In this model, the prices for pollution rights and harvesting rights are determined in stage two jointly with current period production, product-pricing and wage-setting by the world's non-financial business sectors, but before current interest rates or exchange rates are established.

Market for Pollution Rights

Define the home country's current demand for pollution rights, $\bar{P}^{pd}$, by:

(3.50) $\bar{P}^{pd} = \kappa q^{\wedge d}(W_{t-1}, Q_t, q^{*n}_t, K_t, Q^{\wedge}_t, p^p_t, p^x_t) -\mu(h^{nd}_t (\bullet) \cdot N^n_t - h^{qd}_t(\bullet) \cdot N^n_t)$
$$\qquad\qquad\qquad + \quad - \quad - \quad - \quad + \quad - \quad +$$

$$= \bar{P}^{pd}(W_{t-1}, Q_t, q^{*n}_t, K_t, Q^{\wedge}_t, p^p_t, p^x_t).$$
$$\qquad\qquad + \quad - \quad - \quad - \quad + \quad - \quad +$$

Note that $h^{nd}_t (\bullet)$ and $h^{qd}_t(\bullet)$ vary in the same direction unit for unit for changes in all parameters except p^p_t and W_{t-1}. Therefore the desired value of $\mu(\bullet)$ does not change unless either p^p_t or W_{t-1} change. As a result the home non-financial business sector's demand for pollution rights responds to a change in any parameter other than p^p_t or W_{t-1} in proportion to the corresponding change in $q^{\wedge d}_t$. If W_{t-1} were to rise, the amount of labor applied to pollution abatement must fall so that μ' may rise in accordance with (3.19). This effect upon $\bar{P}^{pd}$ reinforces the effect of a rise in W_{t-1} upon $q^{\wedge d}_t$. If, instead, p^p_t were to increase, the amount of labor applied to pollution abatement must rise so that μ' may fall in accordance with (3.19). This effect upon $\bar{P}^{pd}$ reinforces the effect of a rise in p^{p}_{t} upon $q^{\wedge d}_{t}$. Therefore, we easily obtain the signs of the partial derivatives of the home non-financial business sector's demand for pollution rights in the current period.

The foreign non-financial business sector's demand for pollution rights is derived analogously as:

$$(3.51)\ \bar{P}^{p*d} = \kappa^{*} q^{\wedge *d}(\underset{+}{W^{*}_{t-1}}, \underset{-}{Q^{*}_{t}}, \underset{-}{q^{n*}_{t}}, \underset{-}{K^{*}_{t}}, \underset{+}{Q^{\wedge *}_{t}}, \underset{-}{p^{p}_{t}}, \underset{+}{p^{x}_{t}}) - \mu^{*}(h^{*n*d}_{t}(\cdot)N^{*n*}_{t} - h^{*q*d}_{t}(\cdot)N^{*n*}_{t})$$

$$= \bar{P}^{p*d}(\underset{+}{W^{*}_{t-1}}, \underset{-}{Q^{*}_{t}}, \underset{-}{q^{n*}_{t}}, \underset{-}{K^{*}_{t}}, \underset{+}{Q^{\wedge *}_{t}}, \underset{-}{p^{p}_{t}}, \underset{+}{p^{x}_{t}}).$$

We assume that the prices of both pollution and harvesting rights are expressed in terms of the home country's unit of account. Therefore, the relevant prices for these rights from the point of view of the foreign non-financial business sector are $p^{p}_{t}/\varepsilon^{n*}_{t}$ and $p^{x}_{t}/\varepsilon^{n*}_{t}$ respectively, where ε^{n*}_{t} denotes the foreign non-financial business sector's anticipated value for the current period spot rate expressed as the value of the foreign unit of account in terms of home country's unit of account. Since ε^{n*}_{t} is unobservable to an outsider, we do not include it explicitly in the demand function. As discussed above, $\phi \cdot \bar{P}$ denotes the amount of pollution rights offered for sale by the international agent during the current period. Therefore the equilibrium condition for those rights, shown in Figure 3.1, may be written as:

$$(3.52)\ \phi \cdot \bar{P} = \bar{P}^{pd}(\underset{+}{W_{t-1}}, \underset{-}{Q_{t}}, \underset{-}{q^{*n}_{t}}, \underset{-}{K_{t}}, \underset{+}{Q^{\wedge}_{t}}, \underset{-}{p^{p}_{t}}, \underset{+}{p^{x}_{t}}) + \bar{P}^{p*d}(\underset{+}{W^{*}_{t-1}}, \underset{-}{Q^{*}_{t}}, \underset{-}{q^{n*}_{t}}, \underset{-}{K^{*}_{t}}, \underset{+}{Q^{\wedge *}_{t}}, \underset{-}{p^{p}_{t}}, \underset{+}{p^{x}_{t}}).$$

Figure 3.1 **Equilibrium Price of Pollution Rights**

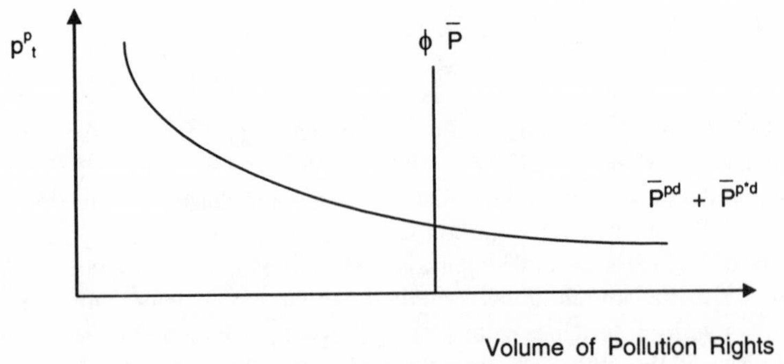

Market for Harvesting Rights

The home country's non-financial business sector's demand for harvesting rights for the renewable resource is shown by (3.32) above; we repeat it here for convenience:

$$(3.53)\ R^{xd}_t = R^{xd}_t(\underset{+}{W_{t-1}}, \underset{-}{Q_t}, \underset{-}{q^{*n}_t}, \underset{-}{K_t}, \underset{-}{Q^{\wedge}_t}, \underset{+}{p^P_t}, \underset{-}{p^x_t}).$$

The analogous demand function for the foreign non-financial business sector is then:

$$(3.54)\ R^{x*d}_t = R^{x*d}_t(\underset{+}{W^*_{t-1}}, \underset{-}{Q^*_t}, \underset{-}{q^{n*}_t}, \underset{-}{K^*_t}, \underset{-}{Q^{\wedge*}_t}, \underset{+}{p^P_t}, \underset{-}{p^x_t})$$

where, once again we have omitted the unobservable ε^{n*}_t. Therefore, the equilibrium condition for harvesting rights for the renewable resource during the current period, illustrated in Figure 3.2, is given by:

$$(3.55)\ G(S_t, \bar{P}) - \Omega = R^{xd}_t(\underset{+}{W_{t-1}}, \underset{-}{Q_t}, \underset{-}{q^{*n}_t}, \underset{-}{K_t}, \underset{-}{Q^{\wedge}_t}, \underset{+}{p^P_t}, \underset{-}{p^x_t})$$
$$+ R^{x*d}_t(\underset{+}{W^*_{t-1}}, \underset{-}{Q^*_t}, \underset{-}{q^{n*}_t}, \underset{-}{K^*_t}, \underset{-}{Q^{\wedge*}_t}, \underset{+}{p^P_t}, \underset{-}{p^x_t}).$$

Figure 3.2 **Equilibrium Price of Harvesting Rights for the Global Renewable Resource**

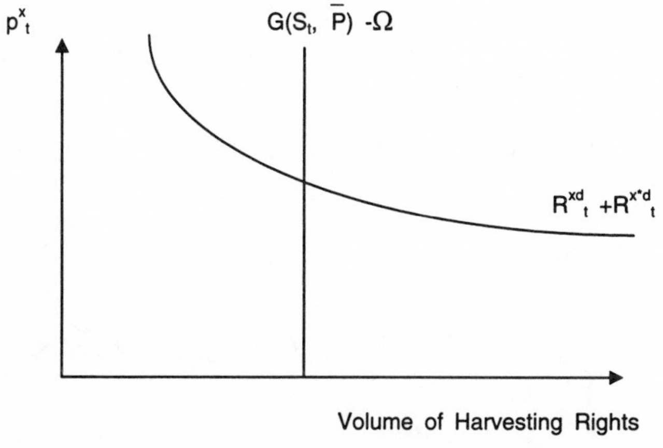

Simultaneous Solution for the Prices of Pollution and Harvesting Rights

We solve (3.52) and (3.55) simultaneously to obtain the equilibrium values for p^p_t and p^x_t. Assuming that the "own" price effects dominate the "cross" price effects in both markets, the analytic solution for these prices takes the following forms:

$$(3.56)\ p^p_t = p^p_t(W_{t-1}, Q_t, q^{*n}_t, K_t, Q^{\wedge}_t, W^*_{t-1}, Q^*_t, q^{n*}_t, K^*_t, Q^{\wedge*}_t, \phi \cdot \bar{P}, G(S_t, \bar{P}) - \Omega)$$
$$\quad\quad + \quad - \quad - \quad - \quad + \quad + \quad - \quad - \quad - \quad + \quad - \quad\quad -$$

$$(3.57)\ p^x_t = p^x_t(W_{t-1}, Q_t, q^{*n}_t, K_t, Q^{\wedge}_t, W^*_{t-1}, Q^*_t, q^{n*}_t, K^*_t, Q^{\wedge*}_t, \phi \cdot \bar{P}, G(S_t, \bar{P}) - \Omega).$$
$$\quad\quad + \quad - \quad - \quad - \quad - \quad + \quad - \quad - \quad - \quad - \quad - \quad\quad -$$

Reduced Form Equations for the Non-Financial Business Sectors' Decision Variables

Substituting (3.56) and (3.57) into (3.28)–(3.34) produces the following reduced form expressions for the corresponding home country variables:

$$(3.58)\ h^n_t = h^n_t(N^n_t, W_{t-1}, Q_t q^{*n}_t, K_t, Q^{\wedge}_t, W^*_{t-1}, Q^*_t, q^{n*}_t, K^*_t, Q^{\wedge*}_t, \phi \cdot \bar{P}, G(S_t, \bar{P}) - \Omega)$$
$$\quad - \quad - \quad - \quad - \quad - \quad - \quad + \quad - \quad - \quad - \quad ? \quad - \quad\quad -$$

$$(3.59)\ h^q_t = h^q_t(W_{t-1}, Q_t, q^{*n}_t, K_t, Q^{\wedge}_t, W^*_{t-1}, Q^*_t, q^{n*}_t, K^*_t, Q^{\wedge*}_t, \phi \cdot \bar{P}, G(S_t, \bar{P}) - \Omega)$$
$$\quad - \quad - \quad - \quad - \quad - \quad + \quad - \quad - \quad - \quad ? \quad - \quad\quad -$$

$$(3.60)\ q_t = q_t(W_{t-1}, Q_t, q^{*n}_t, K_t, Q^{\wedge}_t, W^*_{t-1}, Q^*_t, q^{n*}_t, K^*_t, Q^{\wedge*}_t, \phi \cdot \bar{P}, G(S_t, \bar{P}) - \Omega)$$
$$\quad - \quad - \quad + \quad + \quad + \quad - \quad + \quad + \quad + \quad ? \quad + \quad\quad +$$

$$(3.61)\ p_t = p_t(W_{t-1}, Q_t, q^{*n}_t, K_t, Q^{\wedge}_t, W^*_{t-1}, Q^*_t, q^{n*}_t, K^*_t, Q^{\wedge*}_t, \phi \cdot \bar{P}, G(S_t, \bar{P}) - \Omega)$$
$$\quad + \quad - \quad - \quad - \quad - \quad + \quad - \quad - \quad - \quad ? \quad - \quad\quad -$$

$$(3.62)\ R^x_t = R^x_t(W_{t-1}, Q_t q^{*n}_t, K_t, Q^{\wedge}_t, W^*_{t-1}, Q^*_t, q^{n*}_t, K^*_t, Q^{\wedge*}_t, \phi \cdot \bar{P}, G(S_t, \bar{P}) - \Omega)$$
$$\quad + \quad - \quad - \quad - \quad - \quad - \quad + \quad + \quad + \quad ? \quad + \quad\quad +$$

$$(3.63)\ q^{\wedge}_t = q^{\wedge}_t(W_{t-1}, Q_t, q^{*n}_t, K_t, Q^{\wedge}_t, W^*_{t-1}, Q^*_t, q^{n*}_t, K^*_t, Q^{\wedge*}_t, \phi \cdot \bar{P}, G(S_t, \bar{P}) - \Omega)$$
$$\quad + \quad - \quad - \quad - \quad + \quad - \quad + \quad + \quad + \quad ? \quad + \quad\quad +$$

$$(3.64)\ W_t = W_t(W_{t-1}, Q_t q^{*n}_t, K_t, Q^{\wedge}_t, W^*_{t-1}, Q^*_t, q^{n*}_t, K^*_t, Q^{\wedge*}_t, \phi \cdot \bar{P}, G(S_t, \bar{P}) - \Omega)$$
$$\quad + \quad - \quad - \quad - \quad - \quad + \quad - \quad - \quad - \quad ? \quad - \quad\quad -$$

$$(3.65)\ K^{nde}_{t+1} = K^{nde}_{t+1}(W_{t-1}, Q_t, q^{*n}_t, K_t, Q^{\wedge}_t, W^*_{t-1}, Q^*_t, q^{n*}_t, K^*_t, Q^{\wedge*}_t, \phi \cdot \bar{P}, G(S_t, \bar{P}) - \Omega)$$
$$\quad - \quad + \quad + \quad + \quad - \quad - \quad + \quad + \quad + \quad ? \quad + \quad\quad +$$

$$(3.66)\ N^{nde}_{t+1}=N^{nde}_{t+1}(\underset{+}{W_{t-1}},\underset{-}{Q_t},\underset{-}{q^{*n}_t},\underset{-}{K_t},\underset{-}{\hat{Q}_t},\underset{+}{W^*_{t-1}},\underset{-}{Q^*_t},\underset{-}{q^{n*}_t},\underset{-}{K^*_t},\underset{?}{\hat{Q}^*_t},\underset{-}{\phi\cdot\bar{P}},\underset{-}{G(S_t,\bar{P})-\Omega})$$

$$(3.67)\ R^{xdn}_{t+1}=R^{xdn}_{t+1}(\underset{+}{W_{t-1}},\underset{-}{Q_t},\underset{-}{q^{*n}_t},\underset{-}{K_t},\underset{-}{\hat{Q}_t},\underset{+}{W^*_{t-1}},\underset{-}{Q^*_t},\underset{-}{q^{n*}_t},\underset{-}{K^*_t},\underset{?}{\hat{Q}^*_t},\underset{-}{\phi\cdot\bar{P}},\underset{-}{G(S_t,\bar{P})-\Omega})$$

$$(3.68)\ q^{*ne}_t=q^{*ne}_t(\underset{+}{W_{t-1}},\underset{-}{Q_t},\underset{-}{q^{*n}_t},\underset{-}{K_t},\underset{-}{\hat{Q}_t},\underset{+}{W^*_{t-1}},\underset{-}{Q^*_t},\underset{-}{q^{n*}_t},\underset{-}{K^*_t},\underset{?}{\hat{Q}^*_t},\underset{-}{\phi\cdot\bar{P}},\underset{-}{G(S_t,\bar{P})-\Omega}).$$

In expression (3.58), we assume that the direct effect of a change in the money wage announced last period in the home country, W_{t-1}, upon the total number of hours the home non-financial business sector decides to use its current employees dominates the indirect effect upon that decision stemming from the changes in the current market prices of pollution and harvesting rights induced by a change in W_{t-1}. In expressions (3.58), (3.59) and (3.65)–(3.68), we assume that the direct effects of a change in the initial stock of the home country's non-renewable resource, $\hat{Q}_t$, upon the home non-financial business sector's employment, production, pricing and real resource consumption decisions dominate the indirect effects upon these decisions stemming from the changes in the market prices of pollution and harvesting rights induced by a change in $\hat{Q}_t$. In expression (3.60), we assume that the direct effect of a change in the home non-financial business sector's initial inventory of final goods, Q_t, upon current production by that sector, q_t, dominates the indirect (and opposing) effects upon current production stemming from the changes in the market prices of pollution and harvesting rights induced by a change in Q_t. In expression (3.62), we assume that if both the price of harvesting rights and the price of pollution rights change for the same reason (in particular, due to a change in W^*_{t-1}, Q^*_{t-1}, q^{n*}_t, K^*_t, $\phi\cdot\bar{P}$, or $G(S_t, \bar{P})-\Omega$), the effects of a change in the price of harvesting rights upon the home non-financial business sector's demand for harvesting rights, R^x_t, dominates the effects of change in the price of pollution rights. In expression (3.63), we assume that if both the price of harvesting rights and the price of pollution rights change for the same reason (in particular, due to a change in W^*_{t-1}, Q^*_{t-1}, q^{n*}_t, K^*_t, $\phi\cdot\bar{P}$, or $G(S_t, \bar{P})-\Omega$), the effects of a change in the price of pollution rights upon the home non-financial business sector's demand for pollution rights, $\kappa\hat{q}_t$, dominates the effects of change in the price of harvesting rights. An analogous set of reduced form equations for the foreign non-financial business sector's decision variables are found by substituting (3.56) and (3.57) into (3.39)–(3.45) and making an analogous set of assumptions about relative effects:

$$(3.69)\ h^{*n*}_t=h^{*n*}_t(\underset{-}{N^{*n*}_t},\underset{-}{W^*_{t-1}},\underset{-}{Q^*_t},\underset{-}{q^{n*}_t},\underset{-}{K^*_t},\underset{-}{\hat{Q}^*_t},\underset{+}{W_{t-1}},\underset{-}{Q_t},\underset{-}{q^{*n}_t},\underset{-}{K_t},\underset{?}{\hat{Q}_t},\underset{-}{\phi\cdot\bar{P}},\underset{-}{G(S_t,\bar{P})-\Omega})$$

$$(3.70)\ h^{*q*}_t = h^{*q*}_t(W^*_{t-1}, Q^*_t, q^{n*}_t, K^*_t, Q^{\wedge*}_t, W_{t-1}, Q_t, q^{*n}_t, K_t, Q^{\wedge}_t, \phi\cdot\bar{P}, G(S_t, \bar{P})\text{-}\Omega)$$

\- - - - - + - - - ? - -

$$(3.71)\ q^*_t = q^*_t(W^*_{t-1}, Q^*_t, q^{n*}_t, K^*_t, Q^{\wedge*}_t, W_{t-1}, Q_t, q^{*n}_t, K_t, Q^{\wedge}_t, \phi\cdot\bar{P}, G(S_t, \bar{P})\text{-}\Omega)$$

\- - + + + - + + + ? + +

$$(3.72)\ p^*_t = p^*_t(W^*_{t-1}, Q^*_t, q^{n*}_t, K^*_t, Q^{\wedge*}_t, W_{t-1}, Q_t, q^{*n}_t, K_t, Q^{\wedge}_t, \phi\cdot\bar{P}, G(S_t, \bar{P})\text{-}\Omega)$$

\+ - - - - + - - - ? - -

$$(3.73)\ R^{x*}_t = R^{x*}_t(W^*_{t-1}, Q^*_t, q^{n*}_t, K^*_t, Q^{\wedge*}_t, W_{t-1}, Q_t, q^{*n}_t, K_t, Q^{\wedge}_t, \phi\cdot\bar{P}, G(S_t, \bar{P})\text{-}\Omega)$$

\+ - - - - - + + + ? + +

$$(3.74)\ q^{\wedge*}_t = q^{\wedge*}_t(W^*_{t-1}, Q^*_t, q^{n*}_t, K^*_t, Q^{\wedge*}_t, W_{t-1}, Q_t, q^{*n}_t, K_t, Q^{\wedge}_t, \phi\cdot\bar{P}, G(S_t, \bar{P})\text{-}\Omega)$$

\+ - - - + - + + + ? + +

$$(3.75)\ W^*_t = W^*_t(W^*_{t-1}, Q^*_t, q^{n*}_t, K^*_t, Q^{\wedge*}_t, W_{t-1}, Q_t, q^{*n}_t, K_t, Q^{\wedge}_t, \phi\cdot\bar{P}, G(S_t, \bar{P})\text{-}\Omega)$$

\+ - - - - + - - - ? - -

$$(3.76)\ K^{*n*de}_{t+1} = K^{*n*de}_{t+1}(W^*_{t-1}, Q^*_t, q^{n*}_t, K^*_t, Q^{\wedge*}_t, W_{t-1}, Q_t, q^{*n}_t, K_t, Q^{\wedge}_t, \phi\ \bar{P}, G(S_t, \bar{P})\text{-}\Omega)$$

\- + + + - - + + + ? + +

$$(3.77)\ N^{*n*de}_{t+1} = N^{*n*de}_{t+1}(W^*_{t-1}, Q^*_t, q^{n*}_t, K^*_t, Q^{\wedge*}_t, W_{t-1}, Q_t, q^{*n}_t, K_t, Q^{\wedge}_t, \phi\ \bar{P}, G(S_t, \bar{P})\text{-}\Omega)$$

\+ - - - - + - - - ? - -

$$(3.78)\ R^{xdn*}_{t+1} = R^{xdn*}_{t+1}(W^*_{t-1}, Q^*_t, q^{n*}_t, K^*_t, Q^{\wedge*}_t, W_{t-1}, Q_t, q^{*n}_t, K_t, Q^{\wedge}_t, \phi\cdot\bar{P}, G(S_t, \bar{P})\text{-}\Omega)$$

\+ - - - - + - - - ? - -

$$(3.79)\ q^{n*e}_t = q^{n*e}_t(W^*_{t-1}, Q^*_t, q^{n*}_t, K^*_t, Q^{\wedge*}_t, W_{t-1}, Q_t, q^{*n}_t, K_t, Q^{\wedge}_t, \phi\cdot\bar{P}, G(S_t, \bar{P})\text{-}\Omega).$$

\+ - - - - + - - - ? - -

The importance of (3.56) and (3.57) is that a change in the initial stock of any real asset in either country or a change in the wage rate prevailing in either country affects current output, employment, wages and product prices in both countries through their effects upon the current period prices of pollution and harvesting rights. For instance, a reduction in the initial amount of the non-renewable resource held by the home country, i.e., a reduction in $Q^{\wedge}_t$, has a direct positive effect upon home country employment, product prices and wages and a direct negative effect upon current production of home country goods. However the reduction in $Q^{\wedge}_t$ also causes the home country to increase its demand for harvesting rights and reduce its demand for pollution rights, thereby causing the price of harvesting rights to rise and the price of pollution rights to fall. While the net indirect effects upon the foreign country's employment, production, wages and product prices are not clear, it is the case, nevertheless, that the changes in the prices of these rights potentially affect the levels of these variables. More important, the rise in p^x and the fall in p^p induces the foreign non-financial business sector to substitute its own non-renewable resource for the renewable resource in current period production.

End-of-Period Stock of the Renewable Resource

As mentioned above, the end-of-period stock of the renewable resource, S_{t+1}, is given by:

(3.80) $S_{t+1} = S_t + \Omega$

where, letting τ represent the target rate of growth in the renewable resource, $\tau \cdot S_t = \Omega$. Therefore, "maintainability" is potentially accomplished in this model in the sense that the renewable factor can grow without bound over time even though pollution is generated each period and even though a portion of the renewable resource is extracted each period. At least in principle, this permits the substitution of the renewable resource (as well as labor and physical capital) for the non-renewable resources in future production as the non-renewable resources become depleted. However, in general, over time, depletion of the non-renewable resources will result in higher factor prices and higher product prices. Relative prices will also change in general, since the production functions for public and private goods need not be uniform—nor do the production functions across countries need to be uniform. Real output need not remain unchanged.

National Income, National Product, and Disposable Income

The Home Country

By this point in our analysis, we have determined gross (and net) national product, national income, personal income and disposable income in both countries. In this model, since we ignore depreciation, gross and net production are necessarily equal. Gross national product is defined as the sum of the values added by each of the home country's sectors, where a sector's value added amounts to the value of the goods it produces minus the value of the goods and services it buys from other sectors.

Value Added by the Home Government Sector

In the present model, the households in each country ultimately direct their governments in terms of deciding the volume of public goods to produce. As a first-order approximation, the level of taxes levied by each government therefore reflects the government's economic contribution in the production of public goods. However, to the extent that the government receives income from the operations of its central bank and to the extent that it receives revenue from the international agent's sale of pollution and harvesting rights to its non-financial business sector, the government is able to charge less in taxes than the value of the public goods it produces. On the other hand, since the level of taxes was set in the immediately preceding period before current expenses in providing public goods during the current period become known, the sum of the government's tax and non-tax revenue during the current period overstates the value of its production of public goods by the amount of government saving, $S^g{}_t$, defined as:

$$(3.81)\ S^g{}_t = T_t + \Pi^c{}_t + p^x{}_t R^x{}_t + p^p{}_t\ \bar{P}_t - W_{t-1} h^g{}_t N^g{}_t - B^g{}_t.$$

Therefore, the government's production statement may be represented by:

$$(3.82)\ T_t + \Pi^c{}_t + p^x{}_t R^x{}_t + p^p{}_t\ \bar{P}_t\ - S^g{}_t = W_{t-1} h^g{}_t N^g{}_t\ + B^g{}_t.$$

The left-hand side of (3.82) represents the value of current production by the home government, while the right-hand side denotes the charges against that value. The interest paid by the government, however, represents intermediate services provided by other sectors so that the value added by the government may be represented as:

$$(3.83)\ VA^g{}_t = T_t + \Pi^c{}_t + p^x{}_t R^x{}_t + p^p{}_t\ \bar{P}^p{}_t - S^g{}_t - B^g{}_t = W_{t-1} h^g{}_t N^g{}_t\ .$$

Value Added by the Home Central Bank

The value added by the home country's central bank is equal to the sum of its interest income. The central bank is viewed as distributing its earnings entirely to the home government sector.

$$(3.84)\ VA^c{}_t = \rho_{t-1} A_t + B^c{}_t + \varepsilon_t B^{*c}{}_t = \Pi^c{}_t.$$

Value Added by the Home Private Financial Sector

The value added by the home private financial sector equals the interest it receives during the current period on home and foreign bonds less the interest it pays to the home central bank on advances. Its value added is paid to the households in the home country as wage income, interest income and dividends:

$$(3.85)\ VA^f{}_t = B^f{}_t + \varepsilon\hat{}_{t-1} B^{*f}{}_t - \rho_{t-1} A_t = W_{t-1} h^f{}_t N^f{}_t + r^d{}_{t-1} D_t + \Pi^f{}_t.$$

For simplicity, we assume that the home country's households hold a fixed number of non-marketable equity shares issued by the home financial sector and a fixed number of non-marketable shares issued by the home non-financial business sector; the foreign household sector holds a fixed number of non-marketable shares issued by the foreign financial sector and a fixed number of shares issued by the foreign non-financial business sector. The foreign household sector does not hold any shares in the home country's businesses and the home household sector does not hold any shares in foreign businesses.

Value Added by the Home Non-Financial Business Sector

The value of production by the home non-financial business sector is equal to the value of the privately-produced goods produced in the home country:

(3.86) $p_t q_t = \hat{\varepsilon}_{t-1} p^*_{t-1} q^{*n}_t + B^n_t + p^x_t R^x_t + p^p_t \bar{P}^p_t + W_{t-1} h^n_t N^n_t + \Pi^n_t$.

A portion of the value of this production is paid to other non-household sectors for goods and services purchased from them. Two services purchased from the international body are the rights to pollute and to extract some of the renewable resource. Another service is the use of borrowed funds, so the interest payments by the sector are not considered part of its value added. The difference between the value of the sector's production and its purchases from other (non-household) sectors is the value added by the non-financial business sector:

(3.87) $VA^n_t = p_t q_t - \hat{\varepsilon}_{t-1} p^*_{t-1} q^{*n}_t - B^n_t - p^x_t R^x_t - p^p_t \bar{P}^p_t = W_{t-1} h^n_t N^n_t + \Pi^n_t$.

The sector's value added is paid to the households in the home country as wages and dividends.

Gross and Net National Product

Summing the values added by each of the home country's sectors on the sources side yields a measure for gross (and net) national product:

$$
\begin{aligned}
(3.88)\ GNP_t &= VA^g_t + VA^c_t + VA^f_t + VA^n_t \\
&= W_{t-1} h^g_t N^g_t + (\rho_{t-1} A_t + B^c_t + \varepsilon_t B^{*c}_t) + (B^f_t + \hat{\varepsilon}_{t-1} B^{*f}_t - \rho_{t-1} A_t) \\
&\quad + (p_t q_t - \hat{\varepsilon}_{t-1} p^*_{t-1} q^{*n}_t - p^x_t R^x_t - p^p_t \bar{P}^p_t - B^n_t) \\
&= (p_t q_t - \hat{\varepsilon}_{t-1} p^*_{t-1} q^{*n}_t - p^x_t R^x_t - p^p_t \bar{P}^p_t) + (W_{t-1} h^g_t N^g_t + B^g_t) + (\varepsilon_t B^{*c}_t + \hat{\varepsilon}_{t-1} B^{*f}_t - B^r_t)
\end{aligned}
$$

where we have used the identity $B^g_t - B^r_t = B^c_t + B^f_t - B^n_t$, where B^r_t denotes interest income paid to the rest of the world by the home country. According to (3.88), GNP in the home country is equal to the value of production by the home government and the home non-financial business sector, $W_{t-1} h^g_t N^g_t + B^g_t + p_t q_t$, less the value of imports from the foreign country and from the international agent, $\hat{\varepsilon}_{t-1} p^*_{t-1} q^{*n}_t + p^x_t R^x_t + p^p_t \bar{P}^p_t$, plus net factor income (which in the present model consists entirely of net interest payments) received from abroad, $\varepsilon_t B^{*c}_t + \hat{\varepsilon}_{t-1} B^{*f}_t - B^r_t$.

The value of current output by the home non-financial business sector, $p_t q_t$, necessarily equals the value of its sales to other sectors plus the value of the change in its inventories of all goods:

$$(3.89)\ p_t q_t = p_t c^d_t + p_t(K^{gd}_{t+1} - K^g_t) + p_{t-1} q^{n*}_t$$
$$+ [\, p_t(K^{nd}_{t+1} - K^n_t) + p_t(Q_{t+1} - Q_t) - (v_t - p^p_t \kappa)\hat{q}_t \,]$$

where the four terms on the right-hand side of (3.89) denote, respectively, the (planned and actual) purchases of home country goods by the home household sector, the actual purchases of home country goods by the home government sector, the purchases of home country goods by the foreign non-financial business sector and the "gross" (and "net," since we ignore depreciation) investment expenditure by the home non-financial business sector. The actual investment by this sector equals its planned accumulation to physical capital plus its ex post (but unplanned, if $Q_{t+1} \neq 0$) accumulation of inventories of final goods minus the value of the depletion of its non-renewable resource. Because no explicit market exists for the non-renewable resource, we impute a value to a unit of this resource by calculating the difference between (a) the value of the marginal product of the factor, v_t, and (b) the market price of the right to generate a unit of pollution times the extra pollution generated by the extraction and use of an extra unit of the non-renewable resource, $p^p_t \kappa$; the resulting imputed value of a unit of the non-renewable resource, $v_t - p^p_t \kappa$, is then multiplied by the quantity of the resource extracted to obtain the "market" value of the reduction in inventory. It is important to note that according to (3.22), for the optimizing non-financial business sector, this imputed value equals the present value of the marginal product forgone by extracting the resource. Substituting the right-hand side of (3.89) for $p_t q_t$ in (3.88) yields the following "expenditures approach" measure of the home country's GNP:

$$(3.90)\ GNP_t = p_t c^d_t + [p_t(K^{gd}_{t+1} - K^g_t) + W_{t-1} h^g_t N^g_t + B^g_t]$$
$$+ [p_t(K^{nd}_{t+1} - K^n_t) + p_t(Q_{t+1} - Q_t) - (v_t - p^p_t \kappa)\hat{q}_t]$$
$$+ (p_{t-1} q^{n*}_t - \hat{\varepsilon}_{t-1} p^*_{t-1} q^{*n}_t - p^x_t R^x_t - p^p_t \bar{P}^p_t) + (\varepsilon_t B^{*c}_t + \hat{\varepsilon}_{t-1} B^{*f}_t - B^r_t)$$

where: (i) the three terms in the first line on the right-hand side correspond, respectively, to household consumption, government expenditure on home country goods, wages and interest, and gross (and net) investment by the non-financial business sector, $p_t(K^{nd}_{t+1} - K^n_t) + p_t(Q_{t+1} - Q_t) - (v_t - p^p_t \kappa)\hat{q}_t = p_t i_t$; and (ii) the two terms in the second line correspond, respectively, to net exports of goods and services, $p_{t-1}q^{n*}_t - \hat{\varepsilon}_{t-1}p^*_{t-1}q^{*n}_t - p^x_tR^x_t - p^p_t\,\bar{P}^p_t = p_tx_t$, plus net factor income received from abroad, $\varepsilon_tB^{*c}_t + \hat{\varepsilon}_{t-1}B^{*f}_t - B^r_t$. Therefore, we have:

$$(3.91)\ GNP_t = p_tc_t + p_ti_t + [p_t(K^{gd}_{t+1} - K^g_t) + W_{t-1}h^g_tN^g_t + B^g_t]$$

$$+ p_tx_t + (\varepsilon_tB^{*c}_t + \hat{\varepsilon}_{t-1}B^{*f}_t - B^r_t)$$

in which GNP is now represented by consumption spending plus investment spending plus government spending plus net exports plus net interest income received from abroad. On the "uses" side, GNP_t is equal to:

$$(3.92)\ GNP_t = W_{t-1}h^g_tN^g_t + \Pi^c_t + W_{t-1}h^f_tN^f_t + r^d_{t-1}D_t + \Pi^f_t + W_{t-1}h^n_tN^n_t + \Pi^n_t$$

$$= W_{t-1}h_tN_t + r^d_{t-1}D_t + (\Pi^c_t + \Pi^f_t + \Pi^n_t)$$

where $W_{t-1}h_tN_t = W_{t-1}h^g_tN^g_t + W_{t-1}h^f_tN^f_t + W_{t-1}h^n_tN^n_t$. According to (3.92), the value of GNP equals the sum of wages; interest paid to the households; plus the profits of the central bank, the private financial sector and the non-financial business sector.

Gross Domestic Product

Since the sum inside parentheses constituting the fifth term on the right-hand side of (3.91) denotes the net income earned from the rest of the world, gross domestic product may be represented by:

$$(3.93)\ GDP_t = p_tc^d_t + p_ti_t + [p_t(K^{gd}_{t+1} - K^g_t) + W_{t-1}h^g_tN^g_t + B^g_t] + p_tx_t.$$

National Income, Personal Income and Disposable Income

National income in the home country, NI_t, is defined as the total income currently earned by the home country's nationals. In this model, it equals the value of GNP (and NNP):

$$(3.94)\ NI_t = W_{t-1}h_tN^g_t + W_{t-1}h^f_tN^f_t + W_{t-1}h^n_tN^n_t + r^d_{t-1}D_t + \Pi^f_t + \Pi^n_t$$

$$= W_{t-1}h_tN_t + r^d_{t-1}D_t + \Pi^c_t + \Pi^f_t + \Pi^n_t.$$

While expenditures by the home non-financial business sector to obtain pollution and harvesting rights are not part of the home country's national income, all labor earnings, including those associated with pollution abatement, are included in national income.

Since the only component of the home country's national income that is not currently received by the home country's household sector is the income of the home central bank (which is distributed instead to the government), income currently received by the home country's households in this model, that is, personal income in the home country, PI_t, is given by:

$$(3.95)\ PI_t = W_{t-1}h_tN_t + r^d_{t-1}D_t + \Pi^f_t + \Pi^n_t.$$

Disposable income in the home country, DI_t, is defined as home personal income less personal taxes in the home country:

$$(3.96)\quad \bar{Y}_t = W_{t-1}h_tN_t + r^d_{t-1}D_t + \Pi^f_t + \Pi^n_t - T_t.$$

Ceteris paribus, the payments for harvesting rights and pollution rights by the home non-financial business sector reduces the dividends it pays the home household sector, thereby reducing the home country's disposable income. However, these payments to the international agent are passed on to the home government, which, ceteris paribus, reduces the tax bill of the home country's household sector by the same amount. Therefore, in principle, the payments for harvesting rights and pollution rights produce no net effect upon the disposable income of the household sector; the last two terms on the right-hand side of (3.96) are both smaller by the amount of the payments for extraction and pollution rights by the home country's non-financial business sector and therefore the effects offset one another.

From (3.84), (3.92) and (3.96), current disposable income may also be represented as:

$$(3.97)\quad \bar{Y}_t = GNP_t - T'_t$$

where T'_t represents personal taxes paid by the home household sector plus current interest income received by the home central bank.

The Foreign Country

A similar set of measures of aggregate economic activity exists for the foreign country. In particular, the values added by the foreign government, central bank, private financial sector and private non-financial business sector are given respectively by (expressed in terms of the foreign country's unit of account):

$$(3.98)\ VA^{g*}_t = T^*_t + \Pi^{c*}_t + (p^x_tR^{x*}_t + p^p_t\ \bar{P}^{p*}_t)/\varepsilon_t - S^{g*}_t - B^{g*}_t = W^*_{t-1}h^{g*}_tN^{g*}_t$$

$$(3.99)\ VA^{c*}_t = \rho^*_{t-1}A^*_t + B^{*c*}_t + (B^{c*}_t)/\varepsilon_t = \Pi^{c*}_t$$

$$(3.100)\ VA^{f^*}_t = B^{*f^*}_t + (B^{f^*}_t)/\hat{\varepsilon}_{t-1} - \rho^*_{t-1}A^*_t = W^*_{t-1}h^{*f^*}_tN^{*f^*}_t + r^{d^*}_{t-1}D^*_t + \Pi^{*f^*}_t$$

$$(3.101)\ VA^{n^*}_t = p^*_tq^*_t - (p_{t-1}q^n_t)/\hat{\varepsilon}_{t-1} - B^{*n^*}_t - (p^x_tR^{x^*}_t - p^p_t\ \bar{P}^{p^*}_t)/\varepsilon_t$$

$$= W^*_{t-1}h^{*n^*}_tN^{*n^*}_t + \Pi^{n^*}_t.$$

Summing these values added produces the following measure for the foreign country's GNP:

$$(3.102)\ GNP^*_t = VA^{g^*}_t + VA^{c^*}_t + VA^{f^*}_t + VA^{n^*}_t$$

$$= W^*_{t-1}h^{*g^*}_tN^{*g^*}_t + [\rho^*_{t-1}A^*_t + B^{*c^*}_t + (B^{c^*}_t)/\varepsilon_t] + [B^{*f^*}_t + (B^{f^*}_t)/\hat{\varepsilon}_{t-1}$$

$$-\rho^*_{t-1}A^*_t] + [p^*_tq^*_t - (p_{t-1}q^{n^*}_t)/\hat{\varepsilon}_{t-1} - (p^x_tR^{x^*}_t - p^p_t\ \bar{P}^{p^*}_t)/\varepsilon_t - B^{*n^*}_t]$$

$$= [p^*_tq^*_t - (p_{t-1}q^{n^*}_t)/\hat{\varepsilon}_{t-1} - (p^x_tR^{x^*}_t - p^p_t\ \bar{P}^{p^*}_t)/\varepsilon_t] + (W^*_{t-1}h^{*g^*}_tN^{*g^*}_t + B^{*g^*}_t)$$

$$+ [(B^{c^*}_t)/\varepsilon_t + (B^{f^*}_t)/\hat{\varepsilon}_{t-1} - B^{*r^*}_t]$$

where $B^{*g^*}_t - B^{*r^*}_t = B^{*c^*}_t + B^{*f^*}_t - B^{*n^*}_t$ and where $B^{*r^*}_t$ denotes interest income paid to the rest of the world by the foreign country. The "expenditures approach" to measuring GNP^* yields the following expression:

$$(3.103)\ GNP^*_t = p^*_tc^{*d}_t + [p^*_t(K^{*g^*d}_{t+1} - K^{*g^*}_t) + W^*_{t-1}h^{*g^*}_tN^{*g^*}_t + B^{*g^*}_t]$$

$$+ [p^*_t(K^{*n^*d}_{t+1} - K^{*n^*}_t) + p^*_t(Q^*_{t+1} - Q^*_t) - (v^*_t - p^{p^*}_t\kappa^*)q^{\wedge *}_t]$$

$$+ [p^*_{t-1}q^{*n}_t - (p_{t-1}q^{n^*}_t)/\hat{\varepsilon}_{t-1} - (p^x_tR^{x^*}_t + p^p_t\ \bar{P}^{p^*}_t)/\varepsilon_t] + [(B^{c^*}_t)/\varepsilon_t + (B^{f^*}_t)/\hat{\varepsilon}_{t-1} - B^{*r^*}_t].$$

In a manner analogous to (3.89) and (3.90), we may write (3.103) as:

$$(3.104)\ GNP^*_t = p^*_tc^*_t + p^*_ti^*_t + [p^*_t(K^{*g^*d}_{t+1} - K^{*g^*}_t) + W^*_{t-1}h^{*g^*}_tN^{*g^*}_t + B^{*g^*}_t]$$

$$+ p^*_tx^*_t + [(B^{c^*}_t)/\varepsilon_t + (B^{f^*}_t)/\hat{\varepsilon}_{t-1} - B^{*r^*}_t]$$

$$= W^*_{t-1}h^*_tN^*_t + r^{d^*}_{t-1}D^*_t + (\Pi^{c^*}_t + \Pi^{f^*}_t + \Pi^{n^*}_t).$$

In addition, gross domestic product, national income, personal income and disposable income for the foreign country may be written, respectively, as:

$$(3.105)\ GDP^*_t = p^*_tc^*_t + p^*_ti^*_t + [p^*_t(K^{*g^*d}_{t+1} - K^{*g^*}_t) + W^*_{t-1}h^{*g^*}_tN^{*g^*}_t + B^{*g^*}_t] + p^*_tx^*_t$$

$$(3.106)\ NI^*_t = W^*_{t-1}h^*_tN^*_t + r^{d^*}_{t-1}D^*_t + (\Pi^{c^*}_t + \Pi^{f^*}_t + \Pi^{n^*}_t)$$

(3.107) $PI^*_t = W^*_{t-1}h^*_tN^*_t + r^{d*}_{t-1}D^*_t + \Pi^{f*}_t + \Pi^{n*}_t$

(3.108) $\bar{Y}^*_t = W^*_{t-1}h^*_tN^*_t + r^{d*}_{t-1}D^*_t + \Pi^{f*}_t + \Pi^{n*}_t - T^*_t = GNP^*_t - T^{*\prime}_t$

where $T^{*\prime}_t$ denotes personal taxes paid by the foreign household sector plus current interest income of the foreign central bank.

Product Originating in the International Agent's Sector

For the expository purpose of highlighting the various considerations associated with the production of the renewable resource, we separate this production from both the public and private production within the individual countries. We set up an artificial international agent with the authority to decide the target amount of world-wide growth, Ω, in the renewable resource. As discussed above, the net increment to the renewable resource during a period of time equals its natural growth minus the amount of the resource extracted, with its natural growth positively influenced by the beginning-of-period stock of the resource and negatively influenced the level of pollution at the beginning of the period. The international agent issues permits to extract an amount of the renewable resource equal to the natural growth minus the target growth. We assume as well that the international agent does not permit the level of pollution to rise above the level existing at the beginning of the period. It implements this restriction by issuing permits to pollute equal to the amount that the biosphere is capable of assimilating at the current level of pollution. We abstract from any enforcement costs associated with this activity.

The level of production by the international agent equals the amount of the natural growth in the renewable resource, which we value at the market price of a permit to extract one unit of that resource: $p^x_tG(S_t, \bar{P})$. Therefore, the value added by the international agent, expressed in terms of the home country's unit of account, equals the value of this growth in the renewable resource.

(3.109) $VA^i_t = p^x_tG(S_t, \bar{P})$.

The value added by this sector may also be expressed as the value of its sales to other sectors, $p^p(\bar{P}^p + \bar{P}^{p*}) + p^x(R^x + R^{x*})$, plus the net change in its inventories. The net change in its inventories is equal to the target growth (which is also achieved) in the renewable resource minus the environmental depreciation (degradation) resulting from the sale of the pollution rights, which we value in terms of the value of the pollution rights sold. The revenue which the international agent receives from the sale of pollution rights, $p^p(\bar{P}^p + \bar{P}^{p*})$, represents sales from the initial inventory of "environmental quality" and not from goods produced by that sector during the current period. Therefore the value of the net change in inventories may be represented by $p^x_t\Omega - p^p(\bar{P}^p + \bar{P}^{p*})$, so that the value added by the sector may be expressed on the "sources" side of the value added statement as:

$$(3.110)\ VA^i_t\ (= p^x_t G(S_t,\ \bar{P})) = [p^p(\ \bar{P}^p + \bar{P}^{p*}) + p^x(R^x + R^{x*})]$$

$$+[p^x_t\Omega - p^p(\ \bar{P}^p + \bar{P}^{p*})].$$

When calculating the charges against the international agent's value added, we sum depreciation, transfers to other sectors, and the residual undistributed profits. The value of its depreciation equals $p^p(\ \bar{P}^p + \bar{P}^{p*})$; its transfer payments to other sectors equals $p^x(R^x + R^{x*})$; and its undistributed profits equals $p^x_t\Omega - p^p(\ \bar{P}^p + \bar{P}^{p*})$. Therefore (3.111) represents the income side of the value added:

$$(3.111)\ VA^i_t = p^p(\ \bar{P}^p + \bar{P}^{p*}) + p^x(R^x + R^{x*}) + [\ p^x_t\Omega - p^p(\ \bar{P}^p + \bar{P}^{p*})].$$

Note that while the international agent makes a total out-of-pocket payment to the government sectors equal to $p^p(\ \bar{P}^p + \bar{P}^{p*}) + p^x(R^x + R^{x*})$, only a portion of this payment, $p^x(R^x + R^{x*})$, represents a charge against the product originating in the international sector. The remainder, $p^p(\ \bar{P}^p + \bar{P}^{p*})$, is funded by the depreciation in environmental quality resulting from the sale of pollution rights.

Notes

1. The reduction in the amount of the non-renewable resource the sector demands for the current period, ceteris paribus, increases the amount of that resource available for future production, which increases the amount the sector anticipates producing and selling next period, thereby reducing next period's anticipated marginal revenue. By itself, this would tend to offset the increase in the sector's end-of-period demand for physical capital. We assume that this indirect influence upon K^d_{t+1} is minor relative to the effect discussed in the text.

2. As the sector diverts some current production to building capital goods, the resulting rise in current marginal revenue, by itself, tends to induce the sector to increase current production of privately-produced goods. However, we treat this effect as secondary to the tendency for the sector to reduce current output as it reduces its current use of the non-renewable resource discussed earlier.

CHAPTER FOUR

The Banking Sectors

Introduction

The decision variables discussed to this point with respect to current period production of public and private goods, current labor hours, product prices, wages and the prices of pollution and harvesting rights are established before current interest rates and exchange rates are determined, thereby granting more flexibility to the determination of interest rates and exchange rates, which may vary instantly. Once the household sectors have decided the amount of public goods they want their respective government sectors to produce (and the corresponding level of taxes they are willing to pay) next period and once current period product prices and wage rates have been announced, the government sectors are free to alter their end-of-period demands for labor and capital and their end-of-period ex ante supplies of bonds in response to current bond rates. At the same time, the household sectors are free to alter their current consumption spending and their end-of-period ex ante supplies of labor and demands for currency and checkable deposits in response to changes in current interest rates on checkable deposits. In addition, once the non-financial business sectors have announced current period wages and prices and decided the level of current period output, they do not alter those values for the remainder of the current period. However, these sectors are still free to alter their financial and spending decisions for the current period in light of current bond rates and exchange rates. Therefore, we must revisit the various decision-making units in this model and construct a new set of optimization problems that take the new set of predetermined variables into account. This is done in the present chapter and the next, in which we present formal descriptions of the four banking sectors and then revisit the six non-banking sectors.

In this model, the "stock of money" in each country consists of interest-bearing checkable deposits (denominated in that country's unit of account) held by that country's households at the private financial sector in their country plus non-interest-bearing (coin and) currency issued by that country's central bank (and held either by its households or its private financial sector) and non-interest-bearing deposits held by private banks in the other country at the private financial sector in the country in question. In this model, the "monetary base" in each country consists of the currency issued by that country's central bank plus the volume of deposits (denominated in that country's unit of account) held by that country's private financial sector at its central bank. Each central bank is free to buy or sell interest-earning bonds denominated in either country's unit of account. The bonds denominated in its country's unit of account are issued by that country's government and non-financial business sectors; the bonds denominated in the other country's unit of account are issued by that country's government or non-financial business sector. As a central bank buys or sells these assets it potentially affects the level of its country's monetary base. However, a country's monetary base can also change if the private financial sector in that country alters the amount of debt it owes its central bank (i.e., the level of its "advances" from its central bank). In general, the more a private financial sector borrows from its central bank (while paying that country's "discount rate" as interest on each unit it borrows), the greater that country's monetary base. Therefore, we distinguish a country's "unborrowed monetary base," which its central bank can control completely, from a country's "monetary base," which may vary endogenously with changes in the amount its private financial sector borrows from its central bank.

Home Central Bank

Let:

A_t = the level of advances the home central bank has granted its private financial sector by the beginning of the current period.

B^c_t = the number of home country bonds held by the home central bank at the beginning of the current period.

B^{cd}_{t+1} = the number of home country bonds the home central bank plans to hold by the end of the current period.

B^{*c}_t = the number of foreign bonds held by the home central bank at the beginning of the current period.

B^{*cd}_{t+1} = the number of foreign bonds the home central bank plans to hold by the end of the current period.

Cu_t = the amount of (coin and) currency denominated in the home country's unit of account held by the home country's households at the beginning of the current period.

ε_t = the current period price (value) of the foreign country's unit of account in terms of the home country's unit of account.

MB_t = the amount of the home country's monetary base outstanding at the beginning of the current period ($MB_t = Cu_t + R_t$).

p^b_t = the current period price of home country bonds, denominated in the home country's unit of account.

p^{b*}_t = the current period price of foreign country bonds, denominated in the foreign country's unit of account.

Π^c_t = current period income of the home central bank, all of which is assumed to be distributed to the home country's government sector during the current period.

ρ_{t-1} = the discount rate set by the home central bank last period.

R_t = the volume of reserves held by the home private financial sector at the beginning of the current period (consisting of vault cash denominated in the home country's unit of account plus deposits denominated in the home country's unit of account held by the home private financial sector at the home central bank).

UMB_t = the stock of the home country's unborrowed monetary base outstanding at the beginning of the current period ($UMB_t = MB_t - A_t$).

UMB^s_{t+1} = the volume of the home country's unborrowed monetary base at the end of the current period consistent with the plans of the home country's central bank.

Given that the home central bank incurs no operating costs and that it distributes all of its current income to the home government sector during the current period, the following conditions hold:

(4.1) $\Pi^c_t = \rho_{t-1}A_t + B^c_t + \varepsilon_t B^{*c}_t$

(4.2) $p^b_t(B^{cd}_{t+1} - B^c_t) + \varepsilon_t p^{b*}_t (B^{*cd}_{t+1} - B^{*c}_t) = (UMB^s_{t+1} - UMB_t)$.

According to (3.97), the home central bank may arbitrarily decide any two of: its current period purchases of home country bonds, its current period purchases of foreign country bonds and its addition to the unborrowed monetary base during the current period. In this model, an "open-market purchase by the home central bank" refers to equal increases in $p^b_t(B^{cd}_{t+1} - B^c_t)$ and $(UMB^s_{t+1} - UMB_t)$; a "non-sterilized purchase of foreign exchange by the home central bank" refers to equal increases in $\varepsilon_t p^{b*}_t(B^{*cd}_{t+1} - B^{*c}_t)$ and $(UMB^s_{t+1} - UMB_t)$; and a "sterilized purchase of foreign exchange by the home central bank" refers to an increase in $\varepsilon_t p^{b*}_t(B^{*cd}_{t+1} - B^{*c}_t)$ accompanied by a decrease in $p^b_t(B^{cd}_{t+1} - B^c_t)$ by an equal amount.

Let:

β^c = the home central bank's planned purchase of home country bonds during the current period, a policy parameter.

β^{*c} = the home central bank's planned purchase of foreign country bonds (valued in terms of the home country's unit of account) during the current period, a policy parameter.

Then the home central bank's planned holdings of foreign country bonds by the end of the period may be expressed as:

(4.3) $\varepsilon_t p^{b*}{}_t B^{*cd}{}_{t+1} = \varepsilon_t p^{b*}{}_t B^{*c}{}_t + \beta^{*c}$

while its planned holdings of home country bonds by the end of the current period is given by:

(4.4) $p^b{}_t B^{cd}{}_{t+1} = p^b{}_t B^c{}_t + \beta^c = p^b{}_t B^c{}_t + (UMB^s{}_{t+1} - UMB_t) - \beta^{*c}$.

Foreign Central Bank

Let:

$A^*{}_t$ = the level of advances the foreign central bank has granted its private financial sector by the beginning of the current period.

$B^{c*}{}_t$ = the number of home country bonds held by the foreign central bank at the beginning of the current period.

$B^{c*d}{}_{t+1}$ = the number of home country bonds the foreign central bank plans to hold by the end of the current period.

$B^{*c*}{}_t$ = the number of foreign bonds held by the foreign central bank at the beginning of the current period.

$B^{*c*d}{}_{t+1}$ = the number of foreign bonds the foreign central bank plans to hold by the end of the current period.

$Cu^*{}_t$ = the amount of (coin and) currency denominated in the foreign country's unit of account held by the foreign country's households at the beginning of the current period.

$MB^*{}_t$ = the amount of the foreign country's monetary base outstanding at the beginning of the current period ($MB^*{}_t = Cu^*{}_t + R^*{}_t$).

Π^{c*}_t = current period income of the foreign central bank, all of which is assumed to be distributed to the foreign country's government sector during the current period.

ρ^*_{t-1} = the discount rate set by the foreign central bank last period.

R^*_t = the volume of reserves held by the foreign private financial sector at the beginning of the current period (consisting of vault cash denominated in the foreign country's unit of account plus deposits denominated in the foreign country's unit of account held by the foreign private financial sector at the foreign central bank).

UMB^*_t = the stock of the foreign country's unborrowed monetary base outstanding at the beginning of the current period ($UMB^*_t = MB^*_t - A^*_t$).

UMB^{*s}_{t+1} = the volume of the foreign country's unborrowed monetary base at the end of the current period consistent with the plans of the foreign country's central bank.

Given that the foreign central bank incurs no operating costs and that it distributes all of its current income to the foreign government sector during the current period, the following conditions hold:

$$(4.5)\ \Pi^{c*}_t = \rho^*_{t-1}A^*_t + B^{*c*}_t + B^{c*}_t/\varepsilon_t$$

$$(4.6)\ p^{b*}_t(B^{*c*d}_{t+1} - B^{*c*}_t) + p^b_t(B^{c*d}_{t+1} - B^{c*}_t)/\varepsilon_t = (UMB^{*s}_{t+1} - UMB^*_t).$$

According to (4.6), the foreign central bank may arbitrarily decide any two of: its current period purchases of foreign country bonds, its current period purchases of home country bonds and its addition to the unborrowed monetary base during the current period. In this model, an "open-market purchase by the foreign central bank" refers to equal increases in $p^{b*}_t(B^{*c*d}_{t+1} - B^{*c*}_t)$ and $(UMB^{*s}_{t+1} - UMB^*_t)$; a "non-sterilized purchase of foreign exchange by the foreign central bank" refers to equal increases in $p^b_t(B^{c*d}_{t+1} - B^{c*}_t)/\varepsilon_t$ and $(UMB^{*s}_{t+1} - UMB^*_t)$; and a "sterilized purchase of foreign exchange by the foreign central bank" refers to an increase in $p^b_t(B^{c*d}_{t+1} - B^{c*}_t)/\varepsilon_t$ accompanied by a decrease in $p^{b*}_t(B^{*c*d}_{t+1} - B^{*c*}_t)$ by an equal amount.

Let:

β^{c*} = the foreign central bank's planned purchase of home country bonds (valued in terms of the foreign country's unit of account) during the current period, a policy parameter.

β^{*c*} = the foreign central bank's planned purchase of foreign country bonds (valued in terms of the foreign country's unit of account) during the current period, a policy parameter.

Then the foreign central bank's planned holdings of home country bonds by the end of the period may be expressed as:

$$(4.7)\ p^b_t B^{c*d}_{t+1}/\varepsilon_t = p^b_t B^{c*}_t/\varepsilon_t + \beta^{c*}$$

while its planned holdings of foreign country bonds by the end of the current period is given by:

$$(4.8)\ p^{b*}_t B^{*c*d}_{t+1} = p^{b*}_t B^{*c*}_t + \beta^{*c*} = p^{b*}_t B^{*c*}_t + (UMB^{*s}_{t+1} - UMB^*_t) - \beta^{c*}.$$

Home Private Financial Sector

As outlined in detail below, we view the home private financial sector as purchasing and holding both home and foreign country bonds in order to earn the interest income generated by these bonds. The bonds it holds at the beginning of the current period generate income during the current period. The bonds it buys during the current period will not generate interest income until next period. To finance their purchase, the home private financial sector issues interest-earning checkable deposits denominated in its country's unit of account to its household customers. The sector incurs labor costs associated with servicing both its bond holdings and its checking account liabilities. Furthermore, because the checkable deposits are transferable into the home country's coin and currency on demand, the home private banks hold excess reserves in the form of vault cash and/or deposits held at the home central bank to reduce the transactions costs associated with servicing these accounts. In addition, because both the home private financial sector and its customers engage in transactions involving the exchange of items denominated in one unit of account for items denominated in the other unit of account, the home private financial sector also holds deposits denominated in the foreign country's unit of account at the foreign private financial sector. These deposits reduce the home private financial sector's real resource costs associated with those transactions, but generate no interest income for the sector. The home private financial sector also issues non-interest-earning deposits denominated in the home unit of account to the foreign private financial sector. These deposits generate loanable funds for the home private financial sector, but require real resources to service. The home private financial sector is required to hold reserves equal to the required reserve ratio set by its central bank times the volume of its net deposits. Its net deposits equal its gross deposit liabilities minus the value of deposits it holds at the foreign private financial sector (referred to as deposits "due from" that sector). For the purpose of calculating required reserves, we assume that deposits held at foreign banks are valued in terms of the prevailing spot rate.

Let:

A_t = the value (in terms of the home country's unit of account) of the home private financial sector's advances from the central bank outstanding at the beginning of the current period.

B^f_t = the number of home country bonds the home private financial sector holds at the beginning of the current period.

B^{*f}_t = the number of foreign country bonds the home private financial sector holds at the beginning of the current period.

D_t = the volume of checkable deposits (valued in the home country's unit of account) that the home private financial sector has outstanding at the beginning of the current period (had outstanding at the end of last period).

ε_t = the current period spot rate (value of the foreign country's unit of account in terms of the home country's unit of account).

$\varepsilon^{\wedge}_{t-1}$ = the forward exchange rate that prevailed last period (i.e., the value of the foreign unit of account in terms of the home unit of account in contracts struck last period calling for the exchange during the current period of items denominated in different units of account).

$\varepsilon^{\wedge}_t$ = the current forward exchange rate (i.e., the value of the foreign country's unit of account in terms of the home country's unit of account in current contracts calling for the exchange next period of items denominated in different units of account).

f^+_t = the ratio of the current forward exchange rate to the current spot exchange rate, ($f^+_t = \varepsilon^{\wedge}_t/\varepsilon_t$).

$h^f_t N^f_t$ = the number of hours the home private financial sector uses its current employees.

NW^f_t = the net wealth of the home country's private financial sector, measured in terms of the home country's unit of account.

p^b_t = the current period price (in the home unit of account) of home country bonds.

p^{b*}_t = the current period price (in the foreign unit of account) of foreign country bonds.

p^{b*f}_t = the price (in the foreign unit of account) of foreign bonds that the home private financial sector expected last period would prevail during the current period.

Π^f_t = current period dividends paid by the home private financial sector.

r^d_{t-1} = the interest rate on checkable deposits issued by the home private financial sector and held by the home household sector at the end of last period. This rate is payable during the current period on checkable deposits the home private financial sector had outstanding at the end of last period.

$r^\wedge$ = the required reserve ratio prevailing in the home country.

ρ_{t-1} = the discount rate set by the home central bank last period, payable by the home private financial sector during the current period on each unit of advances outstanding at the end of last period (beginning of the current period).

$\mathfrak{R}_t$ = the volume of (non-interest-bearing) deposits, denominated in the home country's unit of account, that the foreign private financial sector holds at the home private financial sector at the beginning of the current period.

$\mathfrak{R}^*_t$ = the volume of (non-interest-bearing) deposits, denominated in the foreign country's unit of account, that the home private financial sector holds at the foreign private financial sector at the beginning of the current period.

X_t = the volume of excess reserves (valued in terms of the home country's unit of account) held by the home private financial sector at the beginning of the current period.

At the end of last period, the home private financial sector held B^{*f}_t units of foreign bonds. Since each bond pays one unit of foreign money as interest starting the next period after its purchase, and since the home private financial sector expected last period that the current market price of foreign bonds, in the foreign unit of account, would be p^{b*f}_t, last period the home private financial sector covered its anticipated current period return on foreign bonds by selling $(1+p^{b*f}_t)B^{*f}_t$ units of its deposits at the foreign private financial sector forward. However, as the current period opens, the sector holds foreign bonds with a market value (in terms of the foreign unit of account) of $p^{b*}_t B^{*f}_t$, which may be written as $[p^{b*f}_t + (p^{b*}_t - p^{b*f}_t)]B^{*f}_t$ in order to separate the portion of the current market value that was sold forward last period, $p^{b*f}_t B^{*f}_t$, from the portion that was not, $(p^{b*}_t - p^{b*f}_t)B^{*f}_t$. Since the former portion was sold forward at the exchange rate $\varepsilon^\wedge_{t-1}$, the current value of that portion in terms of the home unit of account is given by $\varepsilon^\wedge_{t-1}\, p^{b*f}_t B^{*f}_t$. The latter portion may be sold during the current period on the spot market; therefore, its current value in terms of the home unit of account is given by $\varepsilon_t(p^{b*}_t - p^{b*f}_t)B^{*f}_t$. Consequently, the sector's net wealth at the beginning of the current period may be represented by:

$$(4.9)\ NW^f_t = \varepsilon^{\wedge}_{t-1}[p^{b*f}_t B^{*f}_t + \Re^*_t] + \varepsilon_t(p^{b*}_t - p^{b*f}_t)B^{*f}_t + p^b_t B^f_t + X_t - (D_t + \Re_t)$$

$$+ r^{\wedge}(D_t + \Re_t - \varepsilon_t \Re^*_t) - A_t$$

where $(D_t + \Re_t - \varepsilon_t \Re^*_t)$ represents the sector's net demand deposit liabilities. The sector's required reserves equal the required reserve ratio, $r^{\wedge}$, times these net deposits. For the purpose of calculating its net deposits, the sector's interbank deposits are valued in terms of the current spot rate; however, the sector covered the value of these deposits last period by selling foreign exchange forward last period equal to the amount of these deposits in terms of the foreign country's unit of account. The current period dividends which the home private financial sector pays to the home household sector is given by:

$$(4.10)\ \Pi^f_t = B^f_t + \varepsilon^{\wedge}_{t-1}B^{*f}_t - W_{t-1}h^f_t N^f_t - \rho_{t-1}A_t - r^d_{t-1}D_t.$$

The interest income that the home private financial sector receives this period on foreign bonds was sold forward last period, so that the value of that income this period is given by $\varepsilon^{\wedge}_{t-1}B^{*f}_t$. The current wage expense of the home private financial sector includes current labor costs associated with servicing its current holdings of home and foreign bonds, the checkable deposits held by the home household sector, the forward contracts struck last period by home country importers and the deposits held by the foreign private financial sector at the home private financial sector. The sector presumably neither receives interest income on the deposits it holds at the foreign private financial sector nor pays interest on interbank deposits the foreign private financial sector holds at the home private financial sector.

Let:

A^d_{t+1} = the volume of advances the home private financial sector plans to have outstanding at the end of the current period at the home central bank.

B^{fd}_{t+1} = the number of home country bonds the home private financial sector plans to hold by the end of the current period.

B^{*fd}_{t+1} = the number of foreign country bonds the home private financial sector plans to hold by the end of the current period.

D^s_{t+1} = the volume of interest-earning checkable deposits outstanding at the end of the current period at the home private financial sector consistent with the plans of that sector (i.e., the home private financial sector's ex ante end-of-period supply of checkable deposits).

N^{fd}_{t+1} = the home private financial sector's end of current period demand for employees.

NW^{fd}_{t+1} = the net wealth the home private financial sector plans to hold by the end of the current period, expressed in terms of current period prices.

$\mathfrak{R}^{fs}_{t+1}$ = the volume of (non-interest-bearing) deposits, denominated in the home unit of account, held by the foreign private financial sector at the end of the current period consistent with the plans of the home private financial sector (i.e., the home private financial sector's ex ante end-of-period supply of foreign-bank deposits).

$\mathfrak{R}^{*d}_{t+1}$ = the volume of (non-interest-bearing) deposits, denominated in the foreign country's unit of account, that the home private financial sector plans to hold at the foreign private financial sector at the end of the current period.

X^{d}_{t+1} = the home private financial sector's end-of-period demand for excess reserves (valued in terms of the home country's unit of account).

Then, in current period prices, the net wealth attached to the home private financial sector's balance sheet planned for the end of the current period is given by:

$$(4.11)\ NW^{fd}_{t+1} = p^{b}_{t}B^{fd}_{t+1} + \varepsilon_t p^{b*}_{t}B^{*fd}_{t+1} + X^{d}_{t+1} - A^{d}_{t+1}$$

$$-(1 - r\hat{})(D^{s}_{t+1} + \mathfrak{R}^{fs}_{t+1} - \varepsilon_t R^{*d}_{t+1}).$$

Assuming that the home private financial sector distributes all of its current period income to the home household sector as dividends during the current period, the planned net saving by the home private financial sector necessarily equals zero. Therefore, when both are measured in terms of current period prices, the home private financial sector's net wealth planned for the end of the current period necessarily equals its beginning-of-period net wealth; the right-hand side of (4.9) necessarily equals the right-hand side of (4.11). Setting these two expressions equal to one another, we then obtain the following expression for the home private financial sector's end-of-period demand for home bonds:

$$(4.12)\ p^{b}_{t}B^{fd}_{t+1} = p^{b}_{t}B^{f}_{t} - \varepsilon_t p^{b*}_{t}B^{*fd}_{t+1} + \varepsilon\hat{}_{t-1}[p^{b*f}_{t}B^{*f}_{t} + \mathfrak{R}^{*}_{t}] + \varepsilon_t(p^{b*}_{t} - p^{b*f}_{t})B^{*f}_{t} - (X^{d}_{t+1} - X_t)$$

$$+(A^{d}_{t+1} - A_t) + [(D^{s}_{t+1} - D_t) + (\mathfrak{R}^{fs}_{t+1} - \mathfrak{R}_t) - \varepsilon_t \mathfrak{R}^{*d}_{t+1}]$$

$$-r\hat{}[(D^{s}_{t+1} - D_t) + (\mathfrak{R}^{fs}_{t+1} - \mathfrak{R}_t) - \varepsilon_t(\mathfrak{R}^{*d}_{t+1} - \mathfrak{R}^{*}_{t})].$$

According to (4.12), the amount by which the home private financial sector plans to add to its holdings of home country bonds during the period must be equal to: (a) the amount it plans to borrow from the central bank plus (b) the amount it plans to add to its net deposits liabilities, net of additions to its required reserves, minus the sum of: (c) the amount it plans to add to its holdings of foreign bonds and (d) the amount it plans to add to its holdings of excess reserves.

Let:

p^{bf}_{t+1} = the price of home bonds that the home private financial sector anticipates during the current period will prevail next period.

p^{b*f}_{t+1} = the price of foreign bonds that the home private financial sector anticipates during the current period will prevail next period.

p^{f}_{t+1} = the average price of privately-produced home country goods that the home private financial sector anticipates in the current period will prevail next period.

Π^{fef}_{t+1} = the amount the home private financial sector plans to distribute as dividends next period.

ρ_t = the discount rate the home central bank announces during the current period, payable next period on each unit of advances the home private financial sector has outstanding at the end of the current period.

r^{d}_{t} = the current interest rate on checkable deposits issued by the home private financial sector. This rate is payable next period on checkable deposits the home household sector holds at the end of the current period.

$W_t hN^{fd}_{t+1}$ = the wage expense the home private financial sector expects this period to incur next period.

To close the model, we assume that during the current period, the home private financial sector plans to sell all assets and retire all outstanding liabilities by the end of next period. Therefore, as it formulates its plans this period, the sector plans to distribute to its owners next period all net income from its operations that period plus the value of its net wealth at the beginning of that period, all measured in terms of the prices the sector anticipates will prevail next period. Therefore, we may represent next period's anticipated dividends by the following expression:

$$(4.13)\ \Pi^{fef}_{t+1} = (1 + p^{bf}_{t+1})B^{fd}_{t+1} + \varepsilon^{\wedge}_{t}(1 + p^{b*f}_{t+1})B^{*fd}_{t+1} + X^{d}_{t+1} + \varepsilon^{\wedge}_{t}\Re^{*d}_{t+1}$$

$$- r^{\wedge}\cdot\varepsilon^{f}_{t+1}\Re^{*d}_{t+1} - (1+\rho_t)A^{d}_{t+1} - W_t hN^{fd}_{t+1} - (1 - r^{\wedge} + r^{d}_{t})D^{s}_{t+1} - (1 - r^{\wedge})\Re^{fs}_{t+1}$$

where ε^f_{t+1} = the spot rate that the home private financial sector anticipates will prevail next period and where we have assumed that the home private financial sector sells forward during the current period the volume of interbank deposits it plans to hold by the end of the current period. However, these interbank deposits will reduce next period's required reserves by the required reserve ratio times the anticipated spot value of those deposits next period, since we assume that these deposits will be valued by their market value next period as they are deducted from gross deposit liabilities of the sector at the beginning of that period.

Divide all terms in (4.12) by p^b_t and substitute the right-hand side of the resulting expression for B^{fd}_{t+1} in (4.13) to obtain:

$$(4.14)\ \Pi^{fef}_{t+1} = [(1 + p^{bf}_{t+1})/p^b_t]\ [p^b_t B^f_t - \varepsilon_t p^{b*}_t B^{*fd}_{t+1} + \varepsilon^{\wedge}_{t-1}\ [p^{b*f}_t B^{*f}_t + \Re^*_t]$$

$$+\varepsilon_t(p^{b*}_t - p^{b*f}_t)B^{*f}_t\ -(X^d_{t+1} - X_t) + (A^d_{t+1} - A_t)$$

$$+[(D^s_{t+1} - D_t) + (\Re^{fs}_{t+1} - \Re_t) - \varepsilon_t \Re^{*d}_{t+1}]$$

$$-r^{\wedge}[(D^s_{t+1} - D_t) + (\Re^{fs}_{t+1} - \Re_t) - \varepsilon_t(\Re^{*d}_{t+1} - \Re^*_t)]\ ]$$

$$+\varepsilon^{\wedge}_t(1 + p^{b*f}_{t+1})B^{*fd}_{t+1} + X^d_{t+1} + \varepsilon^{\wedge}_t \Re^{*d}_{t+1} - r^{\wedge}\varepsilon^f_{t+1}\Re^{*d}_{t+1} - (1 + \rho_t)A^d_{t+1}$$

$$-(1-r^{\wedge})\Re^{fs}_{t+1}\ - W_t h N^{fd}_{t+1} - (1 - r^{\wedge} + r^d_t)D^s_{t+1}.$$

We assume that the home private financial sector attempts to maximize its present value, which is the amount that its owners (the home household sector) would have to place in its next best alternative (i.e., checkable deposits, since they are the only income-earning market alternative available to the households in this model) at the beginning of the current period in order to duplicate, period by period, the real income to be generated by the home private financial sector. Therefore, we view the home private financial sector as maximizing:

$$(4.15)\ \Pi^f_t/p_t + \Pi^{fef}_{t+1}/(1 + r^d_t)p^f_{t+1}$$

$$= (1/p_t)[\ B^f_t + \varepsilon^{\wedge}_{t-1}B^{*f}_t - W_{t-1}h^f_t N^f_t - \rho_{t-1}A_t - r^d_{t-1}D_t]$$

$$+[1/(1 + r^d_t)p^f_{t+1}]\{\ [(1 + p^{bf}_{t+1})/p^b_t]\ [p^b_t B^f_t - \varepsilon_t p^{b*}_t B^{*fd}_{t+1} + \varepsilon^{\wedge}_{t-1}\ [p^{b*f}_t B^{*f}_t + \Re^*_t]$$

$$+\varepsilon_t(p^{b*}_t - p^{b*f}_t)B^{*f}_t\ -(X^d_{t+1} - X_t) + (A^d_{t+1} - A_t)$$

$$+[(D^s_{t+1} - D_t) + (\Re^{fs}_{t+1} - \Re_t) - \varepsilon_t \Re^{*d}_{t+1}]$$

$$-r^{\wedge}[(D^s_{t+1} - D_t) + (\Re^{fs}_{t+1} - \Re_t) - \varepsilon_t(\Re^{*d}_{t+1} - \Re^*_t)]]$$

$$+\hat{\varepsilon}_t(1 + p^{b*f}_{t+1})B^{*fd}_{t+1} + X^d_{t+1} + \hat{\varepsilon}_t\Re^{*d}_{t+1} - \hat{r}\varepsilon^f_{t+1}\Re^{*d}_{t+1}$$

$$-(1+\rho_t)A^d_{t+1} - (1-\hat{r})\Re^{fs}_{t+1} - W_t h N^{fd}_{t+1} - (1 - \hat{r} + r^d_t)D^s_{t+1}\}.$$

The objective of the sector is to maximize (4.15), subject to the various real resource constraints facing it. We now develop those constraints.

Bond Management

Current Period

For simplicity, the required volume of clerical operations and administrative tasks associated with the home financial sector's bond portfolio during the current period is assumed to be directly proportional to the volume of each type of bond it holds at the beginning of that period. In particular, let

T^b_t = the number of operations associated with home bonds during the current period.

T^{b*}_t = the number of operations associated with foreign bonds during the current period.

Then, by assumption, the number of operations in each category may be specified as follows:

(4.16) $T^b_t = \alpha_1 \cdot (p^b_t B^f_t)$

(4.17) $T^{b*}_t = \alpha_2 \cdot (\varepsilon_t p^{b*}_t B^{*f}_t)$

where α_1 and α_2 denote positive constants. For simplicity, to determine the quantity of real resources required to undertake the required number of operations in each case, we posit a clerical and administrative services function with labor as the only input. According to this function, as the home private financial sector employs more labor hours to managing a particular portfolio, a greater number of clerical and administrative operations are performed. We posit further that labor displays a positive but diminishing marginal product in providing the required operations.

Let:

h^{bf}_t = the average number of hours the home private financial sector uses its current employees to carry out operations associated with its current portfolio of home country bonds.

h^{b*f}_t = the average number of hours the home private financial sector uses its current employees to carry out operations associated with its current portfolio of foreign country bonds.

N^{bf}_t = the number of people that have been assigned at the beginning of the current period by the home private financial sector to undertake home-bond operations during the current period.

N^{b*f}_t = the number of people that have been assigned at the beginning of the current period by the home private financial sector to undertake foreign-bond operations during the current period.

Then the production functions for clerical and administrative services carried out by the home private financial sector in conjunction with its holdings of home and foreign bonds are given respectively by:

(4.18) $T^b_t = \tau^b(h^{bf}_t N^{bf}_t)$, where $(\tau^b)' > 0$ and $(\tau^b)'' < 0$

(4.19) $T^{b*}_t = \tau^{b*}(h^{b*f}_t N^{b*f}_t)$, where $(\tau^{b*})' > 0$ and $(\tau^{b*})'' < 0$.

Setting the right-hand side of (4.16) equal to the right-hand side of (4.18) yields an implicit function, (4.20), relating the total number of labor hours the home private financial sector must employ during the current period to service a given amount of home country bonds held at the beginning of the current period. A similar implicit function, (4.21), may be obtained relating labor hours to the amount of foreign country bonds the sector holds at the beginning of the current period by setting the right-hand side of (4.17) to the right-hand side of (4.19):

(4.20) $\tau^b(h^{bf}_t N^{bf}_t) = \alpha_1 \cdot (p^b_t B^f_t)$

(4.21) $\tau^{b*}(h^{b*f}_t N^{b*f}_t) = \alpha_2 \cdot (\varepsilon_t p^{b*}_t B^{*f}_t)$.

In each case, using the implicit function rule, we may solve for the number of labor hours the sector requires to achieve the requisite number of clerical and administrative operations associated with its initial bond holdings.

(4.22) $h^{bf}_t N^{bf}_t = \sigma^b(p^b_t B^f_t)$

where $\sigma^b(\cdot) > 0$, $(\sigma^b)' = \alpha_1/(\tau^b)' > 0$, $(\sigma^b)'' = -(\tau^b)'' \cdot \alpha_1/[(\tau^b)']^2 > 0$, and:

(4.23) $h^{b*f}_t N^{b*f}_t = \sigma^{b*}(\varepsilon_t p^{b*}_t B^{*f}_t)$

where $\sigma^{b*}(\bullet) > 0$, $(\sigma^{b*})' = \alpha_2/(\tau^{b*})' > 0$, $(\sigma^{b*})'' = -(\tau^{b*})'' \cdot \alpha_2/[(\tau^{b*})']^2 > 0$. The implication of expressions (4.22) and (4.23) is that for a given money wage, the marginal cost of servicing the beginning-of-period holdings of either home or foreign bonds is an increasing function of the beginning-of-period holdings of those bonds. The increasing marginal cost arises because the marginal product of labor diminishes as the number of operations grows even though the number of operations continues to grow in proportion to the value of the bonds held at the beginning of the period.

Next Period

Let:

T^{b}_{t+1} = the number of clerical and administrative operations the home financial sector expects to undertake next period associated with its holdings of home country bonds at the beginning of that period.

T^{b*}_{t+1} = the number of clerical and administrative operations the home financial sector expects to undertake next period associated with its holdings of foreign country bonds at the beginning of that period.

Again, for simplicity, we assume in each case that the anticipated number of operations the sector expects to undertake next period is directly proportional to the value of the bonds the sector plans to hold at the beginning of that period:

$$(4.24)\ T^{b}_{t+1} = \beta_1 \cdot (p^{b}_{t} B^{fd}_{t+1})$$

$$(4.25)\ T^{b*}_{t+1} = \beta_2 \cdot (\varepsilon_t p^{b*}_{t} B^{*fd}_{t+1})$$

where β_1 and β_2 are positive constants.

Let:

N^{bfd}_{t+1} = the number of people the home private financial sector plans to employ next period to undertake operations associated with its holdings of home country bonds.

N^{b*fd}_{t+1} = the number of people the home private financial sector plans to employ next period to undertake operations associated with its holdings of foreign country bonds.

We assume that the production functions associated with the number of clerical and administrative operations completed next period involving both home and foreign bonds are positive increasing functions of the total number of labor hours the sector applies to these operations. We also assume in each case that the marginal product of labor is diminishing. Therefore, we have:

$$(4.26)\ T^{b}_{t+1} = \zeta^{b}(h \cdot N^{bfd}_{t+1}), \text{ where } \zeta^{b}(\bullet) > 0,\ (\zeta^{b})' > 0, \text{ and } (\zeta^{b})'' < 0$$

$$(4.27)\ T^{b*}_{t+1} = \zeta^{b*}(h \cdot N^{b*fd}_{t+1}), \text{ where } \zeta^{b*}(\bullet) > 0,\ (\zeta^{b*})' > 0, \text{ and } (\zeta^{b*})'' < 0.$$

Combining (4.24) and (4.26) and combining (4.25) and (4.27) we obtain implicit functions for the total number of labor hours the sector requires next period to complete the respective number of operations implied by its holdings of home and foreign bonds at the beginning of next period. Solving these implicit functions for the number of labor hours yields:

$$(4.28)\ h\cdot N^{bfd}_{t+1} = \psi^{b}(p^{b}_{t}B^{fd}_{t+1})$$

where $\psi^{b}(\bullet) < 0$, $(\psi^{b})' = \beta_1/(\zeta^{b})' > 0$, $(\psi^{b})'' = -(\zeta^{b})''\ \beta_1/[(\zeta^{b})']^2$ and

$$(4.29)\ h\cdot N^{b^*fd}_{t+1} = \psi^{b^*}(\varepsilon_t p^{b^*}_{t}B^{*fd}_{t+1})$$

where $\psi^{b^*}(\bullet) < 0$, $(\psi^{b^*})' = \beta_2/(\zeta^{b^*})' > 0$, $(\psi^{b^*})'' = -(\zeta^{b^*})''\ \beta_2/[(\zeta^{b^*})']^2$. Taken together, (4.28) and (4.29) reveal the total number labor of hours the home private financial sector expects to use next period in carrying out operations associated with its holdings of both home and foreign bonds. However, since the planned holdings of home country bonds at the end of the period must conform to restriction (4.12), we re-write (4.28) as:

$$(4.30)\ h\cdot N^{bfd}_{t+1} = \psi^{b}[p^{b}_{t}B^{f}_{t} - \varepsilon_t p^{b^*}_{t}B^{*fd}_{t+1} + \hat{\varepsilon}_{t-1}[p^{b^*f}_{t}B^{f^*}_{t} + \Re^{*}_{t}] + \varepsilon_t(p^{b^*}_{t} - p^{b^*f}_{t})B^{*f}_{t}$$

$$-(X^{d}_{t+1} - X_t) + (A^{d}_{t+1} - A_t) + [(D^{s}_{t+1} - D_t) + (\Re^{fs}_{t+1} - \Re_t) - \varepsilon_t\Re^{*d}_{t+1}]$$

$$-\hat{r}[(D^{s}_{t+1} - D_t) + (\Re^{fs}_{t+1} - \Re_t) - \varepsilon_t(\Re^{*d}_{t+1} - \Re^{*}_{t})]]$$

where $\psi^{b}(\bullet) < 0$, $(\psi^{b})' = \beta_1/(\zeta^{b})' > 0$, $(\psi^{b})'' = -(\zeta^{b})''\ \beta_1/[(\zeta^{b})']^2$.

Checkable-Deposit Liability Management

Current Period

For simplicity, we assume that during the current period the number of transactions associated with the interest-bearing checkable-deposit liabilities held by the home private financial sector's households at the beginning of the current period is directly proportional to the real value of those deposits.

Let:

T^{c}_{t} = the number of transactions during the current period associated with the private financial sector's checkable-deposit liabilities.

Then:

$$(4.31)\ T^{c}_{t} = \nu\cdot(D_t/p_t),\ \text{where } \nu \text{ is a positive constant.}$$

To complete the transactions during the current period dictated by the real volume of its checkable-deposit liabilities, the home private financial sector must employ real resources. For simplicity, we assume that labor is the only real input required and that it displays a positive, but diminishing, marginal product in completing these transactions. Excess reserves held by the private financial sector either as vault cash or as deposits held at the home central bank, however, conserve the time that labor requires to carry out its transactions, for, to the extent that the sector holds excess reserves, a temporary "cash drain" can be met simply by drawing down those reserves, thereby obviating the need to sell another asset or to borrow for the purpose of meeting the cash drain. Therefore, excess reserves provide the same time-saving function for the private financial sector that coin, currency and checkable-deposit balances provide the household sector. Furthermore, since the number of transactions associated with servicing the sector's checkable-deposit liabilities is assumed to be proportional to the real value of these deposits, the real value of the sector's excess reserves will indicate their ability to conserve the sector's transactions time. Consequently, we posit the following production function for completing the transactions associated with the home private financial sector's interest-bearing checkable-deposit liabilities:

(4.32) $T^c_t = \gamma(h^{cf}_t N^{cf}_t, X_t/p_t)$, where $\gamma_1, \gamma_2 > 0$; $\gamma_{11}, \gamma_{22} < 0$; and $\gamma_{12} > 0$,

and where

$h^{cf}_t N^{cf}_t$ = the total number of hours the home private financial sector uses people to service its interest-bearing checkable-deposit liabilities during the current period.

According to (4.32), both labor and real excess reserves are productive in servicing the home private financial sector's checkable-deposit liabilities during the current period; both have diminishing marginal products; and they are technical complements—the marginal product of each factor increases with a greater use of the other factor. Setting the right-hand side of (4.31) equal to the right-hand side of (4.32) yields the following implicit function:

(4.33) $v\cdot(D_t/p_t) = \gamma(h^{cf}_t N^{cf}_t, X_t/p_t)$.

Next, solve (4.33) explicitly for the total labor hours necessary to service the sector's checkable-deposit liabilities:

(4.34) $h^{cf}_t N^{cf}_t = \delta(D_t/p_t, X_t/p_t)$ where $\delta(\bullet) > 0$, $\delta_1 = v/\gamma_1 > 0$, $\delta_2 = -\gamma_2/\gamma_1 < 0$,

$\delta_{11} = -v\gamma_{11}/(\gamma_1)^2 > 0$, $\delta_{22} = -(\gamma_{22}/\gamma_1) + \gamma_2\gamma_{12}/(\gamma_1)^2 > 0$, $\delta_{12} = -v\gamma_{12}/(\gamma_1)^2 < 0$,

$\delta_{21} = -(\gamma_{21}/\gamma_1) + \gamma_2\gamma_{11}/(\gamma_1)^2 < 0$, and $\delta_{11}\cdot\delta_{22} - \delta_{12}\cdot\delta_{21} = v[\gamma_{11}\cdot\gamma_{22} - \gamma_{12}\cdot\gamma_{21}]/(\gamma_1)^3 > 0$.

The current labor requirement function associated with checkable deposits is drawn in Figure 4.1

Figure 4.1 **Current Labor Requirement**

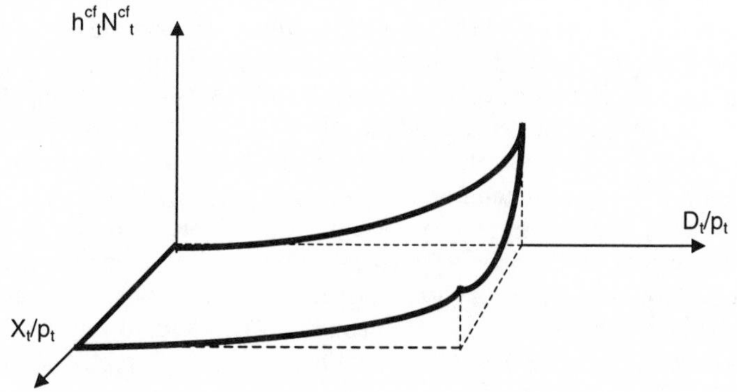

Next Period

In a similar fashion, we may derive next period's anticipated total labor hours devoted to servicing checkable deposits as an increasing function of the real checkable deposits the sector plans to have outstanding by the beginning of that period and as a decreasing function of the real value of the excess reserves it plans to hold by then.

Let:

N^{cfd}_{t+1} = the number of people the home private financial sector plans to employ next period to service its checkable deposit liabilities next period.

Then the total labor hours the sector plans to use next period to service its checkable deposit liabilities may be given by:

(4.35) $h \cdot N^{cfd}_{t+1} = \phi(D^s_{t+1}/p^f_{t+1}, X^d_{t+1}/p^f_{t+1})$

where $\phi_1 > 0$, $\phi_2 < 0$, $\phi_{11}, \phi_{22} > 0$, $\phi_{12} < 0$, and $\phi_{11} \cdot \phi_{22} - (\phi_{12})^2 > 0$.

The graph of the sector's demand for labor for servicing checkable deposits next period is analogous to the one drawn in Figure 4.1.

Servicing Non-Bank Customers

The home private financial sector holds deposits at the foreign private financial sector to reduce the transactions costs associated with servicing its non-bank customers as they trade goods with the foreign country. The home private financial sector holds deposits at the foreign private financial sector (denominated in the foreign country's unit of account) into which its purchases of claims denominated in that unit of account can be deposited and out of which payments can be ordered when it sells claims denominated in that unit of account. In the present model, the home private financial sector may purchase claims in the foreign unit of account when the home non-financial business sector receives a financial claim in that unit of account as payment for goods it exports to the foreign country. The home private financial sector may order payment out of its deposits at the foreign private sector when the home non-financial business sector orders payment out of its deposit at the home bank to pay for goods it imports from the foreign country.

The volume of real imports by the home non-financial business sector presumably reflects the number of payment orders and accompanying documents that must be processed by the home private financial sector in association with its customers' trades with the foreign country. Therefore, to simplify our analysis, we assume that the home private financial sector's real resource cost of servicing its non-bank customers presumably increases in proportion with the level of real imports by its customers, but diminishes at a decreasing rate as the home banks increase their holdings of deposits at the foreign banks. Once again, we assume that labor displays diminishing marginal product as it services these transactions. (By the same token, the foreign banks hold deposits at the home private financial sector to serve their country's importers of home country goods. As mentioned earlier, we assume that no interest is paid on these inter-bank deposits in either country.)

Current Period

Let:

$T^{q^*f}_t$ = the number of transactions the home country's private financial sector must undertake during the current period associated with the current trading activity of the home non-financial business sector.

Then the volume of these transactions is given by:

$$(4.36)\quad T^{q^*f}_t = \eta \cdot q^{*n}_t$$

where η is a positive constant. To complete the number of transactions during the current period dictated by the real volume of these imports, the home private financial sector must employ real resources. For simplicity, we assume that labor is the only real input required and that it displays a positive, but diminishing marginal product in completing these transactions. The real value, in units of foreign goods, of deposits denominated in the foreign country's unit of account held by the home private financial sector at the foreign private financial sector, however, conserves the time that labor requires to carry out its transactions. Therefore, the real value of these deposits provides the same time-saving function for the home private financial sector that real coin, currency and checkable-deposit balances denominated in the home country's unit of account provide the home household sector. Furthermore, since the number of transactions associated with servicing its customers' imports is assumed to be proportional to the real value of these imports, the real value of the home private financial sector's deposits will indicate their ability to conserve the sector's transactions time. Consequently, we posit the following concave production function for completing the transactions associated with the home non-financial business sector's import activity:

(4.37) $T^{q*}_t = \chi(h^{q*f}_t N^{q*f}_t, \Re^*_t/p^*_{t-1})$, where χ_1 , $\chi_2 > 0$; χ_{11}, $\chi_{22} < 0$; and $\chi_{12} = \chi_{21} > 0$

and where

$h^{q*f}_t N^{q*f}_t$ = the total number of hours the home private financial sector uses people to service its transactions associated with the home non-financial sector's current payments for its imports.

According to (4.37), both labor and real deposits denominated in the foreign unit of account are productive in servicing the home non-financial business sector's imports during the current period; both have positive, but diminishing marginal products; and they are technical complements—the marginal product of each factor increases with a greater use of the other factor. Setting the right-hand side of (4.36) equal to the right-hand side of (4.37) yields the following implicit function:

(4.38) $\eta \cdot q^{*n}_t = \chi(h^{q*f}_t N^{q*f}_t, \Re^*_t/p^*_{t-1})$.

Next, solve (4.38) explicitly for the total labor hours necessary to service the home non-financial sector's imports:

(4.39) $h^{q*f}_t N^{q*f}_t = \kappa(q^{*n}_t, \Re^*_t/p^*_{t-1})$

where: $\kappa(\bullet) > 0$, $\kappa_1 = \eta/\chi_1 > 0$, $\kappa_2 = -\chi_2/\chi_1 < 0$, $\kappa_{11} = -\eta\chi_{11}/(\chi_1)^2 > 0$,

$\kappa_{22} = -(\chi_{22}/\chi_1) + \chi_2\chi_{12}/(\chi_1)^2 > 0$, $\kappa_{12} = -\eta\chi_{12}/(\chi_1)^2 < 0$, $\kappa_{21} = -(\chi_{21}/\chi_1) + \chi_2\chi_{11}/(\chi_1)^2 < 0$,

and $\kappa_{11} \cdot \kappa_{22} - \kappa_{12} \cdot \kappa_{21} = \eta[\chi_{11} \cdot \chi_{22} - \chi_{12} \cdot \chi_{21}]/(\chi_1)^3 > 0$.

Next Period

In a similar fashion, we may derive next period's anticipated total labor hours devoted to servicing real imports as an increasing function of the real imports the home non-financial business sector orders during the current period and as a decreasing function of the real value (in terms of the foreign unit of account) of the deposits the home private financial sector plans to hold by the beginning of next period.

Let:

N^{q*fd}_{t+1} = the number of people the home private financial sector plans to employ next period to service its customers' imports next period.

Then the total labor hours the sector plans to use next period to service these imports may be given by:

(4.40) $h \cdot N^{q*fd}_{t+1} = \zeta(q^{*nd}_{t+1}(\bullet), \Re^{*d}_{t+1}/p^{*}_{t})$ where $\zeta_1 > 0$, $\zeta_2 < 0$, ζ_{11}, $\zeta_{22} > 0$,

$\zeta_{12}, \zeta_{21} < 0$, and $\zeta_{11} \cdot \zeta_{22} - \zeta_{12} \cdot \zeta_{21} > 0$.

According to (4.40), ceteris paribus, the greater the number of goods the home non-financial business sector orders this period from the foreign non-financial business sector, the more labor services the home private financial sector requires next period to service its importing customers, as those goods are paid for and shipped. In addition, as the non-financial business sector imports more, the marginal product of real interbank deposits held by the home private financial sector rises, $\zeta_{21} < 0$. Also, holding the number of goods imported constant, the greater the real value of interbank deposits the home private financial sector holds at the foreign private financial sector by the beginning of next period, the fewer labor services it will require on the margin to service those imports, $\zeta_2 < 0$. However, as the sector continues to add to these real balances, their marginal product falls, $\zeta_{22} > 0$, in the sense that the labor-time saved by an extra unit of real balances diminishes (ζ_2 becomes closer to zero) as the real balances increase.

Servicing Deposits Held by the Foreign Private Financial Sector

The deposits held by the foreign banks at the home private financial sector provide the latter with loanable funds, which may then provide it with interest income. But the home private financial sector incurs real resource costs associated with servicing these interbank deposits. We assume that the level of services increases in proportion with the volume of foreign deposits, and that labor displays a positive, but diminishing, marginal product in providing these services.

Current Period

Let:

$\Re_t$ = the level of deposits (denominated in the home country's unit of account) held by the foreign private financial sector at the home private financial sector at the beginning of the current period.

T^{rf}_t = the number of transactions the home private financial sector must undertake during the current period in servicing the foreign private financial sector's current deposits.

We assume that the number of transactions the home private financial sector undertakes during the current period to service the foreign private financial sector's deposits is proportional to the real value of those deposits at the beginning of the current period. Then:

(4.41) $T^{rf}_t = \upsilon\cdot(\Re_t/p_t)$, where υ is a positive constant.

Next, let:

$h^{rf}_t N^{rf}_t$ = the total number of hours the home private financial sector devotes to undertaking the transactions associated with servicing the foreign private sector's deposits. Assuming that labor displays positive, but diminishing, marginal product in undertaking these transactions, the production function for these transactions may be represented by:

(4.42) $T^{rf}_t = \omega(h^{rf}_t N^{rf}_t)$, where $\omega' > 0$ and $\omega'' < 0$.

Setting the right-hand side of (4.41) equal to the right-hand side of (4.42) yields the following implicit function for the sector's demand for labor for servicing the foreign bank deposits as a function of the real value of those deposits:

(4.43) $\upsilon\cdot(\Re_t/p_t) = \omega(h^{rf}_t N^{rf}_t)$.

In principle, this function may be solved explicitly for $h^{rf}_t N^{rf}_t$:

(4.44) $h^{rf}_t N^{rf}_t = \varpi(\Re_t/p_t)$ where $\varpi' = \upsilon/\omega' > 0$ and $\varpi'' = -\upsilon\cdot\omega''/(\omega')^2 > 0$.

The implication of (4.44) is that the larger the volume of deposits held by the foreign private financial sector at the home private financial sector at the beginning of the current period, the greater the marginal (labor) cost of servicing those deposits.

Next Period

Similarly, we may posit the following anticipated labor requirements function for next period:

(4.45) $h\cdot N^{rfd}_{t+1} = \varphi(\Re^s_{t+1} /p^f_{t+1})$ where $\varphi' > 0$ and $\varphi'' > 0$.

where:

$\Re^{fs}_{t+1}$ = the level of deposits held by the foreign private financial sector at the end of the current period at the home private financial sector consistent with the plans of the home private financial sector.

Anticipated Total Labor Requirement for Next Period

The total amount of labor the home private financial business sector plans to use next period is given by the sum:

$$(4.46)\ hN^{fd}_{t+1} = \psi^{b}[p^{b}_{t}B^{f}_{t} - \varepsilon_{t}p^{b*}_{t}B^{*fd}_{t+1} + \hat{\varepsilon}_{t-1}[p^{b*f}_{t}B^{f*}_{t} + \Re^{*}_{t}] + \varepsilon_{t}(p^{b*}_{t} - p^{b*f}_{t})B^{*f}_{t}$$

$$-(X^{d}_{t+1} - X_{t}) + (A^{d}_{t+1} - A_{t}) + [(D^{s}_{t+1} - D_{t}) + (\Re^{fs}_{t+1} - \Re_{t}) - \varepsilon_{t}\Re^{*d}_{t+1}]$$

$$-\hat{r}[(D^{s}_{t+1} - D_{t}) + (\Re^{fs}_{t+1} - \Re_{t}) - \varepsilon_{t}(\Re^{*d}_{t+1} - \Re^{*}_{t})]\,] + \psi^{b*}(\varepsilon_{t}p^{b*}_{t}B^{*fd}_{t+1})$$

$$+\phi(D^{s}_{t+1}/p^{f}_{t+1}, X^{d}_{t+1}/p^{f}_{t+1}) + \zeta(q^{*nd}_{t+1}(\bullet), \Re^{*d}_{t+1}/p^{*}_{t}) + \varphi(\Re^{s}_{t+1}/p^{f}_{t+1}).$$

Home Private Financial Sector's Objective Function

Substituting the right-hand side of (4.46) for hN^{fd}_{t+1} into (4.15) yields the following objective function. Maximize:

$$(4.47)\ \mathbf{Z} = \Pi^{f}_{t}/p_{t} + \Pi^{fef}_{t+1}/(1 + r^{d}_{t})p^{f}_{t+1}$$

$$= (1/p_{t})[B^{f}_{t} + \hat{\varepsilon}_{t-1}B^{*f}_{t} - W_{t-1}h^{f}_{t}N^{f}_{t} - \rho_{t-1}A_{t} - r^{d}_{t-1}D_{t}]$$

$$+[1/(1+r^{d}_{t})p^{f}_{t+1}]\{[(1 + p^{bf}_{t+1})/p^{b}_{t}][p^{b}_{t}B^{f}_{t} - \varepsilon_{t}p^{b*}_{t}B^{*fd}_{t+1} + \hat{\varepsilon}_{t-1}[p^{b*f}_{t}B^{f*}_{t} + \Re^{*}_{t}]$$

$$+\varepsilon_{t}(p^{b*}_{t} - p^{b*f}_{t})B^{*f}_{t} - (X^{d}_{t+1} - X_{t}) + (A^{d}_{t+1} - A_{t}) + [(D^{s}_{t+1} - D_{t}) + (\Re^{fs}_{t+1} - \Re_{t}) - \varepsilon_{t}\Re^{*d}_{t+1}]$$

$$-\hat{r}[(D^{s}_{t+1} - D_{t}) + (\Re^{fs}_{t+1} - \Re_{t}) - \varepsilon_{t}(\Re^{*d}_{t+1} - \Re^{*}_{t})]]$$

$$+\hat{\varepsilon}_{t}(1 + p^{b*f}_{t+1})B^{*fd}_{t+1} + X^{d}_{t+1} + \hat{\varepsilon}_{t}\Re^{*d}_{t+1} - \hat{r}\varepsilon^{f}_{t+1}\Re^{*d}_{t+1} - (1 + \rho_{t})A^{d}_{t+1} - (1 - \hat{r})\Re^{fs}_{t+1}$$

$$-W_{t}[\psi^{b}[p^{b}_{t}B^{f}_{t} - \varepsilon_{t}p^{b*}_{t}B^{*fd}_{t+1} + \hat{\varepsilon}_{t-1}[p^{b*f}_{t}B^{f*}_{t} + \Re^{*}_{t}] + \varepsilon_{t}(p^{b*}_{t} - p^{b*f}_{t})B^{*f}_{t} - (X^{d}_{t+1} - X_{t})$$

$$+(A^{d}_{t+1} - A_{t}) + [(D^{s}_{t+1} - D_{t}) + (\Re^{fs}_{t+1} - \Re_{t}) - \varepsilon_{t}\Re^{*d}_{t+1}]$$

$$-\hat{r}[(D^{s}_{t+1} - D_{t}) + (\Re^{fs}_{t+1} - \Re_{t}) - \varepsilon_{t}(\Re^{*d}_{t+1} - \Re^{*}_{t})]] + \phi(D^{s}_{t+1}/p^{f}_{t+1}, X^{d}_{t+1}/p^{f}_{t+1})$$

$$+\psi^{b*}(\varepsilon_{t}p^{b*}_{t}B^{*fd}_{t+1}) + \zeta(q^{*nd}_{t+1}(\bullet), \Re^{*d}_{t+1}/p^{*}_{t}) + \varphi(\Re^{s}_{t+1}/p^{f}_{t+1})] - (1 - \hat{r} + r^{d}_{t})D^{s}_{t+1}\}$$

with respect to: the sector's (i) end-of-period demands for foreign bonds, excess reserves, advances, and deposits (denominated in the foreign unit of account) at foreign banks, and (ii) end-of-period volumes of checkable deposit liabilities and deposits held by the foreign banks consistent with its plan to maximize its present value. The solution for these variables may then be substituted into expression (4.12) to obtain the sector's end-of-period demand for home country bonds. To obtain this solution, we first specify the first-order conditions associated with the relevant choice variables.

First-Order Conditions

$$(4.48)\quad \frac{\partial Z}{\partial D^{s}_{t+1}} = (1-\hat{r})\cdot\{ [(1+p^{bf}_{t+1})/p^{b}_{t}] -1 -W_t\cdot\psi^{b'}\} -r^{d}_{t} -W_t\cdot\phi_1(1/p^{f}_{t+1}) = 0$$

$$(4.49)\quad \frac{\partial Z}{\partial \varepsilon_t p^{b*}_{t} B^{*fd}_{t+1}} = -\{ [(1+p^{bf}_{t+1})/p^{b}_{t}] -W_t\psi^{b'}\}+\hat{\varepsilon}_t(1+p^{b*f}_{t+1})/(\varepsilon_t p^{b*}_{t})-W_t\psi^{b*\prime}= 0$$

$$(4.50)\quad \frac{\partial Z}{\partial X^{d}_{t+1}} = -\{ [(1+p^{bf}_{t+1})/p^{b}_{t}] -1 -W_t\cdot\psi^{b'}\} -W_t\cdot\phi_2(1/p^{f}_{t+1}) = 0$$

$$(4.51)\quad \frac{\partial Z}{\partial A^{d}_{t+1}} = \{ [(1+p^{bf}_{t+1})/p^{b}_{t}] -1 -W_t\cdot\psi^{b'}\} -\rho_t = 0$$

$$(4.52)\quad \frac{\partial Z}{\partial \varepsilon_t \mathfrak{R}^{*d}_{t+1}} =-(1-\hat{r})\{[(1+p^{bf}_{t+1})/p^{b}_{t}]-W_t\psi^{b'}\}+\hat{\varepsilon}_t/\varepsilon_t -\hat{r}(\varepsilon^{f}_{t+1}/\varepsilon_t)-W_t\zeta_2/\varepsilon_t\, p^{*}_{t}=0$$

$$(4.53)\quad \frac{\partial Z}{\partial \mathfrak{R}^{fs}_{t+1}} = (1-\hat{r})\cdot\{[(1 +p^{bf}_{t+1})/p^{b}_{t}] -1 -W_t\psi^{b'}\} -W_t\, \varphi'(1/p^{f}_{t+1}) = 0.$$

From condition (4.51), the home private financial sector will borrow from the home central bank as long as the home discount rate is below the net return on home country bonds anticipated by the home private financial sector. As the sector adds to its holdings of home country bonds, the marginal product of labor in providing financial services associated with home country bonds falls, causing the marginal cost of holding home country bonds to rise, until the net return on home bonds falls to meet the home discount rate.

For the purpose of facilitating our discussion, let

$\mathfrak{I}^{bf}_{t}$ = the home financial business sector's anticipated net return on home country bonds = $\{[(1 +p^{bf}_{t+1})/p^{b}_{t}] -1 -W_t\psi^{b'}\}$.

Then, according to (4.48), the home private financial sector will desire to experience a growth in its end-of-period checkable-deposit liabilities as long as:

$$(4.54)\ (1-r^{\wedge})\cdot\Im^{bf}_{t} > r^{d}_{t} + W_{t}\cdot\ \phi_{1}(1/p^{f}_{t+1}).$$

The left-hand side of (4.54) indicates the marginal revenue to the home private financial sector resulting from having an additional unit of home checkable deposits outstanding at the end of the current period. By issuing an extra unit of home checkable deposits, the sector can lend the excess reserves generated by that extra unit and earn the net anticipated return on home country bonds on those funds. The right-hand side of (4.54) indicates the marginal cost to the sector of issuing an extra unit of checkable deposits by the end of the current period. The extra unit of checkable deposits means that the sector must pay an extra r^{d}_{t} in interest next period in addition to incurring an additional real resource cost of maintaining and servicing that deposit. The marginal cost of servicing checkable deposits rises as the marginal product of labor falls in providing those services. The optimal level of checkable deposits associated with maximizing the sector's objective occurs where the marginal revenue from an additional unit of checkable deposits equals the marginal cost of adding that unit.

From condition (4.49), the sector adds to its planned end-of-period holdings of foreign bonds up to the point at which:

$$(4.55)\ \Im^{bf}_{t} = \varepsilon^{\wedge}_{t}(1 + p^{b*f}_{t+1})/(\varepsilon_{t}p^{b*}_{t}) - 1 - W_{t}\psi^{b*\prime} = (\varepsilon^{\wedge}_{t}/\varepsilon_{t})\cdot(r^{b*}_{t} + p^{\sim b*f}_{t}) + f_{t} - W_{t}\psi^{b*\prime}$$

where:

$p^{\sim b*f}_{t}$ = the anticipated percentage change in the price of foreign country bonds $= (p^{b*f}_{t+1} - p^{b*}_{t})/(p^{b*}_{t})$.

f_{t} = the forward premium $= (\varepsilon^{\wedge}_{t} - \varepsilon_{t})/\varepsilon_{t} = f^{+}_{t} - 1$, i.e., where the anticipated net return on foreign country bonds, shown by the right-hand side of (4.55), is equal to the anticipated net return on home country bonds.

From condition (4.50), the sector will demand excess reserves for the end of the current period up to the point at which:

$$(4.56)\ \Im^{bf}_{t} = -W_{t}\cdot\phi_{2}(1/p^{f}_{t+1}),$$

in other words, it demands excess reserves up to the point at which the opportunity cost of excess reserves, shown by the anticipated net return on home country bonds, is equal to the value of the marginal product of excess reserves, i.e., the marginal wage expense saved by adding another unit of excess reserves to the sector's end-of-period holdings of that asset.

From (4.52), the sector will want to add to its end-of-period deposits at foreign banks by the end of the current period until:

$$(4.57)\ (1-r^{\wedge})\Im^{bf}_{t} = (\varepsilon^{\wedge}_{t}/\varepsilon_{t}) - 1 - r^{\wedge}[(\varepsilon^{f}_{t+1}/\varepsilon_{t}) - 1] - W_{t}\zeta_{2}/\varepsilon_{t}\, p^{*}_{t}.$$

The left-hand side of (4.57) denotes the marginal cost (in terms of the home country's unit of account) to the home private financial sector of holding a unit of deposits (denominated in the foreign country's unit of account) at the foreign private financial sector at the end of the current period. The marginal cost is less than the net return on home country bonds since the home sector reduces its own required reserves to the extent that it holds deposits at the foreign banks. The net return (in terms of the home country's unit of account) on these deposits at foreign banks is given by the right-hand side of (4.57). First, these deposits are productive in that they conserve the amount of labor time necessary to complete financial transactions associated with the real imports of the home non-financial business sector. The value of the marginal product of these deposits is shown by the term $-W_t\zeta_2/\varepsilon_t\, p^*_t$. In addition, the sector stands to gain financially next period to the extent that the current forward exchange rate exceeds the current spot rate, since the sector plans to buy these deposits at the spot rate this period and trade them at the current forward rate next period. However, for the purpose of reducing next period's required reserves, the sector anticipates that these reserves will be valued at the spot rate it expects will prevail next period, ε^f_{t+1}. To the extent that the next period's expected spot rate exceeds the current spot rate, the sector anticipates it will lose reserves (valued in terms of the home country's unit of account) with the passage of time.

According to expression (4.51), the sector will add to the amount it borrows from the home central bank up to the point at which the net return on home country bonds just equals the given discount rate set by the home central bank:

(4.58) $\Im^{bf}_t = \rho_t$.

From condition (4.53), the home private financial sector will want to issue (non-interest bearing) interbank deposits to the foreign private financial sector as long as the marginal revenue from those deposits, given by the net interest income generated by the excess reserves obtained from those deposits, is at least as great as the marginal cost of servicing those interbank deposits, as shown by the term $W_t\varphi'(1/p^f_{t+1})$:

(4.59) $(1-r^\wedge)\Im^{bf}_t = W_t\varphi'(1/p^f_{t+1})$.

Home Private Financial Sector's Desired End-of-Period Balance Sheet

Totally differentiating (4.48)–(4.53) yields a simultaneous system of six equations in the six unknowns: the level of checkable deposits at the end of the current period consistent with the sector's desire to maximize its present value, $D^s_{t+1,}$ the sector's end-of-period demand for foreign bonds, $\varepsilon_t p^{b*}_t B^{*fd}_{t+1}$, the sector's end-of-period demand for excess reserves, X^d_{t+1}, the sector's end-of-period demand for advances, A^d_{t+1}, the sector's end-of-period demand for deposits held at the foreign private financial sector, $\varepsilon_t \mathfrak{R}^{*d}_{t+1}$, and the level of interbank deposits held by the foreign private financial sector at the end of the current period consistent with the home private financial sector's desire to maximize its present value, $\mathfrak{R}^{fs}_{t+1}$. The qualitative responses of these variables to parametric changes can be obtained by solving for the changes in the dependent variables in response to each of the parametric changes taken separately. Substituting the resulting supply and demand functions back into (4.12) yields the sector's demand for home bonds, $p^b_t B^{fd}_{t+1}$.

Home Country's Bond Rate

From condition (4.58), as long as the home discount rate remains unchanged, so must the net rate of return on home bonds. Therefore, should the home bond rate, r^b_t, increase, the home private financial sector will increase its end-of-period holdings of home bonds until the net rate of return on those bonds has returned to its original level. The sector will finance its purchase of those bonds by increasing its end-of-period advances from the home central bank. Since the net return on home bonds must return to its original level, the sector will not desire to finance any purchases of home bonds either by reducing its end-of-period holdings of excess reserves or its end-of-period holdings of interbank deposits at foreign banks. From (4.56) and (4.57), the value of the marginal products of both of these assets must remain unchanged as well and will do so only if the levels of these balances remain unchanged. Also, from (4.55), if the net rate of return on home bonds remains unchanged, so must the net rate of return on foreign bonds; the sector's end-of-period demand for foreign bonds also remains unchanged. By the same token, from (4.53) and (4.59), the home private financial sector's marginal costs of issuing checkable deposits and interbank deposits held by foreign banks must also remain unchanged; the sector will not want to change the end-of-period levels of these liabilities. Therefore, we have:

$$(4.60)\quad \partial D^s_{t+1}/\partial r^b_t = 0,\ \partial \varepsilon_t p^{b*}_t B^{*fd}_{t+1}/\partial r^b_t = 0,\ \partial X^d_{t+1}/\partial r^b_t = 0,\ \partial A^d_{t+1}/\partial r^b_t > 0,$$

$$\partial \varepsilon_t \mathfrak{R}^{*d}_{t+1}/\partial r^b_t = 0,\ \partial \mathfrak{R}^{fs}_{t+1}/\partial r^b_t = 0,\ \text{and}\ \partial p^b_t B^{fd}_{t+1}/\partial r^b_t > 0$$

with $\partial p^b_t B^{fd}_{t+1}/\partial r^b_t = \partial A^d_{t+1}/\partial r^b_t$.

Foreign Bond Rate

From (4.55) and (4.58), as long as the home discount rate remains unchanged, so must the net return on foreign bonds. Therefore, if the foreign bond rate should increase, the home private financial sector will continue to add to its holdings of foreign bonds until the net return on these bonds falls back to its original level. The sector will finance these purchases with additional advances from the home central bank at the fixed discount rate. Since the sector can borrow an unlimited amount from the home central bank, it compares both the home bond rate and the foreign bond rate to the discount rate rather than to each other. Therefore, when the foreign bond rate rises, the sector does not reduce its demand for home bonds, for to do so would cause the net return on these bonds to rise above the fixed discount rate. Since the net return on home bonds remains unchanged, the sector does not alter its end-of-period demands for excess reserves or deposits it holds at foreign banks, so that the value of the marginal products of these assets may remain unchanged as well. The sector does not alter its end-of-period demands for these assets when the foreign bond rate rises. Also, for the same reason, the sector does not alter its desired end-of-period amounts of checkable deposits and interbank deposit liabilities. Therefore, we have:

$$(4.61)\quad \partial D^{s}_{t+1}/\partial r^{b*}_{t} = 0,\ \partial \varepsilon_t p^{b*}_{t} B^{*fd}_{t+1}/\partial r^{b*}_{t} > 0,\ \partial X^{d}_{t+1}/\partial r^{b*}_{t} = 0,\ \partial A^{d}_{t+1}/\partial r^{b*}_{t} > 0,$$

$$\partial \varepsilon_t \Re^{*d}_{t+1}/\partial r^{b*}_{t} = 0,\ \partial \Re^{fs}_{t+1}/\partial r^{b*}_{t} = 0, \text{ and } \partial p^{b}_{t} B^{fd}_{t+1}/\partial r^{b*}_{t} = 0$$

with $\partial \varepsilon_t p^{b*}_{t} B^{*fd}_{t+1}/\partial r^{b*}_{t} = \partial A^{d}_{t+1}/\partial r^{b*}_{t}$.

Spot Rate

Ceteris paribus, an increase in the spot exchange rate reduces the anticipated market return on foreign bonds purchased by the home private financial sector during the current period because it increases the current market price of a foreign bond in terms of the home country's unit of account. As a result the home private financial sector will reduce its end-of-period demand for foreign bonds. From (4.57), the rise in the spot rate also reduces the anticipated net return on deposits (denominated in the foreign country's unit of account), $(\varepsilon^{\wedge}_{t}/\varepsilon_t) - 1 - r^{\wedge}[(\varepsilon^{f}_{t+1}/\varepsilon_t) - 1] - W_t\zeta_2/\varepsilon_t p^{*}_{t}$, that the home private financial sector holds at foreign banks at the end of the current period because it increases the current price which the sector must pay in terms of the home country's unit of account to purchase a unit of these deposits. Therefore, the sector reduces its end-of-period demands for both foreign bonds and deposits at foreign banks as the spot rate rises. The sector simultaneously reduces its end-of-period demand for advances. Therefore, we have:

$$(4.62)\quad \partial D^{s}_{t+1}/\partial \varepsilon_t = 0,\ \partial \varepsilon_t p^{b*}_{t} B^{*fd}_{t+1}/\partial \varepsilon_t < 0,\ \partial X^{d}_{t+1}/\partial \varepsilon_t = 0,\ \partial A^{d}_{t+1}/\partial \varepsilon_t < 0,$$

$$\partial \varepsilon_t \Re^{*d}_{t+1}/\partial \varepsilon_t < 0,\ \partial \Re^{fs}_{t+1}/\partial \varepsilon_t = 0, \text{ and } \partial p^{b}_{t} B^{fd}_{t+1}/\partial \varepsilon_t = 0$$

with $(\partial \varepsilon_t p^{b*}_{t} B^{*fd}_{t+1}/\partial \varepsilon_t) + (\partial \varepsilon_t \Re^{*d}_{t+1}/\partial \varepsilon_t) = \partial A^{d}_{t+1}/\partial \varepsilon_t$.

Forward Rate

An increase in the forward exchange rate produces effects opposite to those generated by an increase in the spot rate. The higher the forward rate, the greater the net returns from holding foreign bonds and deposits at foreign banks, because these deposits translate into a greater number of units of the home country's unit of account next period. Therefore, we have:

$$(4.63)\quad \partial D^{s}_{t+1}/\partial\varepsilon^{\wedge}_{t} = 0,\ \partial\varepsilon_{t}p^{b*}{}_{t}B^{*fd}{}_{t+1}/\ \partial\varepsilon^{\wedge}_{t} > 0,\ \partial X^{d}_{t+1}/\ \partial\varepsilon^{\wedge}_{t} = 0,\ \partial A^{d}_{t+1}/\ \partial\varepsilon^{\wedge}_{t} > 0,$$

$$\partial\varepsilon_{t}\ \Re^{*d}{}_{t+1}/\ \partial\varepsilon^{\wedge}_{t} > 0,\ \partial\Re^{fs}{}_{t+1}/\ \partial\varepsilon^{\wedge}_{t} = 0,\ \text{and}\ \partial p^{b}{}_{t}B^{fd}{}_{t+1}/\partial\varepsilon^{\wedge}_{t} = 0$$

with $(\partial\varepsilon_{t}p^{b*}{}_{t}B^{*fd}{}_{t+1}/\ \partial\varepsilon^{\wedge}_{t}) + (\partial\varepsilon_{t}\ \Re^{*d}{}_{t+1}/\partial\varepsilon^{\wedge}_{t}) = \partial A^{d}_{t+1}/\partial\varepsilon^{\wedge}_{t}$.

Interest Rate on Home Checkable Deposits

An increase in the interest rate on home checkable deposits increases the marginal cost of issuing these deposits, causing the desired end-of-period amount of this liability to fall. The reduction in its ex ante supply of checkable deposits reduces the value of the marginal product of excess reserves, causing the sector to reduce its end-of-period demand for excess reserves. Ceteris paribus, the sector's end-of-period demands for home and foreign bonds and its end-of-period demand for interbank deposits at foreign banks all remain unchanged. Its ex ante end-of-period supply of interbank deposits to foreign banks also remains unchanged. What happens to the sector's end-of-period demand for advances depends upon the amount by which its ex ante end-of-period supply of checkable deposits falls relative to the amount by which its demand for excess reserves falls. If $(1\text{-}r^{\wedge})$ times the reduction in the supply of checkable deposits exceeds the fall in ex ante excess reserves, the sector's end-of-period demand for advances increases. The reason is that, ceteris paribus, a given reduction in the supply of checkable deposits reduces end-of-period excess reserves by $(1\text{-}r^{\wedge})$ times that amount; if desired excess reserves fall less than that, the sector will increase borrowing to achieve its desired end-of-period balance sheet. In effect, the sector will be substituting funds borrowed from the home central bank for funds borrowed from the household sector to maintain its desired asset holdings. Since, in practice, the volume of excess reserves held by private banks is small relative to the volume of their checkable deposit liabilities, it is unlikely that planned excess reserves will diminish by as much as $(1\text{-}r^{\wedge})$ times the fall in ex ante checkable deposits. Therefore, we assume:

$$(4.64)\ \partial D^{s}_{t+1}/\partial r^{d}_{t} < 0,\ \partial\varepsilon_{t}p^{b*}{}_{t}B^{*fd}{}_{t+1}/\partial r^{d}_{t} = 0,\ \partial X^{d}_{t+1}/\partial r^{d}_{t} < 0,\ \partial A^{d}_{t+1}/\partial r^{d}_{t} > 0,$$

$$\partial\varepsilon_{t}\ \Re^{*d}{}_{t+1}/\partial r^{d}_{t} = 0,\ \partial\Re^{fs}{}_{t+1}/\partial r^{d}_{t} = 0,\ \text{and}\ \partial p^{b}{}_{t}B^{fd}{}_{t+1}/\partial r^{d}_{t} = 0$$

with $\partial A^d_{t+1}/\partial r^d_t = -(1-r^\wedge)(\partial D^s_{t+1}/\partial r^d_t) + (\partial X^d_{t+1}/\partial r^d_t)$.

Home Discount Rate

An increase in the home discount rate increases the opportunity costs associated with every one of the home private financial sector's assets; instead of holding these assets, the sector could reduce the amount of advances it owes the home central bank. In addition, the higher home discount rate increases the sector's return on funds borrowed in the form of checkable deposits and interbank deposits owed to foreign banks rather than borrowing from the home central bank; the sector's ex ante end-of-period deposit liabilities of both types will increase in order to decrease its end-of-period advances. To the extent that this sector increases its ex ante supply of checkable deposits, the value of the marginal product of excess reserves increases. Therefore the rise in the home discount rate indirectly stimulates the sector's demand for excess reserves. However, we assume that the direct effect, produced by the higher opportunity cost of holding excess reserves, dominates so that the net effect upon the sector's demand for excess reserves is negative. Therefore, we have:

$$(4.65)\ \partial D^s_{t+1}/\partial \rho_t > 0,\ \partial \varepsilon_t p^{b*}{}_t B^{*fd}{}_{t+1}/\partial \rho_t < 0,\ \partial X^d_{t+1}/\partial \rho_t < 0,\ \partial A^d_{t+1}/\partial \rho_t < 0,$$

$$\partial \varepsilon_t \Re^{*d}{}_{t+1}/\partial \rho_t < 0,\ \partial \Re^{fs}{}_{t+1}/\partial \rho_t > 0, \text{ and } \partial p^b{}_t B^{fd}{}_{t+1}/\partial \rho_t < 0$$

with

$$\partial A^d_{t+1}/\partial \rho_t = (\partial X^d_{t+1}/\partial \rho_t) + (\partial \varepsilon_t p^{b*}{}_t B^{*fd}{}_{t+1}/\partial \rho_t) + (\partial p^b{}_t B^{fd}{}_{t+1}/\partial \rho_t) + (\partial \varepsilon_t \Re^{*d}{}_{t+1}/\partial \rho_t)$$

$$-(\partial \Re^{fs}{}_{t+1}/\partial \rho_t) - (1-r^\wedge)(\partial D^s_{t+1}/\partial \rho_t)\ .$$

Home Country's Money Wage

An increase in the home money wage reduces the anticipated net marginal return to holding both home and foreign bonds. In addition, it increases the marginal cost of issuing and servicing checkable-deposit and interbank-deposit liabilities. On the other hand, an increase in the home money wage increases the values of the marginal products of excess reserves and interbank deposits due from foreign banks, since excess reserves and deposits due from foreign banks reduce the real resource requirements of the home private financial sector. Therefore the higher W_t happens to be, the lower the sector's demands for interest earning assets, the higher its demands for non-interest earning assets and the lower its ex ante supplies of deposit liabilities. The decreases in the sector's demands for interest earning assets tend to cause its demand for advances to fall as well. However, ceteris paribus, the increases in its demands for excess reserves and deposits due from foreign banks and the decreases in its ex ante supplies of checkable deposits and deposits due to foreign banks all tend to cause the sector to increase its demand for advances. The net effect upon ex ante advances is indeterminate. Therefore, we have:

$$(4.66)\ \partial D^{s}_{t+1}/\partial W_t > 0,\ \partial \varepsilon_t p^{b*}{}_t B^{*fd}{}_{t+1}/\partial W_t < 0,\ \partial X^{d}{}_{t+1}/\partial W_t < 0,\ \partial A^{d}{}_{t+1}/\partial W_t > 0 \text{ or } \leq 0,$$

$$\partial \varepsilon_t \mathfrak{R}^{*d}{}_{t+1}/\partial W_t < 0,\ \partial \mathfrak{R}^{fs}{}_{t+1}/\partial W_t > 0, \text{ and } \partial p^{b}{}_t B^{fd}{}_{t+1}/\partial W_t < 0$$

$$\text{with } \partial A^{d}{}_{t+1}/\partial W_t = (\partial X^{d}{}_{t+1}/\partial W_t) + (\partial \varepsilon_t p^{b*}{}_t B^{*fd}{}_{t+1}/\partial W_t) + (\partial p^{b}{}_t B^{fd}{}_{t+1}/\partial W_t)$$

$$+ (\partial \varepsilon_t \mathfrak{R}^{*d}{}_{t+1}/\partial W_t) - (\partial \mathfrak{R}^{fs}{}_{t+1}/\partial W_t) - (1-r^{\wedge})(\partial D^{s}{}_{t+1}/\partial W_t).$$

Change in p^* *or* $q^{*nd}{}_{t+1}$

An increase in the current period price of privately-produced foreign goods reduces the real value of the deposits the home private sector plans to hold at foreign banks by the end of the current period. This increases the marginal product of those deposits, inducing the home private financial sector to increase its desired end-of-period deposits due from foreign banks. Ceteris paribus, this causes the sector to increase its planned end-of-period level of advances from the home central bank to finance the increase in its interbank deposits at foreign banks.

An increase in the number of foreign privately-produced goods that the home non-financial business sector orders during the current period also increases the marginal product of interbank deposits held by the home private financial sector at foreign banks. Therefore, an increase in $q^{*nd}{}_{t+1}$ also causes the sector to increase its end-of-period demand for deposits due from foreign banks and its demand for advances from the home central bank. Therefore,

$$(4.67)\quad \partial D^{s}{}_{t+1}/\partial p^{*}{}_t = 0,\ \partial \varepsilon_t p^{b*}{}_t B^{*fd}{}_{t+1}/\partial p^{*}{}_t = 0,\ \partial X^{d}{}_{t+1}/\partial p^{*}{}_t = 0,\ \partial A^{d}{}_{t+1}/\partial p^{*}{}_t > 0,$$

$$\partial \varepsilon_t \mathfrak{R}^{*d}{}_{t+1}/\partial p^{*}{}_t > 0,\ \partial \mathfrak{R}^{fs}{}_{t+1}/\partial p^{*}{}_t = 0, \text{ and } \partial p^{b}{}_t B^{fd}{}_{t+1}/\partial p^{*}{}_t = 0,$$

$$\text{with } \partial A^{d}{}_{t+1}/\partial p^{*}{}_t = \partial \varepsilon_t \mathfrak{R}^{*d}{}_{t+1}/\partial p^{*}{}_t.$$

An analogous set of responses is generated by an increase in $q^{*nd}{}_{t+1}$.

Summary

The above analysis yields the following demand and supply functions for the home private financial sector's end-of-period assets and liabilities:

$$(4.68)\ p^{b}{}_t B^{fd}{}_{t+1} = p^{b}{}_t B^{fd}{}_{t+1}(\underset{+}{r^{b}{}_t}, \underset{-}{\rho_t})$$

$$(4.69)\ X^d_{t+1} = X^d_{t+1}(\underset{-}{r^d_t}, \underset{-}{\rho_t})$$

$$(4.70)\ \varepsilon_t p^{b*}_t B^{*fd}_{t+1} = \varepsilon_t p^{b*}_t B^{*fd}_{t+1}(\underset{+}{r^{b*}_t}, \underset{+}{\hat{\varepsilon}_t}, \underset{-}{\varepsilon_t}, \underset{-}{\rho_t})$$

$$(4.71)\ A^d_{t+1} = A^d_{t+1}(\underset{+}{r^b_t}, \underset{+}{r^{b*}_t}, \underset{+}{\hat{\varepsilon}_t}, \underset{-}{\varepsilon_t}, \underset{+}{r^d_t}, \underset{-}{\rho_t}, \underset{+}{p^*_t}, \underset{+}{q^{*nd}_{t+1}})$$

$$(4.72)\ D^s_{t+1} = D^s_{t+1}(\underset{-}{r^d_t}, \underset{+}{\rho_t})$$

$$(4.73)\ \varepsilon_t \Re^{*d}_{t+1} = \varepsilon_t \Re^{*d}_{t+1}(\underset{+}{\hat{\varepsilon}_t}, \underset{-}{\varepsilon_t}, \underset{-}{\rho_t}, \underset{+}{p^*_t}, \underset{+}{q^{*nd}_{t+1}})$$

$$(4.74)\ \Re^{fs}_{t+1} = \Re^{fs}_{t+1}(\underset{+}{\rho_t})$$

where, for simplicity, we have abstracted from the effects associated with changes in W_t. The number of hours the sector uses its current employees is given by:

$$(4.75)\ h^f_t N^f_t = h^f_t N^f_t(\underset{+}{p^b_t B^f_t}, \underset{+}{\varepsilon_t p^{b*}_t B^{*f}_t}, \underset{+}{D_t/p_t}, \underset{-}{X_t/p_t}, \underset{-}{\Re^*_t/p^*_{t-1}}, \underset{+}{\Re_t/p_t}).$$

The sector's end-of-current period demand for employees is represented by:

$$(4.76)\ N^{fd}_{t+1} = N^{fd}_{t+1}(\underset{+}{r^b_t}, \underset{+}{r^{b*}_t}, \underset{+}{\hat{\varepsilon}_t}, \underset{-}{\varepsilon_t}, \underset{-}{r^d_t}, \underset{+}{\rho_t}, \underset{-}{W_t}).$$

In the next section we consider the corresponding functions associated with the foreign country's private financial sector.

Foreign Private Financial Sector

Let:

B^{f*d}_{t+1} = the number of home country bonds the foreign private financial sector plans to hold by the end of the current period.

B^{f*}_t = the number of home country bonds the foreign private financial sector holds at the beginning of the current period.

$B^{*f^*}_t$ = the number of foreign country bonds the foreign private financial sector holds at the beginning of the current period.

$B^{*f^*d}_{t+1}$ = the number of foreign country bonds the foreign private financial sector plans to hold by the end of the current period.

D^{*s}_{t+1} = the volume of interest-earning checkable deposits outstanding at the end of the current period at the foreign private financial sector consistent with the plans of that sector (i.e., the foreign private financial sector's ex ante end-of-period supply of checkable deposits).

$h^{f^*}_t N^{f^*}_t$ = the number of hours the foreign private financial sector uses its current employees.

$N^{f^*d}_{t+1}$ = the foreign private financial sector's end-of-current period demand for employees.

$r^{d^*}_t$ = the current period interest rate on checkable deposits issued by the foreign private financial sector.

$\mathfrak{R}^d_{t+1}$ = the volume of interbank deposits the foreign private financial sector plans to hold at the home private financial sector at the end of the current period.

$\mathfrak{R}^{*f^*s}_{t+1}$ = the volume of interbank deposits (denominated in the foreign country's unit of account) held by the home private financial sector at the foreign private financial sector at the end of the current period consistent with the plans of the foreign private financial sector.

X^*_t = the volume of excess reserves (valued in terms of the foreign country's unit of account) held by the foreign private financial sector at the beginning of the current period.

X^{*d}_{t+1} = the foreign private financial sector's end-of-period demand for excess reserves (valued in terms of the foreign country's unit of account).

Then the foreign country's private financial sector's end-of-period demands for home country bonds, excess reserves, foreign country bonds, and advances, its end-of-period supply of checkable deposits, its end-of-period demand for interbank deposits denominated in the home country's unit of account, and its end-of-period supply of interbank deposits denominated in the foreign country's unit of account (all valued in terms of the foreign country's unit of account) may be shown respectively by the following expressions:

$$(4.77)\ p^b_t B^{f*d}_{t+1}/\varepsilon_t = p^b_t B^{f*d}_{t+1}/\varepsilon_t(\underset{+}{r^b_t},\ \underset{-}{\hat{\varepsilon}_t},\ \underset{+}{\varepsilon_t},\ \underset{-}{\rho^*_t})$$

$$(4.78)\ X^{*d}_{t+1} = X^{*d}_{t+1}(\underset{-}{r^{d*}_t},\ \underset{-}{\rho^*_t})$$

$$(4.79)\ p^{b*}_t B^{*f*d}_{t+1} = p^{b*}_t B^{*f*d}_{t+1}(\underset{+}{r^{b*}_t},\ \underset{-}{\rho^*_t})$$

$$(4.80)\ A^{*d}_{t+1} = A^{*d}_{t+1}(\underset{+}{r^b_t},\ \underset{+}{r^{b*}_t},\ \underset{-}{\hat{\varepsilon}_t},\ \underset{+}{\varepsilon_t},\ \underset{+}{r^{d*}_t},\ \underset{-}{\rho^*_t})$$

$$(4.81)\ D^{*s}_{t+1} = D^{*s}_{t+1}(\underset{-}{r^{d*}_t},\ \underset{+}{\rho^*_t})$$

$$(4.82)\ \Re^d_{t+1}/\varepsilon_t = \Re^d_{t+1}/\varepsilon_t(\underset{-}{\hat{\varepsilon}_t},\ \underset{+}{\varepsilon_t},\ \underset{-}{\rho^*_t},\ \underset{+}{p_t},\ \underset{+}{q^{n*d}_{t+1}})$$

$$(4.83)\ \Re^{*f*s}_{t+1} = \Re^{*f*s}_{t+1}(\underset{+}{\rho^*_t}).$$

The number of hours the sector uses its current employees is given by:

$$(4.84)\ h^{f*}_t N^{f*}_t = h^{f*}_t N^{f*}_t(\underset{+}{p^b_t B^f_t/\varepsilon_t},\ \underset{+}{p^{b*}_t B^{*f}_t},\ \underset{+}{D^*_t/p^*_t},\ \underset{-}{X^*_t/p^*_t},\ \underset{+}{\Re^*_t/p^*_t},\ \underset{-}{\Re_t/p_{t-1}}).$$

The sector's end-of-current period demand for employees is represented by:

$$(4.85)\ N^{f*d}_{t+1} = N^{f*d}_{t+1}(\underset{+}{r^b_t},\ \underset{+}{r^{b*}_t},\ \underset{-}{\hat{\varepsilon}_t},\ \underset{+}{\varepsilon_t},\ \underset{-}{r^{d*}_t},\ \underset{+}{\rho^*_t},\ \underset{-}{W^*_t}).$$

Now that the decisions of the central banks and private financial sectors in both countries have been specified, it is time to specify the optimal behavior of the non-bank sectors in both countries now that product prices, wages, production and employment have been determined. These matters are addressed in Chapter 5.

CHAPTER FIVE

Non-Banking Sectors Revisited

Introduction

By the beginning of this chapter, both government sectors know the amount of public goods they will produce next period, but they still must decide the optimal combination of inputs to use in producing those goods. These decisions rest upon current interest rates and exchange rates, which were not yet known when the respective household sectors selected next period's production of public goods. By the beginning of this chapter, the non-financial business sectors in each country have also announced current period wages and prices and decided current output and employment. But, they have yet to decide their scales of plant with which to begin next period, in particular, their end-of-current period levels of physical capital, the number of people they will employ by the end of the current period, the volume of intermediate goods they will order this period from the other country for delivery and use next period, and their end-of-period stocks of their respective non-renewable resources. These decisions too depend upon current interest rates and exchange rates. The analysis contained in this chapter provides the foundation not only for the non-financial business sectors' participation in the financial markets, but also for their demand for both domestic and foreign goods. The household sectors' decisions analyzed in Chapter 2 in connection with their selection of next period's production of public goods must also be updated now that current wages, prices and disposable incomes are known. In short, the analysis contained in the present chapter, coupled with the analysis of Chapter 4 lays the foundation for the simultaneous determination of current period interest rates, exchange rates, current spending by each sector, and the end-of-period scales of plant by both private and public producers in both countries. The demand and supply functions of the individual sectors derived in Chapters 4 and 5 will be combined in Chapters 6–8 to form markets for checkable deposits, bonds, non-interest bearing money and spot and forward contracts.

Home Government Sector

Once g_{t+1} has been decided by the home country's household sector and once W_t and p_t have been announced by the home non-financial business sector in this model, the home government sector's new problem is to minimize next period's outlays, O_{t+1}, with respect to its effective end-of-period demands for labor, N^{gd}_{t+1}, and physical capital, K^{gd}_{t+1}. At the same time, it determines the value of its effective end-of-period supply of bonds to the home bond market, $p^b_t B^{gs}_{t+1}$. Therefore the home government's new objective is to minimize:

$$(5.1)\ O_{t+1} = W_t hN^{gd}_{t+1} + (1 + p^{bg}_{t+1})B^{gs}_{t+1} - p^g_{t+1}K^{gd}_{t+1}$$

with respect to N^{gd}_{t+1}, B^{gs}_{t+1} and K^{gd}_{t+1} subject to:

$$(5.2)\quad g_{t+1} = g_{t+1}(\ hN^{gd}_{t+1}, K^{gd}_{t+1})$$

where g_{t+1} is known and subject to:

$$(5.3)\quad p^b_t(B^{gs}_{t+1} - B^g_t) = W_{t-1}h^g_t N^g_t + p_t(K^{gd}_{t+1} - K^g_t) + B^g_t\ - T_t - \Pi^c_t - p^x_t R^x_t - p^p_t\ \bar{P}^{pd}.$$

Expression (5.2) details the combinations of workers and physical capital next period that could be used to produce the now predetermined level of public goods next period. Equation (5.3) stipulates the relevant budget constraint for this decision; in particular, it stipulates that, ceteris paribus, the more physical capital the government acquires this period to carry out public goods production next period, the more it must borrow during the current period. From (5.3), the optimal level of B^{gs}_{t+1} is known once the sector solves for N^{gd}_{t+1} and K^{gd}_{t+1}.

Finding the first-order necessary conditions with respect to N^{gd}_{t+1} and K^{gd}_{t+1}, we have:

$$(5.4)\quad \partial O_{t+1}/\partial hN^{gd}_{t+1} \ = \ W_t - \lambda(\ \partial g_{t+1}/\partial hN^{gd}_{t+1})$$

$$(5.5)\ \partial O_{t+1}/\partial K^{gd}_{t+1} \ = \ -p^g_{t+1} + (1+p^{bg}_{t+1})(p_t/p^b_t)\ -\lambda(\ \partial g_{t+1}/\partial K^{gd}_{t+1}).$$

Let $p^{\sim bg}_t = (p^{bg}_{t+1} - p^b_t)/p^b_t$ and let $r^b_t = 1/p^b_t$; then $(1+ p^{bg}_{t+1})(p_t/p^b_t) = p_t(\ r^b_t + 1 + p^{\sim bg}_t)$. Then, rearranging terms and dividing one condition by the other produces the following expression equating the technical rate of substitution of labor for physical capital to the market rate of substitution of labor for capital:

$$(5.6)\ (\partial g_{t+1}/\partial hN^{gd}_{t+1})/(\partial g_{t+1}/\partial K^{gd}_{t+1}) = W_t\ /[(1+r^b_t + p^{\sim bg}_t)p_t - p^g_{t+1}]$$

$$= W_t\ /[(r^b_t + p^{\sim bg}_t - p^{\sim g}_t)p_t]$$

where $p^{\sim g}_t$ denotes the rate of change in the price of home country goods that the home government sector anticipates will take place between the current period and next period, $(p^{\sim g}_t = (p^g_{t+1} - p_t)/p_t)$. According to condition (5.6), the home government will hire people to work next period and add to its end-of-period stock of physical capital up to the point at which the technical rate of substitution of labor for capital, shown by the slope of the isoquant associated with the predetermined value for g_{t+1}, is equal to the market rate of substitution. See Figure 5.1. The denominator of the ratio on the far right-hand side of (5.6) denotes the user cost of physical capital from the point of view of the home government sector. Note that neither $p^{\sim bg}_t$ nor $p^{\sim g}_t$ are observable to an outsider.

On the margin, the higher the money wage announced by the home nonfinancial business sector during the current period, the more the home government will substitute physical capital for labor in next period's production; ceteris paribus, the higher the current interest rate on home country bonds or the higher the current price of privately-produced goods, the more the government will substitute labor for physical capital in next period's production of public goods.

Figure 5.1 **Technical vs. Market Rates of Substitution of Next Period's Labor for Next Period's Capital**

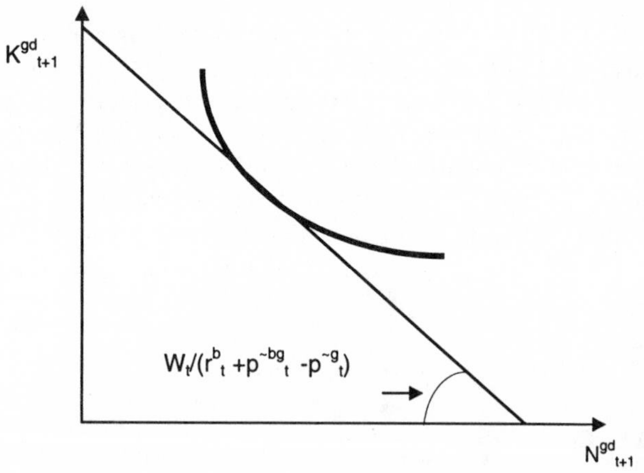

Ceteris paribus, the greater the level of public-goods production which the home household sector has selected for next period, the more of both factors the home government will use in next period's production of those goods. The resulting demand functions for next period's workers and physical capital by the home country are given by:

$$(5.7)\quad N^{gd}_{t+1} = N^{gd}_{t+1}(\underset{-}{W_t}, \underset{+}{p_t}, \underset{+}{r^b_t}, \underset{+}{g_{t+1}})$$

$$(5.8)\quad K^{gd}_{t+1} = K^{gd}_{t+1}(\underset{+}{W_t}, \underset{-}{p_t}, \underset{-}{r^b_t}, \underset{+}{g_{t+1}}).$$

The home government's end-of-period supply of bonds to the home bond market is now:

$$(5.9)\ p^b{}_t B^{gs}{}_{t+1} = W_{t-1} h^g{}_t N^g{}_t + p_t K^{gd}{}_{t+1}(W_t, p_t, r^b{}_t, g_{t+1}) - p_t K^g{}_t + (1+p^b{}_t) B^g{}_t$$

$$- T_t - \Pi^c{}_t - p^x{}_t R^{xd}{}_t - p^p{}_t\ \overline{P}^{pd}.$$

When the home government prepared the public goods menu for the home household sector last period, it specified a level of taxes, T_t, necessary to provide public goods in the current period. As it calculated the taxes it would require, it deducted the amount of revenue it anticipated it would receive this period from the international agent's sale of pollution and extraction rights to the home non-financial business sector. Therefore, the home government's (ex ante) supply of bonds for the end of the current period is affected by the international agent's current sales of pollution and extraction rights to the home non-financial business sector only to the extent that these sales generate more or less income to the home government than it anticipated last period as it prepared the current period's public goods menu.

Foreign Government Sector

Analogously, the foreign government sector's end-of-period demands for workers and physical capital and its end-of-period (ex ante) supply of bonds to the foreign bond market may be derived as:

$$(5.10)\ N^{g*d}{}_{t+1} = N^{g*d}{}_{t+1}(\underset{-}{W^*{}_t}, \underset{+}{p^*{}_t}, \underset{+}{r^{b*}{}_t}, \underset{+}{g^*{}_{t+1}})$$

$$(5.11)\ K^{*g*d}{}_{t+1} = K^{*g*d}{}_{t+1}(\underset{+}{W^*{}_t}, \underset{-}{p^*{}_t}, \underset{-}{r^{b*}{}_t}, \underset{+}{g^*{}_{t+1}})$$

$$(5.12)\ p^{b*}{}_t B^{*g*s}{}_{t+1} = W^*{}_{t-1} h^{g*}{}_t N^{g*}{}_t + p^*{}_t K^{*g*d}{}_{t+1}(W^*{}_t, p^*{}_t, r^{b*}{}_t, g^*{}_{t+1}) - p^*{}_t K^{*g*}{}_t$$

$$+ (1+p^{b*}{}_t) B^{*g*}{}_t - T^*{}_t - \Pi^{c*}{}_t - (p^x{}_t R^{x*d}{}_t + p^p{}_t\ \overline{P}^{p*d})/\varepsilon_t.$$

The foreign government sector's end-of-period supply of foreign bonds constitutes part of the ex ante end-of-period market supply of foreign bonds.

Home Non-Financial Business Sector

Revised Objective Function

Given that the home non-financial business sector has by now decided the values for $h^n{}_t$, $h^q{}_t$, q_t, p_t, $R^x{}_t$, $\hat{q}_t$ and W_t, its former objective function, (3.18), must be modified and solved for the sector's effective end-of-period demand for a total number of workers, $N^{nd}{}_{t+1}$, its end-of-period demand for production workers, $N^{qd}{}_{t+1}$, its demand for the imported factor (to be ordered this period for delivery and use next period), q^{*nd}_{t+1}, and its end-of-period demand for physical capital, K^{nd}_{t+1}. The sector also solves provisionally for the amount of the renewable resource it plans to use next period. However, the sector will be free next period in light of new information and a new planning horizon to alter its current notional demand for the renewable resource for next period, R^{xe}_{t+1}. The sector's new objective function is given by:

$$(5.13)\ \Pi = \Pi^{n}_{t} + \Pi^{ne}_{t+1}/(1+r^{d}_{t})$$

$$= p_t(\bullet)q_t(\bullet) - p_t(\bullet)\{(1+p^{bn}_{t+1})/[p^{bn}_{t}(1+r^{d}_{t})]\}\cdot[(K^{nd}_{t+1}-K^{n}_{t})-Q_t]$$

$$-W_{t-1}h^{n}_{t}N^{n}_{t} - \hat{\varepsilon}_{t-1}p^{*}_{t-1}q^{*n}_{t} - B^{n}_{t} - p^{x}_{t}R^{xd}_{t} - p^{p}_{t}[\kappa\, \hat{q}_{t}(\bullet) - \mu(h^{n}_{t}N^{n}_{t} - h^{q}_{t}N^{n}_{t})]$$

$$+\{R^{e}[q^{ne}(hN^{qd}_{t+1}, q^{*nd}_{t+1}, K^{nd}_{t+1}, R^{xe}_{t+1}, \hat{Q}_{t} - \hat{q}_{t}(\bullet)) + K^{nd}_{t+1}, \beta]$$

$$-W_{t}(\bullet)hN^{nd}_{t+1} - \hat{\varepsilon}^{n}_{t}p^{*}_{t}(\bullet)q^{*nd}_{t+1} - p^{xe}_{t+1}R^{xe}_{t+1} - (1+p^{bn}_{t+1})B^{n}_{t}$$

$$-p^{pe}_{t+1}[\kappa^{e}(\hat{Q}_{t} - \hat{q}_{t}(\bullet)) - \mu^{e}(hN^{nd}_{t+1} - hN^{qd}_{t+1})]\}/(1+r^{d}_{t}).$$

First-Order Conditions

The corresponding first-order necessary conditions are given by:

$$(5.14)\ \partial\Pi/\partial N^{nd}_{t+1} = -W_{t}(\bullet)h + p^{pe}_{t+1}\mu^{e\prime}h = 0$$

$$(5.15)\ \partial\Pi/\partial N^{qd}_{t+1} = R^{e\prime}q^{ne}_{1}h - p^{pe}_{t+1}\mu^{e\prime}h = 0$$

$$(5.16)\ \partial\Pi/\partial q^{*nd}_{t+1} = R^{e\prime}q^{ne}_{2} - \hat{\varepsilon}_{t}p^{*}_{t}(\bullet) = 0$$

$$(5.17)\ \partial\Pi/\partial K^{nd}_{t+1} = R^{e\prime}(q^{ne}_{3}+1) - [(1+p^{bn})/p^{b}_{t}]p_{t}(\bullet) = 0$$

$$(5.18)\ \partial\Pi/\partial R^{xe}_{t+1} = R^{e\prime}q^{ne}_{4} - p^{xe}_{t+1} = 0.$$

Technical vs. Market Rates of Substitution

According to (5.14), the home non-financial business sector desires to add to its stock of employees at the end of the period up to the point at which the extra wages it must pay next period is equal to the value of the marginal product of labor in next period's pollution abatement (holding the number of workers used in producing privately-produced goods, N^{q}_{t+1}, constant, an added worker is necessarily assigned to pollution abatement in this model). Combining (5.14) and (5.15) yields the conventional result that the sector will continue to add to workers for the purpose of producing home privately-produced goods up to the point at which the marginal wage expense is equal to the value of the marginal worker in next period's production of those goods:

(5.19) $R^{e'}q^{ne}_1 h = W_t(\bullet)h.$

Dividing (5.4) by (5.16) yields the condition that the sector demands labor for producing home private goods and the imported factor up to the point at which the technical rate of substitution of home labor for the imported factor, $R^{e'}q^{ne}_1 h/R^{e'}q^{ne}_2$ is equal to the price of labor in terms of the imported factor, $W_t(\bullet)h/\varepsilon^\wedge_t p^*_t(\bullet)$. See Figure 5.2.

Figure 5.2 Technical vs. Market Rates of Substitution of Labor for the Imported Factor

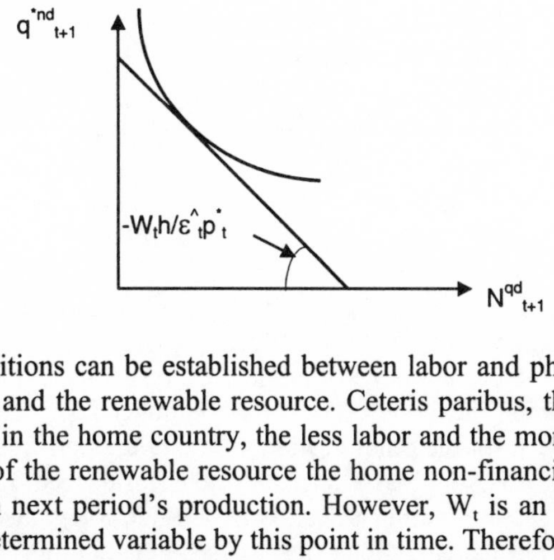

Similar conditions can be established between labor and physical capital and between labor and the renewable resource. Ceteris paribus, the higher the current wage rate in the home country, the less labor and the more physical capital and the more of the renewable resource the home non-financial business sector plans to use in next period's production. However, W_t is an endogenously determined predetermined variable by this point in time. Therefore, the factors that influenced the home non-financial business sector's earlier selection of W_t also affected that sector's notional demands for next period's labor, physical capital, the imported factor and the renewable resource.

From Figure 5.2, it is also clear that a higher current forward exchange rate, $\varepsilon^\wedge_t$, or a higher current period price of the imported factor expressed in terms of the foreign unit of account, p^*_t, ceteris paribus, the sector will tend to substitute labor in next period's production for the imported factor. Similar conditions can be established between the imported factor and physical capital and between the imported factor and the renewable resource. Therefore, ceteris paribus, the higher the current forward exchange rate or the higher the current price of the imported factor in terms of the foreign unit of account, the less of the imported factor demanded and the more labor, physical capital and the renewable resource the sector plans to use in next period's production.[1]

Dividing (5.4) by (5.17) yields the condition that the optimizing sector demands labor for producing home private goods and physical capital up to the point at which the technical rate of substitution of labor for physical capital, $R^{e\prime}q^{ne}{}_1h/R^{e\prime}q^{ne}{}_3$, equals the price of labor in terms of physical capital, $W_th/[R^{e\prime}+(r^b{}_t+1+p^{\sim bn}{}_t)p_t(\bullet)]$, where $(1+p^{bn}{}_{t+1})(p_t(\bullet)/p^b{}_t) = p_t(\bullet)(r^b{}_t+1+p^{\sim bn}{}_t)$. See Figure 5.3.

Figure 5.3 **Technical vs. Market Rates of Substitution of Labor for Physical Capital**

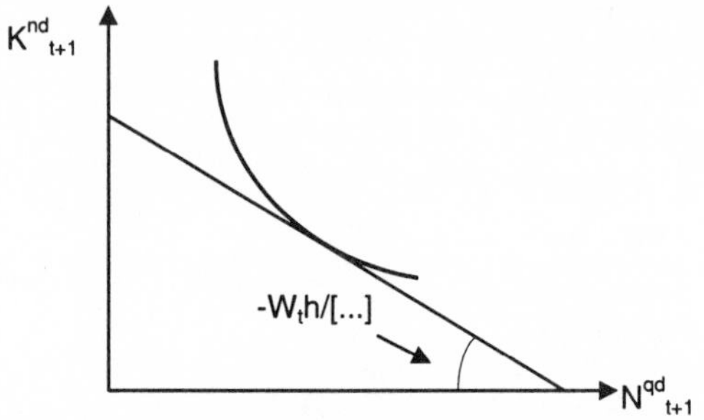

Similar conditions can be established between physical capital and the imported factor and between physical capital and the renewable resource. Ceteris paribus, the higher the current home bond rate, $r^b{}_t$, the less physical capital and the more labor, the more of the imported factor and the more of the renewable resource the home non-financial business sector plans to use in next period's production. While the current price of home country goods is a pre-determined variable at this point, nevertheless it is an endogenously determined pre-determined variable from the point of view of the home non-financial business sector. In other words, the same variables that influenced the home non-financial business sector's earlier selection of a value for p_t also affected that sector's end-of-period demands for labor, physical capital, the imported factor and next period's use of the renewable resource. Therefore, the variables that earlier affected the selection of p_t and these notional demands should appear as the variables also affecting these effective demands in the present stage.

Finally, ceteris paribus, the greater the amount of the non-renewable resource the sector holds at the beginning of next period, $\hat{Q}_t - \hat{q}_t$, the less of all other factors—labor, physical capital, the imported factor and the renewable resource—the sector requires in next period's production. However, the amount of the non-renewable resource the sector elected earlier to use in current production, $\hat{q}_t$, was decided in conjunction with earlier notional demands for these other factors. Therefore, neither W_t, p_t, nor $\hat{q}_t$ should appear explicitly in the effective demand functions for next period's labor, physical capital, or the imported factor; instead, the relevant demand functions are the reduced form expressions for these variables, shown by (3.66), (3.65), and (3.68), but modified to include the new influences of the current home bond rate and the current forward exchange rate. The home private non-financial business sector formulated preliminary plans for N^{nd}_{t+1}, N^{qd}_{t+1}, q^{*nd}_{t+1}, and K^{nd}_{t+1} at the same time that it selected values for W_t, p_t and $q^{\wedge}_{t+1}$ and the foreign non-financial business sector set the value of p^*_t. Therefore, expressions (3.65), (3.66), and (3.68) are still relevant for K^{nd}_{t+1}, N^{nd}_{t+1}, and q^{*nd}_{t+1}, respectively. What is new in the present problem are the influences of the actual values for the home bond rate, r^b_t, and the forward exchange rate, $\varepsilon^{\wedge}_t$, upon these decisions. Therefore, we may write the effective demands for labor, physical capital, and the imported factor as follows:

(5.20) K^{nde}_{t+1}

$$=K^{nde}_{t+1}(\underset{-}{W_{t-1}},\underset{+}{Q_t},\underset{+}{q^{*n}_t},\underset{+}{K_t},\underset{-}{Q^{\wedge}_t},\underset{-}{W^*_{t-1}},\underset{+}{Q^*_t},\underset{+}{q^{n*}_t},\underset{+}{K^*_t},\underset{?}{Q^{\wedge*}_t},\underset{+}{\phi\cdot\bar{P}},\underset{+}{G(S_t,\bar{P})-\Omega},\underset{-}{r^b_t},\underset{+}{\varepsilon^{\wedge}_t})$$

(5.21) N^{nde}_{t+1}

$$=N^{nde}_{t+1}(\underset{+}{W_{t-1}},\underset{-}{Q_t},\underset{-}{q^{*n}_t},\underset{-}{K_t},\underset{-}{Q^{\wedge}_t},\underset{+}{W^*_{t-1}},\underset{-}{Q^*_t},\underset{-}{q^{n*}_t},\underset{-}{K^*_t},\underset{?}{Q^{\wedge*}_t},\underset{-}{\phi\cdot\bar{P}},\underset{-}{G(S_t,\bar{P})-\Omega},\underset{+}{r^b_t},\underset{+}{\varepsilon^{\wedge}_t})$$

(5.22) N^{qdn}_{t+1}

$$=N^{qdn}_{t+1}(\underset{+}{W_{t-1}},\underset{-}{Q_t},\underset{-}{q^{*n}_t},\underset{-}{K_t},\underset{-}{Q^{\wedge}_t},\underset{+}{W^*_{t-1}},\underset{-}{Q^*_t},\underset{-}{q^{n*}_t},\underset{-}{K^*_t},\underset{?}{Q^{\wedge*}_t},\underset{-}{\phi\cdot\bar{P}},\underset{-}{G(S_t,\bar{P})-\Omega},\underset{+}{r^b_t},\underset{+}{\varepsilon^{\wedge}_t})$$

(5.23) q^{*nd}_{t+1}

$$=q^{*nd}_{t+1}(\underset{+}{W_{t-1}},\underset{-}{Q_t},\underset{-}{q^{*n}_t},\underset{-}{K_t},\underset{-}{Q^{\wedge}_t},\underset{+}{W^*_{t-1}},\underset{-}{Q^*_t},\underset{-}{q^{n*}_t},\underset{-}{K^*_t},\underset{?}{Q^{\wedge*}_t},\underset{-}{\phi\cdot\bar{P}},\underset{-}{G(S_t,\bar{P})-\Omega},\underset{+}{r^b_t},\underset{-}{\varepsilon^{\wedge}_t}).$$

From (5.16), an increase in the current forward exchange rate increases the marginal cost of that factor in next period's production of home country goods. The sector reduces its demand for that factor, raising not only its marginal product, but also the marginal revenue from next period's sales of home country goods, since it plans to produce fewer of those goods. As $R^{e\prime}$ rises, the values of the marginal products of the other factors in next period's production of home country goods increase as well; the sector increases its demands for labor, physical capital (and the renewable resource) in next period's production of home country goods. As the sector diverts labor from pollution abatement to the production of home country goods, the value of the marginal product of labor in pollution abatement rises as well. Therefore, the sector also increases its total demand for labor until the value of the marginal product of labor in pollution abatement returns to its original level, with the sector now using just as much labor as before in pollution abatement, but more labor for the purpose of producing home country goods.

From (5.17), an increase in the interest rate on home country bonds increases the marginal cost of diverting a unit of current production of home country goods from sales to other sectors to the accumulation of physical capital within the sector. The sector reduces its demand for physical capital and increases its end-of-period demands for total labor, for labor in the production of home country goods and the imported factor.

Assuming that the home non-financial business sector finances both its ex ante and unintended investment in the bond market during the current period (so that net business saving by this sector equals zero) its end-of-period supply of bonds to the home bond market is given by:

$$(5.24)\ p^b_t B^{ns}_{t+1} = p^b_t B^n_t + p_t\,[K^{nd}_{t+1}(\bullet) - K^n_t] + p_t(Q_{t+1} - Q_t)$$

$$= p^b_t B^n_t + p_t q_t - p_t c^d_t(\bullet) - p_t[K^{gd}_{t+1}(\bullet) - K^g_t] - p_{t-1} q^{n*}_t$$

where the home non-financial business sector's ending inventory is given by:

$$(5.25)\ Q_{t+1} = q_t - (K^{nd}_{t+1} - K^n_t) + Q_t - q^{n*}_t - c^d_t - (K^{gd}_{t+1} - K^g_t) = q_t - y^d_t$$

with y^d_t defined as real consumption by the home households, c^d_t, plus planned real investment by the home non-financial business sector, $(K^{nd}_{t+1} - K^n_t) - Q_t$, plus real exports to the foreign country, q^{n*}_t, plus real purchases of privately-produced goods by the home government, $(K^{gd}_{t+1} - K^g_t)$. See Figure 5.4.

Figure 5.4 **The Keynesian Cross, the Determination of Ending Inventories and the Non-Financial Business Sector's End-of-Period Supply of Home Bonds**

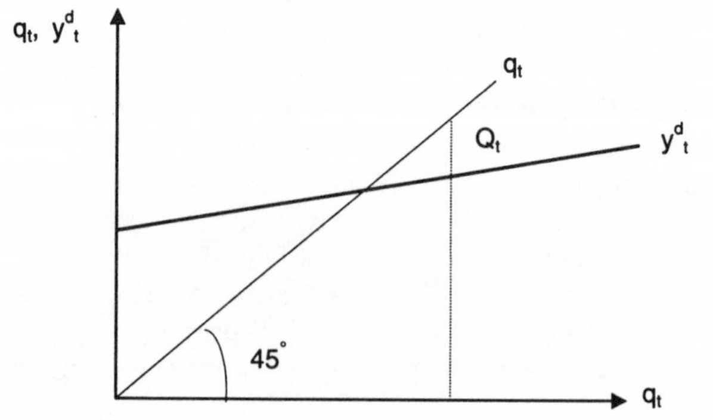

According to (5.24), since the sector pays the factors of production a total amount equal to the value of the sector's current production, it must borrow in the bond market an amount equal to the difference between the value of its current production and its current revenue from its sales to other sectors.[2] As shown above, the sector deducts any current payments for pollution and extraction rights from the dividends it pays its owners. Therefore, its payments for pollution and extraction rights do not enter its (ex ante) end-of-period supply of bonds.

Foreign Non-Financial Business Sector

An analysis of the non-financial business sector in the foreign country, which is directly analogous to that given above, yields a corresponding set of end-of-period demand functions for that sector:

(5.26) K^{*n*de}_{t+1}

$$=K^{*n*de}_{t+1}(\underset{-}{W^*_{t-1}},\underset{+}{Q^*_t},\underset{+}{q^{n*}_t},\underset{+}{K^*_t},\underset{-}{\hat{Q}^{*}_t},\underset{-}{W_{t-1}},\underset{+}{Q_t},\underset{+}{q^{*n}_t},\underset{+}{K_t},\underset{?}{\hat{Q}_t},\underset{+}{\phi\cdot\bar{P}},\underset{+}{G(S_t,\bar{P})-\Omega},\underset{-}{r^{b*}_t},\underset{-}{\hat{\varepsilon}_t})$$

(5.27) N^{*n*de}_{t+1}

$$=N^{*n*de}_{t+1}(\underset{+}{W^*_{t-1}},\underset{-}{Q^*_t},\underset{-}{q^{n*}_t},\underset{-}{K^*_t},\underset{-}{\hat{Q}^{*}_t},\underset{+}{W_{t-1}},\underset{-}{Q_t},\underset{-}{q^{*n}_t},\underset{-}{K_t},\underset{?}{\hat{Q}_t},\underset{-}{\phi\cdot\bar{P}},\underset{-}{G(S_t,\bar{P})-\Omega},\underset{+}{r^{b*}_t},\hat{\varepsilon}_t)$$

(5.28) N^{q*d}_{t+1}

$$=N^{q*d}_{t+1}(\underset{+}{W^*_{t-1}},\underset{-}{Q^*_t},\underset{-}{q^{n*}_t},\underset{-}{K^*_t},\underset{-}{\hat{Q}^{*}_t},\underset{+}{W_{t-1}},\underset{-}{Q_t},\underset{-}{q^{*n}_t},\underset{-}{K_t},\underset{?}{\hat{Q}_t},\underset{-}{\phi\cdot\bar{P}},\underset{-}{G(S_t,\bar{P})-\Omega},\underset{+}{r^{b*}_t},\underset{-}{\hat{\varepsilon}_t})$$

(5.29) q^{n*d}_{t+1}

$$=q^{n*d}_{t+1}(\underset{+}{W^*_{t-1}},\underset{-}{Q^*_t},\underset{-}{q^{n*}_t},\underset{-}{K^*_t},\underset{-}{\hat{Q}^{*}_t},\underset{+}{W_{t-1}},\underset{-}{Q_t},\underset{-}{q^{*n}_t},\underset{-}{K_t},\underset{?}{\hat{Q}_t},\underset{-}{\phi\cdot\bar{P}},\underset{-}{G(S_t,\bar{P})-\Omega},\underset{+}{r^{b*}_t},\underset{+}{\hat{\varepsilon}_t})$$

(5.30) $p^{b*}{}_tB^{*n*s}_{t+1} = p^{b*}{}_tB^{*n*}{}_t + p^*{}_tq^*{}_t - p^*{}_tc^{*d}{}_t(\bullet) - p^*{}_t[K^{*g*d}{}_{t+1}(\bullet) - K^{*g*}{}_t] - p^*{}_{t-1}q^{*n}{}_t.$

Assuming the direct impact of a smaller initial stock of the foreign non-financial business sector's non-renewable resource upon its demand for the home country's privately-produced good dominates, the sector will increase this demand as it attempts to substitute it (and other factors) for the non-renewable resource in future production. A greater stock of pollution rights or a greater volume of extraction rights issued by the international agent causes the sector to reduce its orders this period for the home country's privately-produced good.

Home Household Sector

In this section we revise the analysis of the home household sector presented on pages 14–24 to account for the fact that this sector has already selected both the level of public goods to be produced by the home government next period and the level of next period's taxes in the home country. In addition, by this time the home non-financial business sector has also already announced the current period price of home privately-produced goods and the current wage rate (which will not be actually paid until next period). Also, except for the relatively minor amount of labor the home non-financial business sector decides to use this period to search for employees for next period, the home household sector also knows by this point the wage income it will receive this period. Therefore, for all intents and purposes, the home household sector by this time already knows its current disposable income.

With the current wage rate already announced, the current economic behavior of the home household sector depends upon whether it expects the home country's three employers will want to hire more or fewer people to work next period than the home household sector wishes to supply. In the present model, no one knows before the end of the current period how many people will actually become employed next period, because the non-financial business sector's demand for labor for the end of the current period becomes jointly determined during the current period with current interest rates and exchange rates. Therefore, two alternative cases exist with respect to the formulation of the home household sector's plans at this stage. In the "full-employment" case, the home households anticipate that their ex ante end-of-period supply of labor will be no larger than the home employers' end-of-period market demand for labor. In this case, the home households formulate their plans as if they are unconstrained with respect to their end-of-period supply of labor. In the "unemployment" case, the home households anticipate that their ex ante end-of-period supply of labor may exceed the amount of labor their employers will want to employ by the end of the period. In this case the home households take their estimate of the home country's end-of-period market demand for labor as a constraining parameter.

Full-Employment Case

Utility Maximization

In this case, the home household sector attempts to maximize present utility with respect to current consumption, future consumption, its end-of-period portfolio, and the number of people that will be employed by the end of the current period. This optimization problem closely corresponds to the one depicted in (2.12) on page 19, except that the sector now knows the current values for current product prices and wages and also knows the levels of g_{t+1} and T_{t+1}. Therefore, we have the following maximization problem facing the home household sector in the present stage of decision-making. Maximize:

$$(5.31)\ U = U_1(c^d_t) + U_2(g_t) + U_3(\bar{h}N - h^h_tN_t) + U_4[\bar{\tau}(c^d_t, D_t/p_t, Cu_t/p_t)] + U_5(c^{he}_{t+1})$$

$$+U_6(g_{t+1}) + U_7(\hat{h}N - hN^s_{t+1})$$

$$+U_8\{\tau[c^{he}_{t+1}, D^d_{t+1}/p^{he}_{t+1}, (\bar{Y}_t - p_tc^d_t - D^d_{t+1} + D_t + Cu_t)/p^{he}_{t+1}]\}$$

$$+\lambda[W_thN^s_{t+1} + \Pi^h_{t+1} + r^d_tD^d_{t+1} + \bar{Y}_t - p_tc^d_t + D_t + Cu_t - T_{t+1} - p^{he}_{t+1}c^{he}_{t+1}].$$

First-Order Conditions

At this stage, the first-order necessary conditions for utility maximization with respect to current consumption, future consumption, end-of-period checkable deposits, the end-of-period supply of labor, and the Lagrange multiplier are given by (5.32)–(5.36).

$$(5.32)\ [U'_1 + U'_4 \cdot \bar{\tau}_1 - U'_8\tau_3(p_t/p^h_{t+1})] - \lambda p_t = 0.$$

The sum inside brackets in (5.32) denotes the net marginal present utility from an extra unit of current consumption. As the sector increases current consumption one unit, present utility is affected three ways. First, the increase in current consumption directly raises present utility, since $U'_1 > 0$. Second, the increase in current consumption increases current transactions time, $\bar{\tau}_1 > 0$, which decreases present utility, since $U'_4 < 0$. Third, ceteris paribus, a unit increase in current consumption necessarily reduces the amount of currency the home household sector plans to hold by the end of the current period by p_t. Therefore, the anticipated purchasing power of the sector's end-of-period currency holdings over home country goods next period falls by (p_t/p^h_{t+1}). This raises next period's anticipated transactions time, shown by $-\tau_3(p_t/p^h_{t+1})$ where $\tau_3 < 0$, and reduces present utility by $-U'_8\tau_3(p_t/p^h_{t+1})$, since $U'_8 < 0$. Since both λ and p_t are positive, (5.32) stipulates that if the home household sector decides to consume during the current period, the net marginal present utility of that consumption must be positive.

$$(5.33)\ [U'_5 + U'_8\tau_1] - \lambda p^h_{t+1} = 0.$$

The sum inside brackets in (5.33) denotes the net marginal present utility of an extra unit of consumption planned by the home household sector for next period, where U'_5 denotes the direct increase in present utility from that consumption and $U'_8\tau_1 < 0$ depicts the reduction in present utility due to the anticipated increase in transactions time. With both λ and p^h_{t+1} positive, (5.33) stipulates that if the home household sector decides to consume next period, the net marginal present utility of that consumption must also be positive.

$$(5.34)\ U'_8\cdot(\tau_2 - \tau_3)/p^h_{t+1} + \lambda r^d_t = 0.$$

As shown by (5.34), as the home household sector increases its planned end-of-period holdings of checkable deposits by one unit, it adds $1/p^h_{t+1}$ units to its anticipated real balances of checkable deposits for the end of the period, thereby reducing next period's anticipated transactions time by τ_2/p^h_{t+1}, where $\tau_2/p^h_{t+1} < 0$. By itself, this increases present utility by $U'_8\cdot\tau_2/p^h_{t+1}$. However, ceteris paribus, as the sector adds a unit to its planned end-of-period holdings of checkable deposits, it necessarily reduces its planned end-of-period holdings of home currency by the same amount. The reduction in the planned holdings of currency reduces present utility by $-U'_8\cdot\tau_3/p^h_{t+1}$, where $\tau_3/p^h_{t+1} < 0$. Since both λ and r^d_t are positive, (5.34) stipulates that the present-utility-maximizing sector plans to add to the amount of checkable deposits it holds by the end of the current period until the non-market return on an extra unit of home checkable deposits falls sufficiently below the non-market return on an extra unit of home currency, so that the sum of the market and non-market returns on home checkable deposits just equals the non-market return on home currency.

$$(5.35)\ U'_7\cdot(-h) + \lambda W_t h = 0.$$

According to (5.35), the home household sector increases its end-of-period supply of labor until the marginal reduction in present utility due to the foregone leisure time next period equals the value of the extra wage income generated by that extra unit of labor.

$$(5.36)\ W_t h N^s_{t+1} + \Pi^h_{t+1} + r^d_t D^d_{t+1} + \overline{Y}_t - p_t c^d_t + D_t + Cu_t - T_{t+1} - p^{he}_{t+1} c^{he}_{t+1} = 0.$$

Expression (5.36) merely restates the home household sector's budget constraint.

Subjective vs. Market Rates of Substitution

Chapter 2 contains an analysis of the subjective and market rates of substitution relevant to the home household sector's choice of public goods. In the present stage of our analysis, however, this selection has already occurred. Therefore, we now present a new set of conditions which highlight the parameters affecting the home household sector's choices between current consumption and future consumption, between current consumption and checkable deposits held at the end of the current period, between current consumption and future work, and between future work and checkable deposits held at the end of the current period. These choices are made with next period's public goods, next period's taxes, current disposable income, current product prices and current wage rates already known to the home household sector.

Subjective vs. Market Rates of Substitution between Current and Future Consumption. Rearranging terms and then dividing (5.32) by (5.33) yields:

$$(5.37)\ [U'_1 + U'_4 \cdot \bar{\tau}_1 - U'_8 \tau_3 (p_t/p^h_{t+1})] / [U'_5 + U'_8 \tau_1] = p_t / p^h_{t+1}$$

where the left-hand side of (5.37) depicts the subjective rate of substitution of current consumption for future consumption and where the right-hand side represents the market rate of substitution, i.e., the amount of future consumption the home household sector must sacrifice to purchase an additional unit of privately produced goods in the current period. See Figure 5.5.

According to condition (5.37), if the anticipated future price of home country goods is held constant, the home household sector elects to decrease its demand for current consumption of home goods as the current price of home country goods increases. The sector elects to substitute some future consumption for some current consumption as current product price rises.

Figure 5.5 **Subjective vs. Market Rates of Substitution of Current Consumption for Future Consumption**

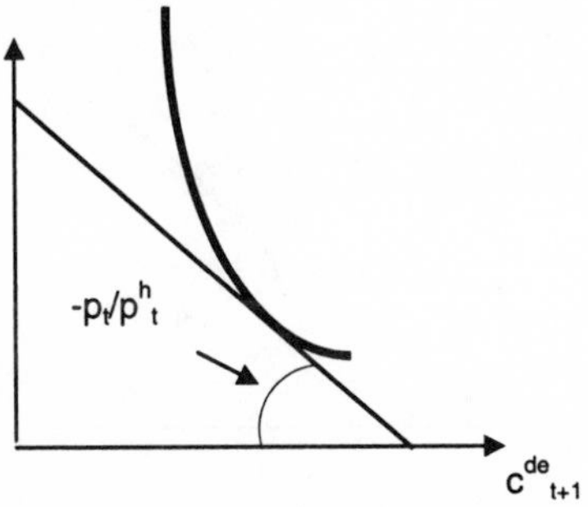

Subjective vs. Market Rates of Substitution between Current Consumption and End-of-Period Checkable Deposits. Rearranging terms and then dividing (5.32) by (5.34) yields:

$$(5.38)\ [U'_1 + U'_4 \cdot \bar{\tau}_1 - U'_8 \tau_3 (p_t/p^h_{t+1})] / [U'_8 \cdot (\tau_2 - \tau_3)/p^h_{t+1}] = -p_t / r^d_t$$

where the left-hand side of (5.38) depicts the subjective rate of substitution of current consumption for checkable deposits held at the end of the current period and where the right-hand side represents the market rate of substitution, i.e., the amount of checkable deposits held at the end of the period that the home household sector must sacrifice to purchase an additional unit of privately-produced goods in the current period. Both the subjective and market rates of substitution in this case are negative. Ceteris paribus, an increase in checkable deposits held at the end of the current period decreases present utility because it means the sector must hold less currency at that time, which decreases the ability of its money holdings to save transactions time next period. Therefore, if the household sector decides to add to its end-of-period holdings of checkable deposits, it must also decide to increase current consumption, ceteris paribus, if it intends to keep present utility constant. By the same token, if the sector decides to add to its end-of-period holdings of checkable deposits (at the expense of currency holdings) it will be able to purchase p_t/r^d_t more goods during the current period without jeopardizing its purchasing power over home country goods next period. See Figure 5.6.

Ceteris paribus, the higher the current price of home goods, the less current consumption and the smaller the end-of-period checkable deposits demanded by the home household sector (with disposable income unchanged, the sector will then add to end-of-period holdings of currency).

Figure 5.6 **Subjective vs. Market Rates of Substitution of Current Consumption for End-of-Period Checkable Deposits**

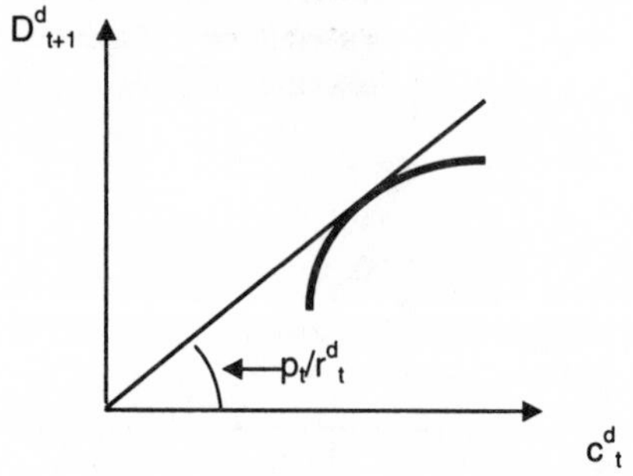

Subjective vs. Market Rates of Substitution between Current Consumption and Future Labor. Rearranging terms and then dividing (5.32) by (5.35) yields:

$$(5.39)\ [U'_1 + U'_4 \cdot \bar{\tau}_1 - U'_8\tau_3(p_t/p^h_{t+1})] \,/\, U'_7 \cdot (-h) = -p_t/W_t h$$

where the left-hand side of (5.39) depicts the subjective rate of substitution of current consumption for future labor and where the right-hand side represents the market rate of substitution, i.e., the amount of labor next period the home household sector must sacrifice to purchase an additional unit of privately-produced goods in the current period. Both the subjective and market rates of substitution in this case are negative. See Figure 5.7.

Figure 5.7 **Subjective vs. Market Rates of Substitution of Current Consumption for Future Labor**

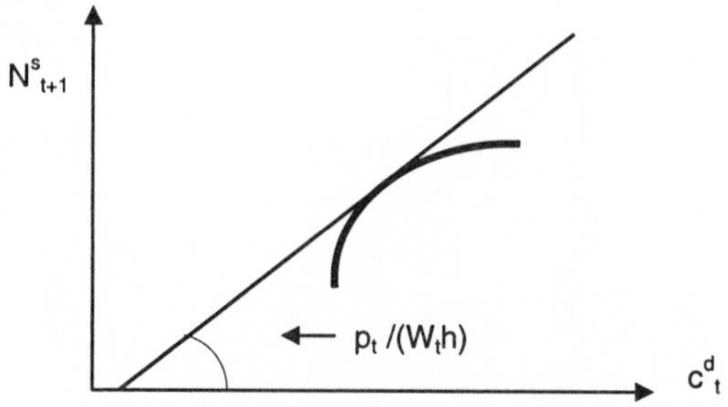

Ceteris paribus, an increase in labor next period decreases present utility. Therefore, if the household sector decides to add to its labor next period, it must also decide to increase current consumption, ceteris paribus, if it intends to keep present utility constant. By the same token, if the sector decides to add to its labor next period it will be able to purchase $p_t/(W_t \cdot h)$ more goods during the current period without jeopardizing its purchasing power over home country goods next period. Ceteris paribus, the higher current product prices, the smaller the household sector's demand for current consumption and the smaller its supply of labor for next period. On the other hand, the higher the current wage rate, the greater its current consumption spending and the greater its supply of workers for next period.

Subjective vs. Market Rate of Substitution between End-of-Period Checkable Deposits and Future Labor. Rearranging terms and then dividing (5.34) by (5.35) yields:

(5.40) $(U'_8 \cdot (\tau_2 - \tau_3)/p^h_{t+1})/ U'_7 \cdot (-h) = r^d_t /(W_t h)$

where the left-hand side of (5.40) depicts the subjective rate of substitution of checkable deposits held at the end of the current period for future labor and where the right-hand side represents the market rate of substitution, i.e., the amount of labor next period the home household sector must sacrifice to add an additional unit to checkable deposits it holds at the end of the current period. Both the subjective and market rates of substitution in this case are positive. Ceteris paribus, an increase in checkable deposits held at the end of the current period decreases present utility. Therefore, if the household sector decides to add to its end-of-period holdings of checkable deposits, it must also decide to decrease its supply of labor for next period, ceteris paribus, if it intends to keep present utility constant. By the same token, if the sector decides to add to its end-of-period holdings of checkable deposits it will be able to decrease the labor

Figure 5.8 **Subjective vs. Market Rates of Substitution of End-of-Period Checkable Deposits for Future Labor**

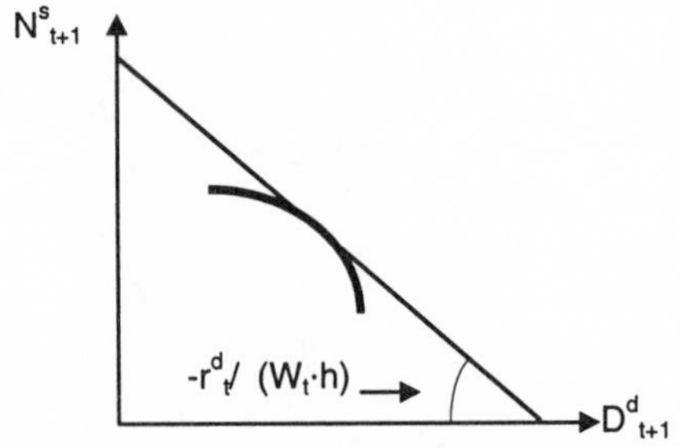

it supplies next period by $r^d_t/(W_t \cdot h)$ without jeopardizing its purchasing power over home country goods next period. See Figure 5.8.

Home Household Sector's Demand and Supply Functions

Totally differentiating necessary conditions (5.32)–(5.36) yields a system of five simultaneous equations in λ and the decision variables c^d_t, c^d_{t+1}, D^d_{t+1}, and N^s_{t+1}. The solution for Cu^d_{t+1} is found by substituting the solutions for c^d_t and D^d_{t+1} into:

$$(5.41)\ Cu^d_{t+1} = \overline{Y}_t - p_t c^d_t - D^d_{t+1} + D_t + Cu_t.$$

The important observable parameters facing the home household sector at the beginning of the current period are the current price of home privately-produced goods, p_t, the current interest rate on home checkable deposits, r^d_t, the current money wage rate, W_t, current disposable income and financial wealth, $\overline{Y}_t + D_t + Cu_t$, and next period's net taxes, T_t. We discuss the effects of each of these parameters upon the home household sector's decisions in the current period. However, it is important to note that the values of p_t, W_t and $\overline{Y}_t$ observed by the home households at this stage were each determined earlier in the current period by the home non-financial business sector (at least in part). The values of these three variables, in turn, depended upon the volume of pollution and extraction rights issued by the international agent as well as upon the home non-financial business sector's initial stock of its non-renewable resource. Therefore, while these environmental parameters do not directly affect the home household sector's current economic behavior, they do affect that behavior indirectly.

Direct Effects via the Current Price of Home Privately-Produced Goods. Holding constant the home household sector's unobservable anticipated rate of inflation, or, in other words, the ratio p_t/p^h_t, the higher the current price of privately-produced goods, ceteris paribus, the substitution effects associated with the resulting increases in the absolute values of the market ratios on the right-hand sides of conditions (5.38) and (5.39) indicate that the household sector will tend to decrease current consumption, its end-of-period demand for checkable deposits, and its end-of-period supply of labor. To the extent that the sector's demand for current consumption is price-elastic, then, from (5.41), the sector will increase its end-of-period demand for currency.

However, a change in the current price of privately-produced goods (accompanied by a proportionate rise in the anticipated future price level) affects not only relative prices between consumption, checkable deposits and leisure, but also the real values of the sector's end-of-period demands for currency and checkable deposits and therefore the productivity of those holdings of currency and checkable deposits as well. In particular, from (5.34), an increase in p^h_{t+1} directly reduces the marginal disutility associated with holding an extra unit of checkable deposits rather than currency at the end of the period, $U'_8 \cdot (\tau_2 - \tau_3)/p^h_{t+1}$, by raising the denominator in the expression for that marginal disutility. By itself, this will tend to make the indifference curve drawn in Figure 5.6 steeper, inducing the sector to add to both current consumption and its end-of-period holdings of checkable deposits on the margin, but also to make the indifference curve drawn in Figure 5.8 flatter, causing the sector to reduce its supply of labor and increase its demand for checkable deposits on the margin.

However, the effect that dominates the literature is the one that recognizes the fact that an increase in the price level, by reducing the volume of real money balances, increases the marginal product of money in undertaking transactions. Hence, in terms of our model, both τ_2 and τ_3 increase in absolute value. In economies in which the volume of checkable deposits is large relative to the volume of currency in circulation, the fall in the real holdings of checkable deposits will exceed the fall in the real holdings of currency for a given change in the price level. In this case the difference, $\tau_2 - \tau_3$, which, from (5.34), is positive, becomes less positive. This also reduces the absolute value of $U'_8 \cdot (\tau_2 - \tau_3)/p^h_{t+1}$, thereby reinforcing the effects discussed in the immediately preceding paragraph.

For the purpose of the following discussion, we assume that an increase in p_t (holding expected inflation unchanged) causes the home household sector to decrease its demand for current consumption, $p_t c^d_t$, to increase its end-of-period demands for both currency and checkable deposits, and to decrease its end-of-period supply of labor.

Direct Effect of a Change in the Current Wage Rate. The higher the wage rate announced by the home non-financial business sector at the beginning of the current period, the lower the market rates of substitution of current consumption and end-of-period checkable deposits for next period's labor. From conditions (5.37) and (5.38), the home household sector tends to consume more in the current period, reduce its end-of-period demand for checkable deposits and increase its end-of-period supply of labor in response to an increase in W_t. Assuming that the home households elect to save less via both currency and checkable deposits during the current period the higher W_t, then an increase in W_t also reduces the sector's end-of-period demand for currency as well.

Direct Effect of a Change in Current Disposable Income and Initial Financial Wealth. The higher the current disposable income received by the home household sector during the current period or the larger its initial holdings of currency or checkable deposits, the more current and future consumption the sector demands and the less labor it supplies for next period. To finance the extra future consumption while supplying less labor, the sector must save more during the current period. Therefore, the sector's marginal propensity to consume during the current period in response to a rise in current disposable income is less than one. Ceteris paribus, the sector's decision to consume more next period causes the marginal products of both currency and checkable deposits held at the beginning of next period to rise, inducing the sector to increase its end-of-period demands for both types of money; we take this effect upon the sector's end-of-period demand for checkable deposits to dominate.

While the home household sector takes the observed values of p_t, W_t and $\bar{Y}_t$ as given at this point, these variables were nevertheless essentially largely chosen by the non-financial business sector based upon conditions facing that sector at the beginning of the current period. Therefore, we need to reckon with the reduced form equations for p_t, q_t, and W_t, since these expressions ultimately determine the consumption, labor and financial decisions of the home household sector. In other words, we need to express the home household sector's current period decisions in terms of the parameters appearing in the reduced form expressions for p_t, q_t and W_t.

Effects of a Change in the Interest Rate on Home Checkable Deposits. From conditions (5.38) and (5.40) respectively, the higher the current interest rate on checkable deposits, the lower the absolute value of the market rate of substitution of current consumption for checkable deposits held at the end of the current period and the greater the market rate of substitution of end-of-period checkable deposits for future labor. The first of these causes the home household sector to increase its current consumption and its end-of-period demand for checkable deposits; the second causes the home household sector to increase its end-of-period demand for checkable deposits and to decrease its supply of labor for next period. The rise in the demand for current consumption and in the end-of-period demand for checkable deposits, from (5.41), implies that the sector's end-of-period demand for home currency falls. To the extent that the sector decides to consume more during the current period, the marginal utility of future consumption also rises. Therefore, although the sector reduces its end-of-period demand for currency, it nevertheless plans to save more during the current period in order to finance its greater consumption next period in spite of the fall in its supply of future labor.

Future Taxes. Although next period's taxes to be paid by the home household sector appear in the revised budget constraint facing the home household sector as a predetermined variable at this stage, nevertheless, the sector made tentative plans with respect to current consumption, its end-of-period demand for checkable deposits, its end-of-period demand for currency and its supply of labor for next period at the same time that it selected the optimal combination of public goods and net taxes for next period. Therefore, what is important at this stage is not the level of taxes the households have agreed to pay next period, but the factors that influenced that decision, which simultaneously involved the sector deciding tentatively upon current consumption, next period's labor and its planned portfolio for the end of the period. In other words, we should consider the reduced form expression for T_{t+1} presented in Chapter 3 in discussing the home household sector's current decisions. In particular, at the time that the home household sector formulated its plans with respect to T_{t+1} in Chapter 3 it considered the same factors we have just discussed. The only difference is that, whereas earlier the household sector relied upon expected values, by the present time the actual values of current prices, wages and disposable incomes are known. Therefore T_{t+1} does not enter as a separate parameter in the present discussion.

Modified Expressions for the Home Household Sector's Demand and Supply Functions. From the discussion to this point, we obtain the following demand and supply functions for the home household sector.

$$(5.42)\quad c^d_t = c^d_t(\underset{+}{\bar{Y}_t}, \underset{+}{D_t}, \underset{+}{Cu_t}, \underset{+}{W_t}, \underset{-}{r^d_t}, \underset{-}{p_t})$$

$$(5.43)\quad Cu^d_{t+1} = Cu^d_{t+1}(\underset{+}{\bar{Y}_t}, \underset{+}{D_t}, \underset{+}{Cu_t}, \underset{-}{W_t}, \underset{-}{r^d_t}, \underset{+}{p_t})$$

$$(5.44)\quad D^d_{t+1} = D^d_{t+1}(\underset{+}{\bar{Y}_t}, \underset{+}{D_t}, \underset{+}{Cu_t}, \underset{-}{W_t}, \underset{+}{r^d_t}, \underset{+}{p_t})$$

$$(5.45)\quad N^s_{t+1} = N^s_{t+1}(\underset{-}{\bar{Y}_t}, \underset{-}{D_t}, \underset{-}{Cu_t}, \underset{+}{W_t}, \underset{-}{r^d_t}, \underset{-}{p_t}).$$

However, these functions do not include the information acquired to this point with respect to the determination of current disposable income, wages and prices. From (3.97), current changes in the home country's disposable income, $\bar{Y}_t$, reflect current movements in home GNP and current changes in net personal taxes paid by the home household sector. From (3.88), current changes in the home country's GNP reflect changes in the value of current product by the home country's non-financial business sector and current changes in spending by the home government sector net of its income from the international agent related to current sales of pollution and extraction rights to the home non-financial business sector. Lagging (2.5) one period, changes in current net taxes paid by the home household sector reflect the home government sector's previous estimates of its current period outlays net of its anticipated revenue associated with the international agent's sale of pollution and extraction rights during the current period to the home non-financial sector. Assuming that the government sector was capable of accurately forecasting current period revenue from the sale of these rights, we may reasonably approximate any current changes in home GNP and home disposable income by the current change in $p_t q_t$. Therefore, we need to incorporate into expressions (5.42)–(5.45) the reduced forms for q_t, p_t, and W_t obtained earlier. Recalling these reduced form equations from Chapter 3:

$$(3.60)\quad q_t = q_t(W_{t-1}, Q_t, q^{*n}_t, K_t, Q^{\wedge}_t, W^*_{t-1}, Q^*_t, q^{n*}_t, K^*_t, Q^{\wedge*}_t, \phi\cdot \bar{P}, G(S_t, \bar{P}) - \Omega)$$

− − + + + − + + + ? + +

$$(3.61)\quad p_t = p_t(W_{t-1}, Q_t, q^{*n}_t, K_t, Q^{\wedge}_t, W^*_{t-1}, Q^*_t, q^{n*}_t, K^*_t, Q^{\wedge*}_t, \phi\cdot \bar{P}, G(S_t, \bar{P}) - \Omega)$$

+ − − − − + − − − ? − −

$$(3.64)\quad W_t = W_t(W_{t-1}, Q_t, q^{*n}_t, K_t, Q^{\wedge}_t, W^*_{t-1}, Q^*_t, q^{n*}_t, K^*_t, Q^{\wedge*}_t, \phi\cdot \bar{P}, G(S_t, \bar{P}) - \Omega)$$

+ − − − − + − − − ? − −

and substituting (3.60), (3.61), and (3.64) into (5.42)–(5.45) yields:

$$(5.46)\quad c^d_t = c^d_t(D_t, Cu_t, r^d_t, Q^{\wedge}_t, \phi\cdot \bar{P}, G(S_t, \bar{P}) - \Omega)$$

+ + − + + +

$$(5.47)\quad Cu^d_{t+1} = Cu^d_{t+1}(D_t, Cu_t, r^d_t, Q^{\wedge}_t, \phi\cdot \bar{P}, G(S_t, \bar{P}) - \Omega)$$

+ + − + + +

$$(5.48)\quad D^d_{t+1} = D^d_{t+1}(D_t, Cu_t, r^d_t, Q^{\wedge}_t, \phi\cdot \bar{P}, G(S_t, \bar{P}) - \Omega)$$

+ + + + + +

$$(5.49)\quad N^s_{t+1} = N^s_{t+1}(D_t, Cu_t, r^d_t, Q^{\wedge}_t, \phi\cdot \bar{P}, G(S_t, \bar{P}) - \Omega)$$

− − − − − −

where, to focus upon environmental issues, we have inserted only the initial stock of the home non-financial business sector, the volume of pollution rights and the volume of extraction rights issued by the international agent.

Since the home non-financial business sector produces in the elastic portion of its forecasted product demand curve, to the extent that the home non-financial business sector correctly forecasted this demand curve, an increase in pollution or extraction rights or an increase in the home non-financial business sector's initial inventory of its non-renewable resource tends to increase the value of current GNP and disposable income in the home country, even though the home non-financial business sector also tends to reduce current product price. Therefore, an increase in the sector's initial inventory of the non-renewable resource or an increase in the volume of pollution or extraction rights operating through current disposable income causes the household sector's current demand for consumption, end-of-period currency holdings and end-of-period holdings of checkable deposits to rise and for the household to reduce its supply of labor for next period. The tendency for the home non-financial sector to set product price lower reinforces the effect of the increase in disposable income upon the home household sector's demand for current real consumption. The tendency for the home non-financial business sector to reduce current wage rates reinforces the effects of the increase in disposable income upon the home household sector's end-of-period demands for currency and checkable deposits and upon that sector's supply of labor. Hence, the reason for the signs presented in (5.46)–(5.49). The following restrictions on these signs in (5.46)–(5.49) hold by virtue of condition (5.41):

$$(5.50)\ (\partial Cu^d_{t+1}/\partial r^d_t) + (\partial D^d_{t+1}/\partial r^d_t) = -p_t(\partial c^d_t/\partial r^d_t)$$

$$(5.51)\ (\partial Cu^d_{t+1}/\partial \hat{Q}_t) + (\partial D^d_{t+1}/\partial \hat{Q}_t) + p_t(\partial c^d_t/\partial \hat{Q}_t) = (\partial \bar{Y}_t/\partial \hat{Q}_t)$$

$$(5.52)\ (\partial Cu^d_{t+1}/\partial \phi \cdot \bar{P}) + (\partial D^d_{t+1}/\partial \phi \cdot \bar{P}) + p_t(\partial c^d_t/\partial \phi \cdot \bar{P}) = (\partial \bar{Y}_t/\partial \phi \cdot \bar{P})$$

$$(5.53)\ (\partial Cu^d_{t+1}/\partial[G(S_t, \bar{P}) - \Omega]) + (\partial D^d_{t+1}/\partial[G(S_t, \bar{P}) - \Omega])$$
$$+ p_t(\partial c^d_t/\partial[G(S_t, \bar{P}) - \Omega]) = (\partial \bar{Y}_t/\partial[G(S_t, \bar{P}) - \Omega])$$

$$(5.54)\ (\partial Cu^d_{t+1}/\partial Cu_t) + (\partial D^d_{t+1}/\partial Cu_t) + p_t(\partial c^d_t/\partial Cu_t) = 1$$

$$(5.55)\ (\partial Cu^d_{t+1}/\partial D_t) + (\partial D^d_{t+1}/\partial D_t) + p_t(\partial c^d_t/\partial D_t) = 1.$$

These functions constitute a few of the basic building blocks in the derivations of the various market demand and supply functions used in the present model.

Involuntary Unemployment Case

If the home household sector feels that the home employers' market demand for workers for next period constitutes an effective constraint upon the home households, then labor supply function (5.49) is no longer relevant. In this case, also, the amount of labor the home households anticipate their employers will demand for next period now enters as a parameter in demand functions (5.46)–(5.48) and affects these demands in manner similar to a change in W_t in expressions (5.43)–(5.45).

Foreign Household Sector

Let:

c^{*d}_t = the foreign household sector's current period demand for goods produced by the foreign non-financial business sector.

Cu^{*d}_{t+1} = the foreign household sector's end-of-period demand for foreign country (coin and) currency.

D^{*d}_{t+1} = the foreign household sector's end-of-period demand for checkable deposits at the foreign private financial sector.

N^{*s}_{t+1} = the foreign households' ex ante supply of labor to the foreign labor market.

Then, in a manner analogous to the above discussion, the foreign household sector's demand for goods, its end-of-period demands for currency and checkable deposits and its end-of-period supply of labor are given respectively by:

$$(5.56)\ c^{d*}_t = c^{d*}_t(\underset{+}{D^*_t},\ \underset{+}{Cu^*_t},\ \underset{-}{r^{d*}_t},\ \underset{+}{Q^{\wedge *}_t},\ \underset{+}{\phi\cdot \bar{P}},\ \underset{+}{G(S_t,\ \bar{P}) - \Omega})$$

$$(5.57)\ Cu^{*d}_{t+1} = Cu^{*d}_{t+1}(\underset{+}{D^*_t},\ \underset{+}{Cu^*_t},\ \underset{-}{r^{d*}_t},\ \underset{+}{Q^{\wedge *}_t},\ \underset{+}{\phi\cdot \bar{P}},\ \underset{+}{G(S_t,\ \bar{P}) - \Omega})$$

$$(5.58)\ D^{*d}_{t+1} = D^{*d}_{t+1}(\underset{+}{D^*_t},\ \underset{+}{Cu^*_t},\ \underset{+}{r^{d*}_t},\ \underset{+}{Q^{\wedge *}_t},\ \underset{+}{\phi\cdot \bar{P}},\ \underset{+}{G(S_t,\ \bar{P}) - \Omega})$$

$$(5.59)\ N^{*s}_{t+1} = N^{*s}_{t+1}(\underset{-}{D^*_t},\ \underset{-}{Cu^*_t},\ \underset{-}{r^{d*}_t},\ \underset{-}{Q^{\wedge *}_t},\ \underset{-}{\phi\cdot \bar{P}},\ \underset{-}{G(S_t,\ \bar{P}) - \Omega})$$

where the following restrictions hold by virtue of the foreign household sector's counterpart to condition (5.41):

$$(5.60)\ (\partial Cu^{*d}_{t+1}/\partial r^{*d}_t) + (\partial D^{*d}_{t+1}/\partial r^{*d}_t) = -p^*_t(\partial c^{*d}_t/\partial r^{*d}_t)$$

$$(5.61)\ (\partial Cu^{*d}_{t+1}/\partial Q^{\wedge *}_t) + (\partial D^{*d}_{t+1}/\partial Q^{\wedge *}_t) + p^*_t(\partial c^{*d}_t/\partial Q^{\wedge *}_t) = (\partial \bar{Y}^*_t/\partial Q^{\wedge *}_t)$$

(5.62) $(\partial Cu^{*d}_{t+1}/\partial\phi\cdot \bar{P}) + (\partial D^{*d}_{t+1}/\partial\phi\cdot \bar{P}) + p^*_t(\partial c^{*d}_t/\partial\phi\cdot \bar{P}) = (\partial \bar{Y}^*_t/\partial\phi\cdot \bar{P})$

(5.63) $(\partial Cu^{*d}_{t+1}/\partial[G(S_t, \bar{P}) - \Omega]) + (\partial D^{*d}_{t+1}/\partial[G(S_t, \bar{P}) - \Omega])$

$+p^*_t(\partial c^{*d}_t/\partial[G(S_t, \bar{P}) - \Omega]) = (\partial \bar{Y}^*_t/\partial[G(S_t, \bar{P}) - \Omega])$

(5.64) $(\partial Cu^{*d}_{t+1}/\partial Cu^*_t) + (\partial D^{*d}_{t+1}/\partial Cu^*_t) + p^*_t(\partial c^{*d}_t/\partial Cu^*_t) = 1$

(5.65) $(\partial Cu^{*d}_{t+1}/\partial D^*_t) + (\partial D^{*d}_{t+1}/\partial D^*_t) + p^*_t(\partial c^{*d}_t/\partial D^*_t) = 1.$

The third and final step in the analysis involves generating equilibrium conditions for the home country's (interest-earning) checkable deposits, bonds and non-interest bearing money (currency and interbank deposits due to foreign banks), the foreign country's checkable deposits, bonds and non-interest bearing money (currency and interbank deposits due to home banks), and spot and forward contracts for foreign exchange using the demand and supply functions specified above to obtain the various market demand and supply curves. Even though the government and non-financial business sectors in the two countries and the international agent are the only ones directly involved in the markets for pollution and extraction rights, the existence of renewable and non-renewable resources and the concomitant pollution- and extraction-right prices impact all other markets through their effects, in particular, upon current period product prices, output and wage incomes. These variables, in turn, affect current interest rates as well as current spot and forward exchange rates, which potentially affect future production and resource allocation in both countries.

Notes

1. Since p^*_t was set earlier by the foreign non-financial business sector in response to some of the same parameters that influenced the home non-financial business sector's reduced form expressions (79)–(89), it does not belong as a separate parameter in the home non-financial business sector's effective demand functions developed in this section.

2. This explains why, later, when we sum over the constraints of the various sectors in the home country we obtain a restriction upon the excess demands in the various financial markets which is independent of any explicit measure of the current excess supply in the market for privately-produced goods. The home non-financial business sector absorbs any excess supply of goods as an unintended addition to its inventories, with the value of that unintended inventory accumulation being revealed in the home bond market.

CHAPTER SIX

Markets for Checkable Deposits and Bonds

Introduction

In the present chapter, we combine the various sectoral demand and supply functions for financial assets that we have derived in preceding chapters to form competitive markets for checkable deposits in both the home and foreign countries as well as competitive markets for the bonds issued in both the home and foreign countries. We are able to solve for equilibrium interest rates in these four markets in a block-recursive fashion, since, in this model, current interest rates on checkable deposits affect current bond rates, but current bond rates do not affect current rates on checkable deposits. Once we have presented the equilibrium conditions for home and foreign bonds separately, we derive a locus, depicting, for a given spot rate, the combinations of the forward exchange rate and the home and foreign bond rates consistent with simultaneous equilibrium in both bond markets.

Checkable Deposits

According to the assumptions of our model, neither the market demand for checkable deposits nor the market supply of those deposits in either country depends upon current bond rates or upon the spot or forward exchange rate. Therefore, in the first step we solve for the equilibrium interest rates on checkable deposits in both countries. Since neither the private financial intermediaries nor the households in either country are directly involved in the decisions pertaining to the generation of pollution or the extraction of natural resources in this model, the prices of pollution and harvesting rights do not enter directly into either the market demand or supply of checkable deposits in either country.

Equilibrium in the Home Country's Market for Checkable Deposits

The equilibrium condition for the home country's checkable deposits is given by:

$$(6.1)\ D^d_{t+1}(\underset{+}{D_t}, \underset{+}{Cu_t}, \underset{+}{r^d_t}, \underset{+}{Q^{\wedge}_t}, \underset{+}{\phi\cdot \bar{P}}, \underset{+}{G(S_t, \bar{P})-\Omega}) = D^s_{t+1}(\underset{-}{r^d_t}, \underset{+}{\rho_t})$$

where the left-hand side of (6.1) denotes the home household sector's end-of-period demand for checkable deposits, expression (5.48) presented above, and where the right-hand side of (6.1) denotes the volume of checkable deposits the home private financial business sector would like to have outstanding by the end of the current period, expression (4.72) specified above. See Figure 6.1.

Solving for the interest rate on the home country's checkable deposits yields:

$$(6.2)\ r^d_t = r^d_t(\underset{-}{D_t}, \underset{-}{Cu_t}, \underset{-}{Q^{\wedge}_t}, \underset{-}{\phi\cdot \bar{P}}, \underset{-}{G(S_t, \bar{P})-\Omega}, \underset{+}{\rho_t}).$$

From expressions (3.58)–(3.64), the greater the home non-financial business sector's initial stock of the non-renewable resource, $Q^{\wedge}_t$, the greater is the value of current output, p_tq_t, by the home non-financial business sector and the lower the money wage, W_t, this sector announces in the current period. In addition, the greater the amount of pollution that the international agent permits, $\phi\cdot \bar{P}$, or the greater the amount of the renewable resource the agent allows to be extracted during the period, $G(\bullet)$ -Ω, the greater is the value of current output, p_tq_t, by the home non-financial business sector and the lower the money wage, W_t, this sector announces in the current period. The rise in p_tq_t translates into a higher current disposable income, $\bar{Y}_t$, even though current labor hours diminish. For these reasons, an increase in any one of $Q^{\wedge}_t$, $\phi\cdot \bar{P}$, or $G(\bullet)$ -Ω, indirectly causes the demand for the home country's checkable deposits to rise, pushing interest rates lower on those deposits.

Figure 6.1 **Equilibrium Interest Rate on Home Checkable Deposits**

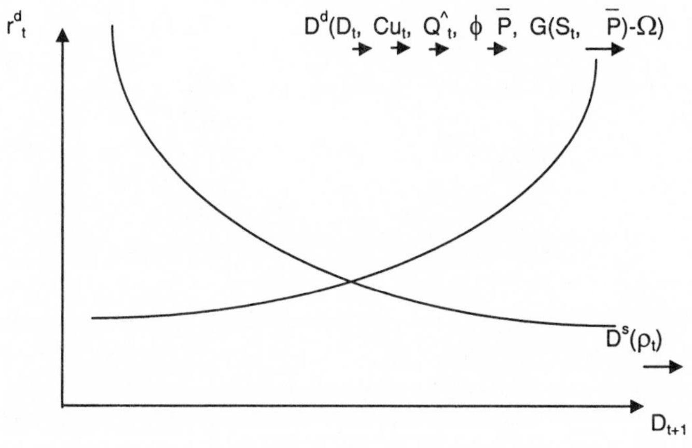

Equilibrium in the Foreign Country's Market for Checkable Deposits

Analogously, as illustrated in Figure 6.2, the equilibrium condition for the foreign country's market for checkable deposits is given by:

$$(6.3)\ D^{*d}_{t+1}\,(\underset{+}{D^{*}_{t}},\ \underset{+}{Cu^{*}_{t}},\ \underset{+}{r^{d*}_{t}},\ \underset{+}{Q^{\wedge*}_{t}},\ \underset{+}{\phi\cdot\ \overline{P}},\ \underset{+}{G(S_{t},\ \overline{P})\ -\Omega}) = D^{*s}_{t+1}(\underset{-}{r^{d*}_{t}},\ \underset{+}{\rho^{*}_{t}})$$

so that the expression for the equilibrium interest rate on the foreign country's checkable deposits is given by:

$$(6.4)\ r^{*d}_{t} = r^{*d}_{t}(\underset{-}{D^{*}_{t}},\ \underset{-}{Cu^{*}_{t}},\ \underset{-}{Q^{\wedge*}_{t}},\ \underset{-}{\phi\ \overline{P}},\ \underset{-}{G(S_{t},\ \overline{P})-\Omega},\ \underset{+}{\rho^{*}_{t}}).$$

Figure 6.2 **Equilibrium Interest Rate on Foreign Checkable Deposits**

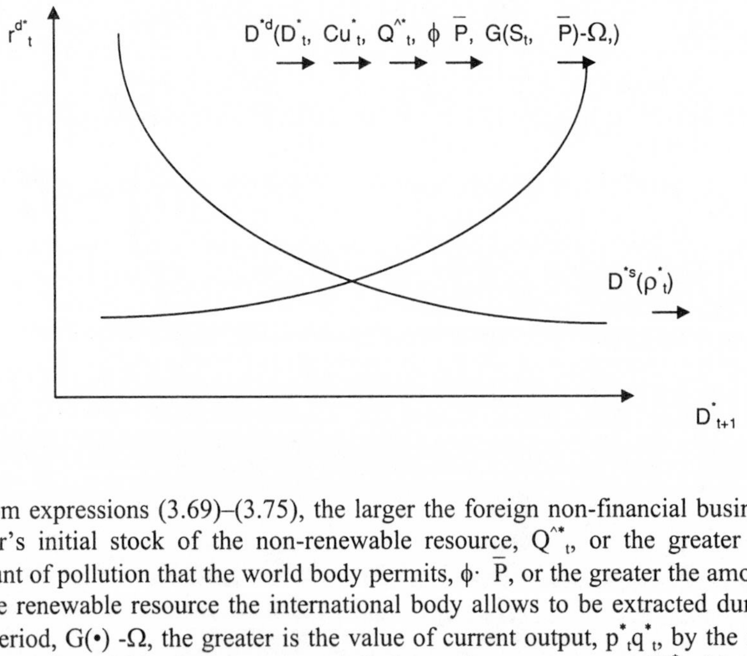

From expressions (3.69)–(3.75), the larger the foreign non-financial business sector's initial stock of the non-renewable resource, $Q^{\wedge*}_{t}$, or the greater the amount of pollution that the world body permits, $\phi\cdot\ \overline{P}$, or the greater the amount of the renewable resource the international body allows to be extracted during the period, $G(\bullet)\ -\Omega$, the greater is the value of current output, $p^{*}_{t}q^{*}_{t}$, by the foreign non-financial business sector and the lower the money wage, W^{*}_{t}, this sector announces in the current period. The rise in $p^{*}_{t}q^{*}_{t}$ translates into a higher current disposable income, $\overline{Y}^{*}_{t}$, even though current labor hours diminishes. For these reasons, an increase in any one of $Q^{\wedge*}_{t}$, $\phi\cdot\ \overline{P}$, or $G(\bullet)\ -\Omega$, causes the end-of-period demand for the foreign country's interest-earning checkable deposits to rise, pushing interest rates lower on those deposits.

The Bond Markets

Home Country Bonds

The market demand for home country bonds for the end of the period, $p^b{}_t B^d{}_{t+1}$, consists of the end-of-period demands for these bonds by the central banks and private financial sectors in both countries. The home and foreign central banks' demands for home country bonds are assumed to be exogenously determined policy variables, respectively given by (4.4) and (4.7). The home private financial sector's demand for bonds issued by borrowers in the home country, expression (4.68), depends upon the interest rate on home bonds and the discount rate set by the home central bank. The foreign private financial sector's demand for home bonds, expression (4.77), depends upon the interest rate on home bonds, the ratio of the forward exchange rate to the spot rate and the discount rate set by the foreign central bank. The stocks of the renewable and non-renewable resources or the prices of pollution and harvesting rights directly affect none of these decisions. Therefore the market demand for home country bonds, presented in (6.5) in terms of the home country's unit of account, is not directly related to these variables.

$$(6.5)\ p^b{}_t B^d{}_{t+1} = [p^b{}_t B^c{}_t + (UMB^s{}_{t+1} - UMB_t) - \beta^{*c}] + (p^b{}_t B^{c*}{}_t + \varepsilon_t \beta^{c*}) + p^b{}_t B^{fd}{}_{t+1}(\underset{+}{r^b{}_t}, \underset{-}{\rho_t})$$

$$+\varepsilon_t[p^b{}_t B^{f*d}{}_{t+1}/\varepsilon_t(\underset{+}{r^b{}_t}, \underset{-}{f^+}, \underset{-}{\rho^*{}_t})].$$

The market supply of home country bonds, expression (6.6) below, equals the sum of the end-of-period (ex ante) supplies of bonds by the home country's government, expression (5.9), and non-financial business sectors, expression (5.24). The home government finances its current deficit via the home bond market. The non-financial business sector issues bonds during the current period to finance the value of its current product and initial inventory not purchased by the other sectors. Because the price that it charges for current output and the amount of current product it produces both depend upon the initial stocks of the renewable and non-renewable resources as well as upon the volumes of pollution rights and harvesting rights granted by the international agent, the market supply of home country bonds also will be directly influenced by these variables. In particular, the greater the amount of pollution or harvesting rights offered for sale by the international agent, the greater will be the level of production and the smaller will be the product price announced by the home country's non-financial business sector. Holding the sector's forecast of the demand curve for its product constant, since the sector decides to produce in the elastic portion of this forecasted demand curve, the value of the product of the home country's non-financial business sector will rise (assuming that the forecast of the actual demand curve is approximately correct) if the initial stock of its non-renewable resource should rise or if the international body were to increase the volume of pollution or harvesting rights it issues during the current period. By itself, the rise in the value of current product by the home non-financial business sector increases its supply of bonds to the home bond market. However, the rise in the value of its current output also tends to increase the disposable income of the home country's household sector dollar for dollar, inducing the sector to increase its expenditures upon the non-financial business sector's product. But, since the households also increase their saving during the current period as their disposable income rises, their consumption demand will not rise as much as the value of current output. Therefore, the net effect is that the non-financial business sector will increase its end-of-period supply of bonds to the home bond market as the initial stock of its non-renewable resource rises or as the international body increases the volume of pollution or harvesting rights.

By similar reasoning, a fall in the initial stock of the home non-financial business sector's non-renewable resource causes that sector to reduce current production and raise product price, so that its end-of-period supply of bonds to the home bond market falls.

Note that while the government's planned purchases of privately-produced home country goods represents a part of current government borrowing, this spending also diminishes the amount of borrowing the home non-financial business sector must undertake this period, unit for unit. The reason is that the more goods the home government buys from the home non-financial business sector during the current period, ceteris paribus, the smaller the home non-financial business sector's inventory of unsold goods by the end of the period and hence the smaller the amount of the sector's unplanned inventory investment it needs to finance in the home bond market. Therefore, the net effect on the end-of-period market supply of home country bonds of a change in government spending on privately produced home country goods is zero. Such is not the case for government outlays for labor, however, even though these wage payments are part of the home household sector's current disposable income. Ceteris paribus, a unit increase in the wages paid by the home government to its household sector causes the government to borrow an extra unit in the home bond market. The home household sector will increase its spending on privately-produced home country goods as a result of the increase in the wage it receives from its government, causing the home non-financial business sector's ending inventory to fall and reducing the amount the sector must borrow in the home bond market. But the increase in household spending will be smaller than the rise in the wage income. Therefore, the reduction in the home non-financial business sector's end-of-period supply of bonds will be smaller in absolute value than the increase in the government sector's end-of-period supply of bonds.

Ceteris paribus, every dollar of spending by either the home household sector or the foreign non-financial business sector on privately-produced home country goods reduces the end-of-period market supply of home country bonds by an equivalent amount. For every unit of this spending, the home non-financial business sector's end-of-period inventory falls by the same amount; there are no further direct effects on the home bond market since, in this model, neither the home household sector nor the foreign non-financial business sector finances any of its spending in the home bond market.[1]

$$
\begin{aligned}
(6.6)\; p^b_t B^s_{t+1} &= W_{t-1}h^g_t N^g_t + p_t(\bullet)K^{gd}_{t+1}(\bullet) - p_t(\bullet)K^g_t + (1+p^b_t)B^g_t - T_t - \Pi^c_t - p^x_t R^{xd}_t \\
&\quad - p^p_t\, \bar{P}^{pd} + p^b_t B^n_t + p_t(\bullet)q_t(\bullet) - p_t(\bullet)c^d_t(\bullet) - p_t(\bullet)[K^{gd}_{t+1}(\bullet) - K^g_t] - p_{t-1}q^{n*}_t \\
&= W_{t-1}h^g_t N^g_t + (1+p^b_t)B^g_t - T_t - \Pi^c_t - p^x_t R^{xd}_t - p^p_t\, \bar{P}^{pd} + p^b_t B^n_t \\
&\quad + p_t(\underset{-}{\hat{Q}_t}, \underset{-}{\phi}\cdot \bar{P}, \underset{-}{G(S_t, \bar{P}) - \Omega})\cdot q_t(\underset{+}{\hat{Q}_t}, \underset{+}{\phi}\cdot \bar{P}, \underset{+}{G(S_t, \bar{P}) - \Omega}) \\
&\quad - p_t(\underset{-}{\hat{Q}_t}, \underset{-}{\phi}\cdot \bar{P}, \underset{-}{G(S_t, \bar{P}) - \Omega})\cdot c^d_t(\underset{+}{D_t}, \underset{+}{Cu_t}, \underset{-}{r^d_t}, \underset{+}{\hat{Q}_t}, \underset{+}{\phi}\cdot \bar{P}, \underset{+}{G(S_t, \bar{P}) - \Omega}) - p_{t-1}q^{n*}_t \\
&= W_{t-1}h^g_t N^g_t + (1+p^b_t)B^g_t - T_t - \Pi^c_t - p^x_t R^{xd}_t - p^p_t\, \bar{P}^{pd} + p^b_t B^n_t - p_{t-1}q^{n*}_t \\
&\quad + B^s(\underset{+}{\hat{Q}_t}, \underset{+}{\phi}\cdot \bar{P}, \underset{+}{G(S_t, \bar{P}) - \Omega})
\end{aligned}
$$

where $B^s(\bullet) \equiv p_t(\bullet)q_t(\bullet) - p_t(\bullet)c^d_t(\bullet)$. For the purpose of this study, we have ignored the effects of non-environmental factors upon p_t, q_t, and c^d_t and we have assumed the direct effects of the environmental factors upon current home consumption due to the corresponding changes in home gross domestic product and current disposable income more than offset the indirect effect upon current consumption operating through the interest rate on home checkable deposits.

Home Bond Market Equilibrium

From (6.5) and (6.6), the equilibrium condition in the home bond market, shown in Figure 6.3, is given by:

$$
\begin{aligned}
(6.7)\; & [p^b_t B^c_t + (UMB^s_{t+1} - UMB_t) - \beta^{*c}] + (p^b_t B^{c*}_t + \varepsilon_t \beta^{c*}) + p^b_t B^{fd}_{t+1}(\underset{+}{r^b_t}, \underset{-}{\rho_t}) \\
&\quad + \varepsilon_t[p^b_t B^{f*d}_{t+1}/\varepsilon_t(\underset{+}{r^b_t}, \underset{-}{f^+}, \underset{-}{\rho^*_t})] = W_{t-1}h^g_t N^g_t + (1+p^b_t)B^g_t - T_t - \Pi^c_t \\
&\quad - p^x_t R^{xd}_t - p^p_t\, \bar{P}^{pd} + p^b_t B^n_t - p_{t-1}q^{n*}_t + B^s(\underset{+}{\hat{Q}_t}, \underset{+}{\phi}\cdot \bar{P}, \underset{+}{G(S_t, \bar{P}) - \Omega}).
\end{aligned}
$$

Figure 6.3 **Equilibrium Interest Rate on Home Country Bonds**

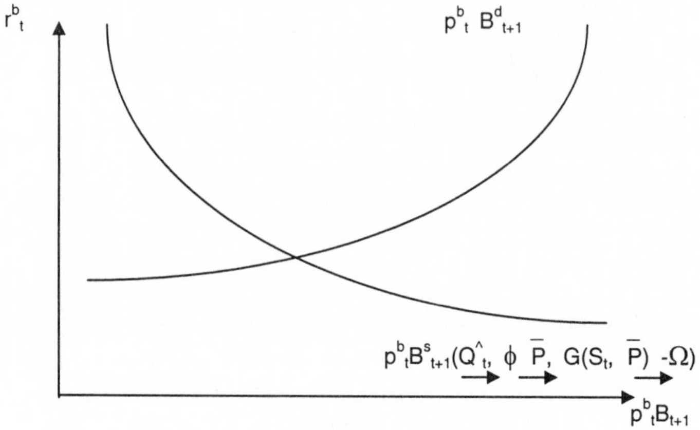

Letting $r^b_t = 1/p^b_t$, we may depict the market demand and supply curves, as well as the equilibrium interest rate on home country bonds in Figure 6.3.

The B Plane

Eventually we must solve simultaneously for the equilibrium home bond rate, the foreign bond rate, the spot rate and the forward rate. To facilitate achieving that solution, we linearize (6.7) and represent this equilibrium condition as a plane in $(r^b_t, r^{b*}_t, \hat{\varepsilon}_t)$ space. See Figure 6.4.Letting $ES^b = p^b_tB^s_{t+1} - p^b_tB^d_{t+1}$, the linearized expression may be represented as:

$$(6.8)\ \underset{-}{(\partial ES^b/\partial r^b_t)}dr^b_t + \underset{-}{(\partial ES^b/\partial \varepsilon_t)}d\varepsilon_t + \underset{+}{(\partial ES^b/\partial \hat{\varepsilon}_t)}d\hat{\varepsilon}_t + \underset{\pm}{(\partial ES^b/\partial x^b_t)}dx^b_t = 0$$

where dx^b_t denotes a change in any variable other than r^b_t, r^{b*}_t, ε_t, or $\hat{\varepsilon}_t$ that affects the excess supply of home country bonds. Then the B plane may be drawn as in Figure 6.4. The greater the amount of pollution or harvesting rights offered for sale by the international body, the greater the market supply of home country bonds ($dx^b > 0$). In either case, the home bond market equilibrium plane drawn in $(r^b_t, r^{b*}_t, \hat{\varepsilon}_t)$ space shifts outward with respect to the r^b_t axis. The smaller the home country's non-financial business sector's initial stock of the non-renewable resource, the smaller the market supply of home country bonds ($dx^b < 0$). In this case, the home bond market equilibrium plane drawn in $(r^b_t, r^{b*}_t, \hat{\varepsilon}_t)$ space shifts inward with respect to the r^b_t axis toward the origin.

Figure 6.4 **The B Plane**

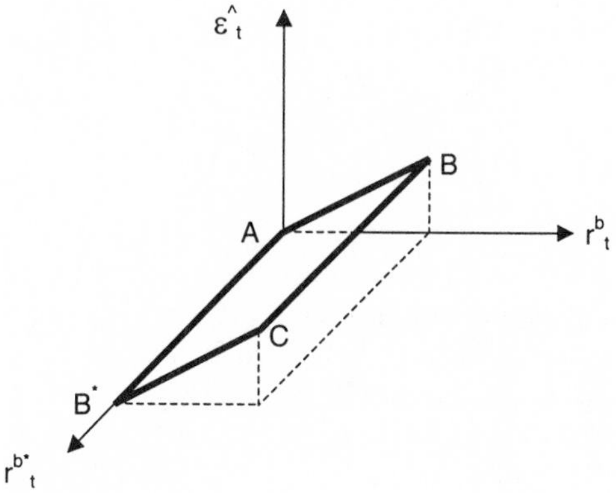

Foreign Country Bonds

The market demand for foreign country bonds (expressed in terms of the home country's unit of account) consists of the sum of the end-of-period demands for foreign bonds by the home and foreign central banks and by the home and foreign private financial sectors. These demand functions (expressed in terms of their own country's unit of account) were presented respectively above by expressions (4.3), (4.8), (4.70), and (4.79). Therefore, we may express the end-of-period market demand for foreign bonds with (6.9):

$$(6.9)\ \varepsilon_t p^{b*}_t B^{*d}_{t+1} = \varepsilon_t[p^{b*}_t B^{*c*}_t + (UMB^{*s}_{t+1} - UMB^*_t) - \beta^{c*}]$$

$$+ \varepsilon_t p^{b*}_t B^{*c}_t + \beta^{*c} + \varepsilon_t p^{b*}_t B^{*f*d}_{t+1}(\underset{+}{r^{b*}_t}, \underset{-}{\rho^*_t})$$

$$+ \varepsilon_t p^{b*}_t B^{*fd}_{t+1}(\underset{+}{r^{b*}_t}, \underset{+}{f^+}, \underset{-}{\rho_t}).$$

The market supply of foreign bonds consists of the sum of the foreign government and non-financial business sectors' end-of-period supplies, (5.10) and (5.30) respectively:

$$(6.10)\ \varepsilon_t p^{b*}_t B^{*s}_{t+1} = \varepsilon_t[W^*_{t-1} h^{g*}_t N^{g*}_t + (1+p^{b*}_t)B^{g*}_t - T^*_t - \Pi^{c*}_t - p^x_t R^{x*d}_t - p^p_t\ \bar{P}^{p*d}]$$

$$+ \varepsilon_t\, p^{b*}_t B^{*n*}_t\ - \varepsilon_t p^*_{t-1} q^{*n}_t$$

$$+ p^*_t(\underset{-}{Q^{\wedge*}_t}, \underset{-}{\phi\cdot\ \bar{P}}, G(S_t,\ \underset{-}{\bar{P}}) - \Omega)\cdot q^*_t(\underset{+}{Q^{\wedge*}_t}, \underset{+}{\phi\cdot\ \bar{P}}, G(S_t,\ \underset{+}{\bar{P}}) - \Omega)$$

$$-\varepsilon_t p^*_t(\underset{-}{Q^{\wedge*}_t}, \underset{-}{\phi\cdot \bar{P}}, \underset{-}{G(S_t, \bar{P}) - \Omega})\cdot c^{d*}_t(\underset{+}{D^*_t}, \underset{+}{Cu^*_t}, \underset{-}{r^{d*}_t}, \underset{+}{Q^{\wedge*}_t}, \underset{+}{\phi\cdot \bar{P}}, \underset{+}{G(S_t, \bar{P}) - \Omega})$$

$$= \varepsilon_t[W^*_{t-1}h^{g*}_t N^{g*}_t + (1+p^{b*}_t)B^{g*}_t - T^*_t - \Pi^{c*}_t - p^x_t R^{x*d}_t - p^p_t \bar{P}^{p*d}] + \varepsilon_t p^{b*}_t B^{*n*}_t$$

$$-\varepsilon_t p^*_{t-1} q^{*n}_t + B^{*s}(\underset{+}{Q^{\wedge*}_t}, \underset{+}{\phi\cdot \bar{P}}, \underset{+}{G(S_t, \bar{P}) - \Omega})$$

where $B^{*s}(\bullet) \equiv p^*_t(\bullet)q^*_t(\bullet) - p^*_t(\bullet)c^{d*}_t(\bullet)$. For the purpose of this study, we have ignored the effects of non-environmental factors upon p^*_t, q^*_t, and c^{d*}_t and we have assumed the direct effects of the environmental factors upon current foreign consumption due to the corresponding changes in foreign GNP and current disposable income more than offset the indirect effect upon current consumption operating through the interest rate on foreign checkable deposits.

Foreign Bond Market Equilibrium

Foreign bond market equilibrium is given by (6.11):

$$(6.11)\ \varepsilon_t[p^{b*}_t B^{*c*}_t + (UMB^{*s}_{t+1} - UMB^*_t) - \beta^{c*}] + \varepsilon_t p^{b*}_t B^{*c}_t + \beta^{*c}$$

$$+\varepsilon_t p^{b*}_t B^{*f*d}_{t+1}(\underset{+}{r^{b*}_t}, \underset{-}{\rho^*_t}) + \varepsilon_t p^{b*}_t B^{*fd}_{t+1}(\underset{+}{r^{b*}_t}, \underset{+}{f}, \underset{-}{\rho_t})$$

$$= \varepsilon_t[W^*_{t-1}h^{g*}_t N^{g*}_t + (1+p^{b*}_t)B^{g*}_t - T^*_t - \Pi^{c*}_t - p^x_t R^{x*d}_t - p^p_t \bar{P}^{p*d}] + \varepsilon_t p^{b*}_t B^{*n*}_t$$

$$-\varepsilon_t p^*_{t-1} q^{*n}_t + B^{*s}(\underset{+}{Q^{\wedge*}_t}, \underset{+}{\phi\cdot \bar{P}}, \underset{+}{G(S_t, \bar{P}) - \Omega}).$$

Letting $r^{b*}_t = 1/p^{b*}_t$, we may depict the market demand and supply curves, as well as the equilibrium interest rate on foreign country bonds in Figure 6.5.

Figure 6.5 **Equilibrium Interest Rate on Foreign Country Bonds**

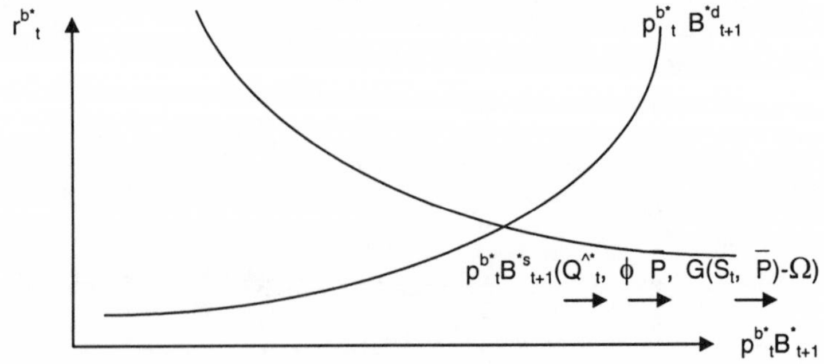

The B Plane*

As mentioned above, eventually we must solve simultaneously for the equilibrium home bond rate, the foreign bond rate, the spot rate and the forward rate. To facilitate obtaining that solution, we linearize (6.11) and represent this equilibrium condition as a plane in $(r^b_t, r^{b*}_t, \hat{\varepsilon}_t)$ space. Letting $ES^{b*} = p^{b*}_t B^{*s}_{t+1} - p^{b*}_t B^{*d}_{t+1}$, the linearized expression may be represented as:

$$(6.12)\ \underset{-}{(\partial ES^{b*}/\partial r^{b*}_t)}dr^{b*}_t + \underset{+}{(\partial ES^{b*}/\partial \varepsilon_t)}d\varepsilon_t + \underset{-}{(\partial ES^{b*}/\partial \hat{\varepsilon}_t)}d\hat{\varepsilon}_t + \underset{\pm}{(\partial ES^{b*}/\partial x^{b*}_t)}dx^{b*}_t = 0$$

where dx^{b*}_t denotes a change in any variable other than r^b_t, r^{b*}_t, ε_t, or $\hat{\varepsilon}_t$ that affects the excess supply of foreign country bonds. Then the B* plane may be drawn as in Figure 6.6.

Figure 6.6 **The B* Plane**

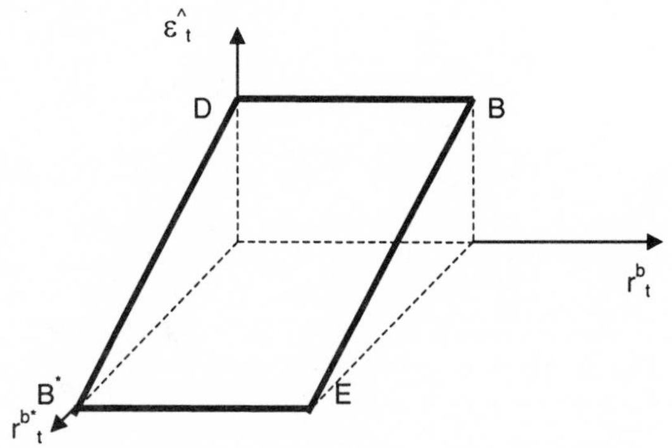

An increase in the volume of pollution or harvesting rights issued by the international body increases the foreign country's non-financial business sector's end-of-period supply of bonds to the foreign bond market ($dx^{b*}_t > 0$). An increase in either of these amounts therefore shifts the plane depicting equilibrium in the foreign bond market in $(r^b_t, r^{b*}_t, \hat{\varepsilon}_t)$ space, i.e., the B* plane, outward with respect to the r^{b*}_t axis. A decrease in the foreign non-financial business sector's initial stock of its non-renewable resource decreases the foreign country's' non-financial business sector's end-of-period supply of bonds to the foreign bond market ($dx^{b*}_t < 0$). A decrease in this amount therefore shifts the plane depicting equilibrium in the foreign bond market in $(r^b_t, r^{b*}_t, \hat{\varepsilon}_t)$ space, i.e., the B* plane, inward with respect to the r^{b*}_t axis toward the origin.

The BB* Locus

Refer to the intersection of the B plane with the B* plane as the BB* locus, as shown in Figure 6.7. This locus satisfies both (6.8) and (6.12) simultaneously.

Figure 6.7 **The BB* Locus**

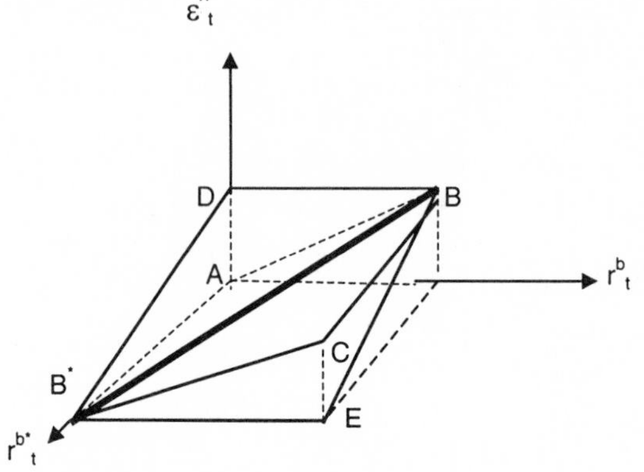

Projection of the BB Locus upon the* $(r^b_t, \hat{\varepsilon}_t)$ *Plane*

The slope of the projection of the BB* locus upon the $(r^b_t, \hat{\varepsilon}_t)$ plane is given by:

(6.13) $d\hat{\varepsilon}_t / dr^b_t = -(\partial ES^b/\partial r^b_t)/(\partial ES^b/\partial \hat{\varepsilon}_t) > 0.$

The (horizontal) shift in the projection of BB* upon the $(r^b_t, \hat{\varepsilon}_t)$ plane in response to a change in the spot rate is given by:

(6.14) $dr^b_t / d\varepsilon_t = -(\partial ES^b/\partial \varepsilon_t)/(\partial ES^b/\partial r^b_t) < 0.$

Therefore, an increase in the spot rate, ceteris paribus, shifts this projection to the left. The (horizontal) shift in the projection of BB* upon the $(r^b_t, \hat{\varepsilon}_t)$ plane in response to a change in a variable other than r^b_t, r^{b*}_t, ε_t, or $\hat{\varepsilon}_t$ that affects the excess supply of home country bonds is given by:

(6.15) $dr^b_t/dx^b_t = -(\partial ES^b/\partial x^b_t)/(\partial ES^b/\partial r^b_t).$

From (6.15), we see that the projection of the BB* locus upon the $(r^b_t, \hat{\varepsilon}_t)$ plane, shown in the right-hand panel of Figure 6.8, shifts inward relative to the r^b_t axis if the home non-financial business sector's initial stock of its non-renewable resource decreases because this causes the market supply of home country bonds to decrease, making the signed ratio on the right-hand side of (6.15) positive.

Figure 6.8 **Projections of the BB* Locus upon the (r^b_t, $\hat{\varepsilon}_t$) and (r^{b*}_t, $\hat{\varepsilon}_t$) Planes**

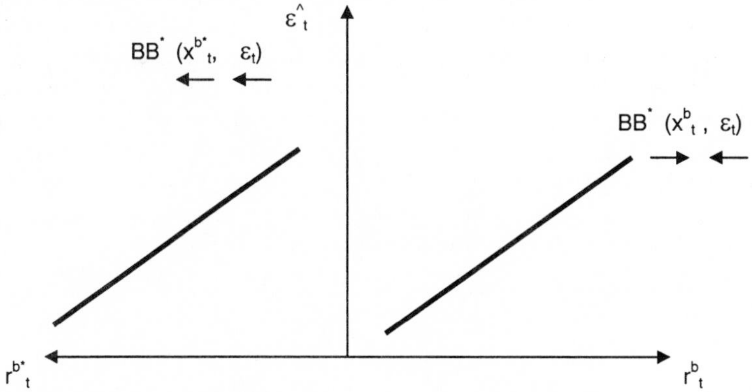

Furthermore, an increase in either the volume of pollution rights or the volume of harvesting rights for the global renewable resource causes the excess supply of home bonds to grow and shifts the BB* locus outward relative to the r^b_t axis.

Projection of the BB Locus upon the (r^{b*}_t, $\hat{\varepsilon}_t$) Plane*

The slope of the projection of the BB* locus upon the (r^{b*}_t, $\hat{\varepsilon}_t$) plane is given by:

(6.16) $d\hat{\varepsilon}_t / dr^{b*}_t = -(\partial ES^{b*}/\partial r^{b*}_t)/ (\partial ES^{b*}/\partial \hat{\varepsilon}_t) < 0.$

The (horizontal) shift in the projection of BB* upon the (r^{b*}_t, $\hat{\varepsilon}_t$) plane in response to a change in the spot rate is given by:

(6.17) $dr^{b*}_t / d\varepsilon_t = -(\partial ES^{b*}/\partial \varepsilon_t)/ (\partial ES^{b*}/\partial r^{b*}_t) > 0.$

Therefore, an increase in the spot rate, ceteris paribus, shifts this projection to the left in the left-hand panel of Figure 6.8. The (horizontal) shift in the projection of BB* upon the (r^{b*}_t, $\hat{\varepsilon}_t$) plane in response to a change in a variable other than r^b_t, r^{b*}_t, ε_t, or $\hat{\varepsilon}_t$ that affects the excess supply of foreign country bonds is given by:

(6.18) $dr^{b*}_t /dx^{b*}_t = -(\partial ES^{b*}/\partial x^{b*}_t)/(\partial ES^{b*}/\partial r^{b*}_t).$

From (6.18), we see that the projection of the BB* locus upon the (r^{b*}_t, $\hat{\varepsilon}_t$) plane, shown in the left-hand panel of Figure 6.8, shifts inward (rightward) relative to the r^{b*}_t axis if the foreign non-financial business sector's initial stock of its non-renewable resource decreases because this causes the market supply of foreign country bonds to decrease, making the signed ratio on the right-hand side of (6.18) positive.

If the international agent increases either the volume of pollution rights or the volume of harvesting rights it issues during the current period, the projections of the BB* locus upon both the $(r^b_t, \hat{\varepsilon}_t)$ and $(r^{b*}_t, \hat{\varepsilon}_t)$ planes shift outward relative to the corresponding interest rate axes, since the non-financial business sectors in both countries will increase current production. (They will also lower product price, but they produce in the elastic portion of their forecasted demand curves, so that their anticipated marginal revenue is positive. This in turn implies that—even though consumption rises with the rise in national income—each non-financial business sector will increase its end-of-period supply of bonds to its own bond market.) In either case, an excess supply is created in both bond markets.

Note

1. It is important to keep in mind that the value of the home non-financial business sector's payments for pollution and harvesting rights is essentially subtracted from the home household sector's current tax payment to its government sector. Therefore, a change in the non-financial business sector's payment to the home government causes taxes to change by the same amount in the opposite direction, thereby leaving unaffected the end-of-period market supply of home country bonds. Also, since the demand function for the home non-financial business sector's product is elastic in the range in which the sector sets product price, we assume that p_tq_t changes in the same direction as q_t. Furthermore, since the household's marginal propensity to consume is less than unity, the amounts $B^s(\bullet) \equiv p_tq_t - p_tc^d_t$ and $p^b_tB^s_{t+1}$ also change, ceteris paribus, in the same direction as q_t.

CHAPTER SEVEN

Spot and Forward Markets for Foreign Exchange

Introduction

In this chapter we continue our analysis of the financial markets in our global economy model by combining the various sectoral demand and supply functions for financial assets associated with trading a good or asset denominated in one country's unit of account for a good or asset denominated in the other country's unit of account. These transactions are divided into spot contracts, in which parties agree to trade assets denominated in different units of account during the current period, and forward contracts, in which agents agree during the current period to exchange goods or assets denominated in different units of account next period. First, we derive separate equilibrium conditions for the spot and forward markets and discuss the factors affecting each of these conditions. Then we combine these equilibrium conditions, producing an SF locus, showing for a given spot rate the combinations of the forward exchange rate and the home and foreign bond rates consistent with simultaneous equilibrium in the spot and forward markets. Then we discuss the impacts of environmental factors upon these simultaneous equilibria.

Spot Market

Spot Market Demand

The spot market consists of spot contracts to trade assets denominated in different units of account. In the present model, we view desired spot purchases of assets denominated in the foreign unit of account as constituting a spot demand for foreign exchange. In the present model, both the home country's central bank and the home private financial sector desire to purchase assets denominated in the foreign unit of account in the spot market during the current period as they purchase foreign bonds during the current period. In addition, the home private financial sector purchases interbank deposits at the foreign private financial sector during the current period. Also, the foreign private financial sector must convert its previously unanticipated capital gain on its beginning-of-period holdings of home country bonds into foreign exchange on the spot market, while the foreign central bank presumably converts into foreign exchange the entire current market value plus interest it receives during the current period on home country bonds it purchased last period. The total value of these demands for foreign exchange, S^d_t, measured in terms of the home country's unit of account, is given by (7.1):

$$(7.1)\ S^d_t = \varepsilon_t p^{b*}_t B^{*fd}_{t+1}(\underset{+}{r^{b*}_t}, \underset{+}{f^{+}_t}, \underset{-}{\rho_t}) + \varepsilon_t p^{b*}_t B^{*c}_t + \beta^{*c}$$

$$+\varepsilon_t \Re^{*d}_{t+1}(\underset{+}{\hat{\varepsilon}_t}, \underset{-}{\varepsilon_t}, \underset{-}{\rho_t}, \underset{+}{p^*_t(\cdot)}, \underset{+}{q^{*nd}_{t+1}(\cdot)})$$

$$+(p^b_t - p^{bf*}_t)B^{f*}_t + (1+p^b_t)B^{c*}_t$$

where $p^*_t(\bullet)$ and $q^{*nd}_{t+1}(\bullet)$ are given by (3.72) and (5.23), respectively:

$$(3.72)\ p^*_t = p^*_t(\underset{+}{W^*_{t-1}}, \underset{-}{Q^*_t}, \underset{-}{q^{n*}_t}, \underset{-}{K^*_t}, \underset{-}{Q^{\wedge *}_t}, \underset{+}{W_{t-1}}, \underset{-}{Q_t}, \underset{-}{q^{*n}_t}, \underset{-}{K_t}, \underset{?}{\hat{Q}_t}, \underset{-}{\phi \cdot \bar{P}}, \underset{-}{G(S_t, \bar{P}) - \Omega})$$

$$(5.23)\ q^{*nd}_{t+1}$$

$$= q^{*nd}_{t+1}(\underset{+}{W_{t-1}}, \underset{-}{Q_t}, \underset{-}{q^{*n}_t}, \underset{-}{K_t}, \underset{-}{\hat{Q}_t}, \underset{+}{W^*_{t-1}}, \underset{-}{Q^*_t}, \underset{-}{q^{n*}_t}, \underset{-}{K^*_t}, \underset{?}{Q^{\wedge *}_t}, \underset{-}{\phi \cdot \bar{P}}, \underset{-}{G(S_t, \bar{P}) - \Omega}, \underset{+}{r^b_t}, \underset{-}{\hat{\varepsilon}_t}).$$

A change in the volume of either pollution rights, $\phi \cdot \bar{P}$, or harvesting rights, $G(S_t, \bar{P}) - \Omega$, directly affects not only the product price announced by the foreign non-financial business sector, but also the amount that the home non-financial business sector wants to import from the foreign country. In particular, the greater the amount of either of these rights, the more the foreign non-financial business sector plans to produce of foreign private goods and, given its forecast of the market demand curve for its product, the lower the price it charges for its product. In addition, the greater the volume of pollution rights or harvesting rights, the more the home non-financial business sector plans to substitute either its own non-renewable resource or the global renewable resource for the good it imports from the foreign country in producing privately-produced home country goods.

A reduction in the volume of the non-renewable resource held by the foreign non-financial business sector at the beginning of the current period, $Q^{\wedge *}_t$, directly affects the product price that the foreign non-financial business sector announces at the beginning of the current period because it reduces the amount that the sector decides to produce this period. Given the sector's forecast of the demand curve for its product, the sector also announces a higher price for its product this period. A reduction in $Q^{\wedge *}_t$ produces a less direct and a less obvious effect upon the home non-financial business sector's demand for the foreign good. For the fall in $Q^{\wedge *}_t$ also causes the foreign country to increase its demand for harvesting rights and to reduce its demand for pollution rights. These price changes affect the relative prices of the home country's factors of production, inducing it to substitute the factor it imports for the renewable resource but to substitute its own non-renewable resource for the imported factor. Therefore, a reduction in the volume of the non-renewable resource held by the foreign non-financial business sector causes the price of foreign goods to increase, but produces an indeterminate effect upon the home country's demand for the foreign good.

On the other hand, a reduction in the amount of the non-renewable resource that the home non-financial business sector holds at the beginning of the current period definitely increases the sector's demand for the imported factor. But, as the sector reduces its demand for pollution rights and increases its demand for harvesting rights, it produces effects upon the prices of those rights that have conflicting effects upon the product price that the foreign non-financial business sector announces this period.

Therefore, we conclude that an increase in the volume of pollution rights, $\phi \cdot \bar{P}$, or harvesting rights, $G(S_t, \bar{P}) - \Omega$, causes value of the home private financial sector's demand for interbank deposits due from the foreign financial sector to fall. In addition, assuming that the rise in the foreign price level dominates the indirect effects upon the home non-financial business sector's demand for foreign goods when $Q^{\wedge *}_t$ falls, a reduction in the volume of the non-renewable resource held by the foreign non-financial business sector causes the home private financial sector's demand for interbank deposits due from the foreign financial sector to increase. Finally, assuming that the increase in the home non-financial business sector's demand for the imported factor due to a fall in $Q^{\wedge}_t$ dominates the impact of a fall in $Q^{\wedge}_t$ upon the foreign sector's product price, then a reduction in $Q^{\wedge}_t$ causes the home private financial sector to increase its demand for interbank deposits due from foreign banks

$$(7.2)\ \varepsilon_t \Re^{*d}_{t+1}(\underset{-}{Q^{\wedge}_t}, \underset{-}{Q^{\wedge *}_t}, \underset{-}{\phi \cdot \bar{P}}, \underset{-}{G(S_t, \bar{P}) - \Omega}, \underset{+}{\varepsilon^{\wedge}_t}, \underset{-}{\varepsilon_t}, \underset{-}{\rho_t})$$

so that the market demand for foreign exchange in the spot market, measured in terms of the home country's unit of account, is negatively related to the volume of pollution and harvesting rights and the volumes of the non-renewable resources held by both countries.

Spot Market Supply

Analogously, both the foreign central bank and the foreign private financial sector supply foreign exchange to the spot market during the current period as they demand home country bonds. In addition, the foreign private financial sector purchases interbank deposits denominated in the home country's unit of account at the home private financial sector during the period. Also, the home private financial sector converts its previously unanticipated capital gain on foreign bonds it purchased last period into assets denominated in the home country's unit of account by selling foreign exchange in the spot market. Finally, the home central bank presumably sells foreign exchange in the spot market during the current period equal to the current market value plus the interest income it receives this period on foreign bonds it purchased last period. Therefore, the market supply of foreign exchange to the spot market, S^s_t, is given by (7.3).

$$(7.3)\quad S^s_t = \varepsilon_t[p^b_t B^{f*d}_{t+1}/\varepsilon_t(\underset{+}{r^b_t}, \underset{-}{f^+_t}, \underset{-}{\rho^*_t})] + p^b_t B^{c*}_t + \varepsilon_t \beta^{c*}$$

$$+\varepsilon_t[\Re^d_{t+1}/\varepsilon_t(\underset{-}{\hat{\varepsilon}_t}, \underset{+}{\varepsilon_t}, \underset{-}{\rho^*_t}, \underset{+}{p_t(\bullet)}, \underset{+}{q^{n*d}_{t+1}(\bullet)})] + \varepsilon_t(p^{b*}_t - p^{b*f}_t)B^{*f}_t + \varepsilon_t(1+p^{b*}_t)B^{*c}_t$$

where $p_t(\bullet)$ and $q^{n*d}_{t+1}(\bullet)$ are given by (3.61) and (5.29), respectively:

$$(3.61)\quad p_t = p_t(\underset{+}{W_{t-1}}, \underset{-}{Q_t}, \underset{-}{q^{*n}_t}, \underset{-}{K_t}, \underset{-}{\hat{Q}_t}, \underset{+}{W^*_{t-1}}, \underset{-}{Q^*_t}, \underset{-}{q^{n*}_t}, \underset{-}{K^*_t}, \underset{?}{\hat{Q}^*_t}, \underset{-}{\phi\cdot\bar{P}}, \underset{-}{G(S_t, \bar{P}) - \Omega})$$

$$(5.29)\quad q^{n*d}_{t+1}$$

$$= q^{n*d}_{t+1}(\underset{+}{W^*_{t-1}}, \underset{-}{Q^*_t}, \underset{-}{q^{n*}_t}, \underset{-}{K^*_t}, \underset{-}{\hat{Q}^*_t}, \underset{+}{W_{t-1}}, \underset{-}{Q_t}, \underset{-}{q^{*n}_t}, \underset{-}{K_t}, \underset{?}{\hat{Q}_t}, \underset{-}{\phi\cdot\bar{P}}, \underset{-}{G(S_t, \bar{P}) - \Omega}, \underset{+}{r^{b*}_t}, \underset{+}{\hat{\varepsilon}_t}).$$

A change in the volume of pollution rights, $\phi\cdot\bar{P}$, or harvesting rights, $G(S_t, \bar{P}) - \Omega$, directly affects both the product price that the home non-financial business sector announces and the amount that the foreign non-financial business sector wants to import from the home country. In particular, the greater the volume of either of these rights, the more the home non-financial business sector plans to produce of home private goods and, given its forecast of the market demand curve for its product, the lower the price it charges for its product. In addition, the greater the volume of pollution rights or harvesting rights, the more the foreign non-financial business sector plans to substitute either its own non-renewable resource or the global renewable resource for the good it imports from the home country in producing privately-produced foreign country goods.

A reduction in the volume of the non-renewable resource held by the home non-financial business sector at the beginning of the current period, $\hat{Q}_t$, directly affects the product price that the home non-financial business sector announces at the beginning of the current period because it reduces the amount that the sector decides to produce this period. Given the sector's forecast of the demand curve for its product, the sector also announces a higher price for its product this period. A reduction in $\hat{Q}_t$ produces a less direct and a less obvious effect upon the foreign non-financial business sector's demand for the home good. For the fall in $Q^{\wedge}_{t}$ also causes the home country's non-financial business sector to increase its demand for harvesting rights and to reduce its demand for pollution rights. These price changes affect the relative prices of the foreign country's factors of production, inducing it to substitute the factor it imports for the renewable resource but to substitute its own non-renewable resource for the imported factor. Therefore, a reduction in the volume of the non-renewable resource held by the home non-financial business sector causes the price of home goods to increase, but produces an indeterminate effect upon the foreign country's demand for the home good.

On the other hand, a reduction in the amount of the non-renewable resource that the foreign non-financial business sector holds at the beginning of the current period definitely increases the sector's demand for the imported factor. But, as the sector reduces its demand for pollution rights and increases its demand for harvesting rights, it produces effects upon the prices of those rights that have conflicting effects upon the product price that the home non-financial business sector announces this period.

Therefore, we conclude that an increase in the volume of pollution rights, $\phi \cdot \bar{P}$, or harvesting rights, $G(S_t, \bar{P}) - \Omega$, causes value of the foreign private financial sector's demand for interbank deposits due from the home financial sector to fall. In addition, assuming that the rise in the home price level dominates the indirect effects upon the foreign non-financial business sector's demand for home goods when $Q^{\wedge}_{t}$ falls, a reduction in the volume of the non-renewable resource held by the home non-financial business sector causes the foreign private financial sector to increase its demand for interbank deposits due from the foreign financial sector. Finally, assuming that the increase in the foreign non-financial business sector's demand for the imported factor due to a fall in $Q^{\wedge *}_{t}$ dominates the impact of a fall in $Q^{\wedge *}_{t}$ upon the home sector's product price, then a reduction in $Q^{\wedge *}_{t}$ causes the foreign private financial sector to increase its demand for interbank deposits due from foreign banks:

$$(7.4)\ \Re^{d}_{t+1}/\varepsilon_t(\underset{-}{Q^{\wedge}_{t}},\ \underset{-}{Q^{\wedge *}_{t}},\ \underset{-}{\phi \cdot \bar{P}},\ \underset{-}{G(S_t,\ \bar{P}) - \Omega},\ \underset{+}{\varepsilon^{\wedge}_{t}},\ \underset{-}{\varepsilon_t},\ \underset{-}{\rho_t})$$

so that the market supply of foreign exchange in the spot market, measured in terms of the home country's unit of account, is also negatively related to the volume of pollution and harvesting rights and the volumes of the non-renewable resources held by both countries.

Spot Market Equilibrium

Spot market equilibrium, shown in Figure 7.1, is denoted by expression (7.5):

$$(7.5)\ \varepsilon_t p^{b*}{}_{t} B^{*fd}_{t+1}(\underset{+}{r^{b*}_{t}},\ \underset{+}{f^{+}_{t}},\ \underset{-}{\rho_t}) + \varepsilon_t p^{b*}{}_{t} B^{*c}_{t} + \beta^{*c}$$

$$+\varepsilon_t \Re^{*d}_{t+1}(\underset{+}{\hat{\varepsilon}_t}, \underset{-}{\varepsilon_t}, \underset{-}{\rho_t}, \underset{-}{\hat{Q}_t}, \underset{-}{\hat{Q}^{*}_t}, \underset{-}{\phi \cdot \bar{P}}, G(S_t, \bar{P}) - \Omega) + (p^b_t - p^{bf*}_t)B^{f*}_t + (1+p^b_t)B^{c*}_t$$

$$= \varepsilon_t[p^b_t B^{f*d}_{t+1}/\varepsilon_t(\underset{+}{r^b_t}, \underset{-}{f^{+}_t}, \underset{-}{\rho^{*}_t})] + p^b_t B^{c*}_t + \varepsilon_t \beta^{c*}$$

$$+\varepsilon_t[\Re^{d}_{t+1}/\varepsilon_t(\underset{-}{\hat{\varepsilon}_t}, \underset{+}{\varepsilon_t}, \underset{-}{\rho^{*}_t}, \underset{-}{\hat{Q}_t}, \underset{-}{\hat{Q}^{*}_t}, \underset{-}{\phi \cdot \bar{P}}, \underset{-}{G(S_t, \bar{P}) - \Omega})]$$

$$+\varepsilon_t(p^{b*}_t - p^{b*f}_t)B^{*f}_t + \varepsilon_t(1+p^{b*}_t)B^{*c}_t.$$

Figure 7.1 **Equilibrium Spot Rate**

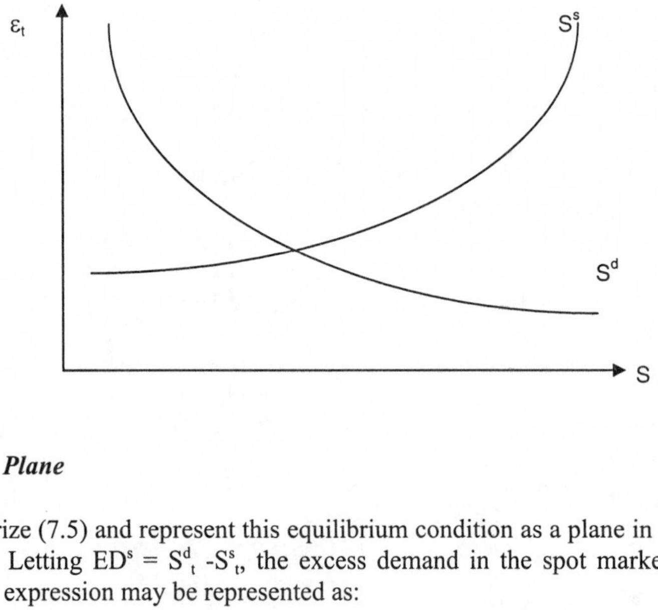

The S Plane

Linearize (7.5) and represent this equilibrium condition as a plane in $(r^b_t, r^{b*}_t, \hat{\varepsilon}_t)$ space. Letting $ED^s = S^d_t - S^s_t$, the excess demand in the spot market, the linearized expression may be represented as:

$$(7.6)\ \underset{-}{(\partial ED^s/\partial r^b_t)}dr^b_t + \underset{+}{(\partial ED^s/\partial r^{b*}_t)}dr^{b*}_t + \underset{-}{(\partial ED^s/\partial \varepsilon_t)}d\varepsilon_t$$

$$+\underset{+}{(\partial ED^s/\partial \hat{\varepsilon}_t)}d\hat{\varepsilon}_t + \underset{\pm}{(\partial ED^s/\partial x^s_t)}dx^s_t = 0$$

where dx^s_t denotes a change in any variable other than r^b_t, r^{b*}_t, ε_t, or $\hat{\varepsilon}_t$ that affects the excess demand for spot contracts. Then the S plane may be drawn as in Figure 7.2.

Figure 7.2 **The S Plane**

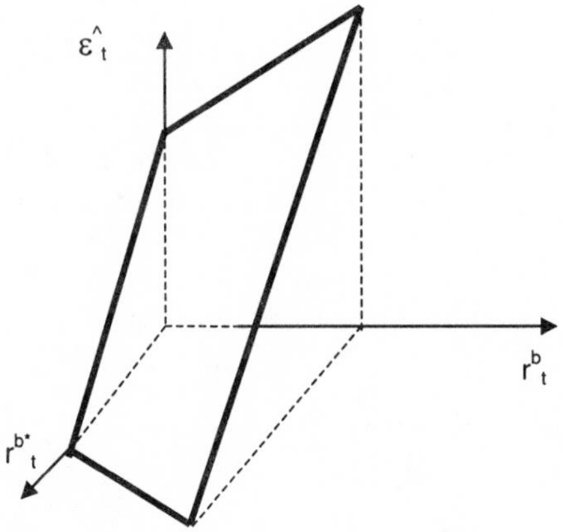

The resource constraints introduced in this study exert no direct influence upon the position of the S plane. In particular, although the foreign country must buy the home country's currency in the spot market to pay the international agent for the pollution and harvesting rights it buys, the international agent passes the revenue it receives from the foreign non-financial business sector to that country's government sector, which converts it back into assets denominated in the foreign country's currency. Therefore, the supply of foreign exchange to the spot market by the foreign non-financial business sector for the purpose of buying pollution and harvesting rights is exactly offset by the demand for foreign exchange by that country's government sector as it redeems the revenue from the international agent's sale of these rights to its non-financial business sector for assets denominated in its own unit of account.

However, the resource constraints do affect the S plane indirectly to the extent that a change in one or more of these constraints affect the private financial sectors' end-of-period demands for interbank deposits. For example, an increase in either the volume of pollution rights or the volume of harvesting rights associated with the global renewable resource causes both the home and foreign private non-financial business sectors to reduce their real demands for the goods they import from each other. Also, the private financial sector in each country reduces its demand for interbank deposits held with the other country's private financial sector. Each private financial sector holds these deposits in order to reduce transaction time associated with facilitating the imports of their own country's non-financial business sector; as these imports decline, not as many deposits are required. As each private financial sector's demand for interbank deposits falls, both the market demand and market supply of foreign exchange in the spot market fall. Because we have no a priori reason to assume that either one of these effects dominates, in the interest of simplifying the analysis, we simply ignore the effects of changes in pollution or harvesting rights operating through the demands for interbank deposits in the spot market.

A reduction in the initial stock of the non-renewable resource held by the home non-financial business sector causes the sector to increase its demand for the imported factor, q^{*nd}_{t+1}, and to raise the price of its own product, p_t; assuming that the effect upon the sector's demand for the factor it imports from the foreign country dominates, the spot demand for foreign exchange increases as the home private financial sector builds up its interbank balances due from the foreign banks in order to service its importing non-financial business sector. Therefore, as $Q^{\wedge}_t$ falls, ceteris paribus, we assume that the excess demand in the spot market increases.

A reduction in the initial stock of the non-renewable resource held by the foreign non-financial business sector induces the sector to increase its demand for the factor it imports from the home country, q^{n*d}_{t+1}, and to raise the price of its own product, p^*_t; assuming that the effect upon the demand for the home country's good dominates the effect upon the price charged by the foreign country, the spot supply of foreign exchange increases as the foreign private financial sector increases its demand for interbank deposits due from the home private financial sector in anticipation of a larger volume of imports by the foreign non-financial business sector next period. Therefore, we assume that as $Q^{\wedge*}_t$ diminishes it creates an excess supply in the spot market.

Forward Market

Forward Market Demand

The forward market consists of forward contracts to exchange assets denominated in different units of account. In this model, a one period lag exists between the time the non-financial business sector in each country orders goods produced by the private firms in the other country and the time these sectors receive, pay for, and apply these goods to their own production process. Therefore, during the current period, the non-financial business sector in each country orders from its counterpart in the other country the number of privately-produced goods it plans to use next period in its own production. The price of the good ordered has already been announced in terms of the unit of account of the producer's country. Because the non-financial business sectors will not pay for the goods they order from each other this period until they actually receive the goods next period, each sector hedges against the possibility that the value of the goods they order will rise in the interim in terms of the purchaser's unit of account, necessitating a larger payment for these goods next period than the current spot exchange rate indicates. The home non-financial business sector, for example, hedges during the current period by buying foreign exchange forward, i.e., for future delivery. In this way, the home non-financial business sector locks into a price of foreign country money in terms of its own unit of account during the current period, referred to as the forward exchange rate, which it agrees to pay next period. In this model, the sector buys an amount of foreign exchange forward equal to the amount it needs to finance its outlays, expressed in terms of the other country's unit of account, on the imported input next period. Expression (5.23) gives its real demand for foreign goods (in terms of those goods).

During the current period, the foreign country's private financial sector also demands foreign exchange in the forward market. The volume of home country bonds the sector decides to hold by the end of the current period (expressed in (4.77) in terms of the foreign country's unit of account) will yield a total return next period, expressed in terms of the home country's unit of account, equal to the interest payments on those bonds plus next period's market value of the bonds. During the current period, the foreign private financial sector presumably protects ("covers") the anticipated total return in terms of its own country's unit of account by buying foreign exchange forward during the current period equal to the value of next period's anticipated total return. In a similar manner, the foreign private financial sector also presumably covers during the current period the value of the interbank deposits they plan to hold at the home private financial sector (denominated in the home unit of account) by the end of the current period.

Based upon these considerations, the market demand for foreign exchange in the forward market during the current period may be represented, in terms of the home country's unit of account, by (7.7):

$$(7.7)\ F^d_t = \hat{\varepsilon}_t p^*_t(\underset{-}{Q^{\hat{}*}_t},\ \underset{-}{\phi\cdot\bar{P}},\ \underset{-}{G(S_t,\ \bar{P})-\Omega})\cdot q^{*nd}_{t+1}(\underset{-}{\hat{Q}_t},\ \underset{-}{\phi\cdot\bar{P}},\ \underset{-}{G(S_t,\ \bar{P})-\Omega},\ \underset{+}{r^b_t},\ \underset{-}{\hat{\varepsilon}_t})$$

$$+[(1+p^{bf*}_{t+1})/p^b_t]\varepsilon_t[p^b_t B^{f*d}_{t+1}/\varepsilon_t(\underset{+}{r^b_t},\ \underset{-}{f^+_t},\ \underset{-}{\rho^*_t})]$$

$$+\varepsilon_t[\Re^d_{t+1}/\varepsilon_t(\underset{-}{\hat{\varepsilon}_t},\underset{+}{\varepsilon_t},\underset{-}{\rho^*_t},p_t(\underset{-}{\hat{Q}_t},\underset{-}{\phi\cdot\bar{P}},\underset{-}{G(S_t,\ \bar{P})-\Omega}),q^{n*d}_{t+1}(\underset{-}{Q^{\hat{}*}_t},\underset{-}{\phi\cdot\bar{P}},\underset{-}{G(S_t,\ \bar{P})-\Omega},\underset{+}{r^{b*}_t},\underset{+}{\hat{\varepsilon}_t}))].$$

Forward Market Supply

By the same token, the foreign private non-financial business sector hedges its current period order for the good produced by the home non-financial business sector—expression (5.29) depicts its real demand for that good—by selling foreign exchange forward during the current period equal to the current market value of that order. Also, the home private financial sector sells foreign exchange forward during the current period equal to the anticipated total return next period on foreign bonds it buys during the current period plus the value of the interbank deposits it plans to hold at the foreign private financial sector by the end of the current period. The sector's end-of-period demand for foreign bonds, expressed in terms of the home country's unit of account, is given by (5.30). Therefore the current market supply of foreign exchange in the forward market, in terms of the home country's unit of account, is given by (7.8):

$$(7.8)\quad F^s_t = p_t(\hat{Q}_t, \phi\cdot\bar{P}, G(S_t, \bar{P})-\Omega)\cdot q^{n*d}_{t+1}(\hat{Q}^*_t, \phi\cdot\bar{P}, G(S_t, \bar{P})-\Omega, r^{b*}_t, \hat{\varepsilon}_t)$$

\- - - - - - + +

$$+\hat{\varepsilon}_t[\varepsilon_t \Re^{*d}_{t+1}(\hat{\varepsilon}_t, \varepsilon_t, \rho_t, p^*_t(\hat{Q}^*_t, \phi\cdot\bar{P}, G(S_t, \bar{P})-\Omega),$$

\+ - - - - -

$$q^{*nd}_{t+1}(\hat{Q}_t, \phi\cdot\bar{P}, G(S_t, \bar{P})-\Omega, r^b_t, \hat{\varepsilon}_t))]/\varepsilon_t$$

\- - - + -

$$+\hat{\varepsilon}_t\cdot[1+p^{b*f}_{t+1}][\varepsilon_t p^{b*}_t B^{*fd}_{t+1}/(r^{b*}_t, f^+_t, \rho_t)]/\varepsilon_t p^{b*}_t.$$

\+ + -

Forward Market Equilibrium

From the above discussion, equilibrium in the forward market, shown in Figure 7.3, is denoted by (7.9):

$$(7.9)\quad \hat{\varepsilon}_t p^*_t(\hat{Q}^*_t, \phi\cdot\bar{P}, G(S_t, \bar{P})-\Omega)\cdot q^{*nd}_{t+1}(\hat{Q}_t, \phi\cdot\bar{P}, G(S_t, \bar{P})-\Omega, r^b_t, \hat{\varepsilon}_t)$$

\- - - - - - + -

$$+[(1+p^{bf*}_{t+1})/p^b_t]\varepsilon_t[p^b_t B^{f*d}_{t+1}/\varepsilon_t(r^b_t, f^+_t, \rho^*_t)]$$

\+ - -

$$+\varepsilon_t[\Re^d_{t+1}/\varepsilon_t(\hat{\varepsilon}_t, \varepsilon_t, \rho^*_t, p_t(\hat{Q}_t, \phi\cdot\bar{P}, G(S_t, \bar{P})-\Omega),$$

\- + - - - -

$$q^{n*d}_{t+1}(\hat{Q}^*_t, \phi\cdot\bar{P}, G(S_t, \bar{P})-\Omega, r^{b*}_t, \hat{\varepsilon}_t))]$$

\- - - + +

$$= p_t(\hat{Q}_t, \phi\cdot\bar{P}, G(S_t, \bar{P})-\Omega)\cdot q^{n*d}_{t+1}(\hat{Q}^*_t, \phi\cdot\bar{P}, G(S_t, \bar{P})-\Omega, r^{b*}_t, \hat{\varepsilon}_t)$$

\- - - - - - + +

$$+\hat{\varepsilon}_t[\varepsilon_t \Re^{*d}_{t+1}(\hat{\varepsilon}_t, \varepsilon_t, \rho_t, p^*_t(\hat{Q}^*_t, \phi\cdot\bar{P}, G(S_t, \bar{P})-\Omega),$$

\+ - - - - -

$$q^{*nd}_{t+1}(\hat{Q}_t, \phi\cdot\bar{P}, G(S_t, \bar{P})-\Omega, r^b_t, \hat{\varepsilon}_t))]/\varepsilon_t + \hat{\varepsilon}_t\cdot[1+p^{b*f}_{t+1}][\varepsilon_t p^{b*}_t B^{*fd}_{t+1}/(r^{b*}_t, f^+_t, \rho_t)]/\varepsilon_t p^{b*}_t.$$

\+ + - - - - + -

Figure 7.3 **Equilibrium Forward Rate**

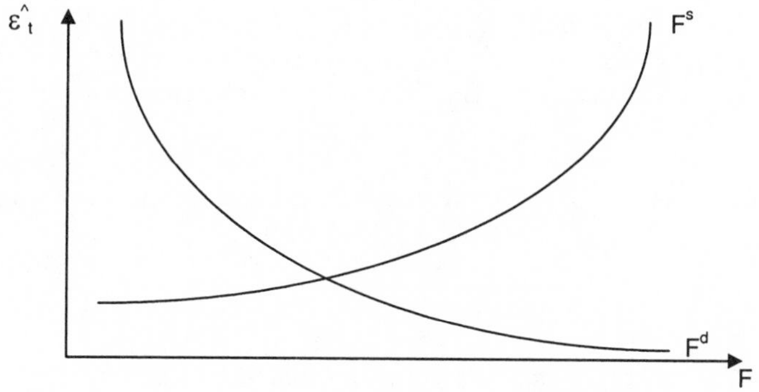

In the following discussion we ignore the effects of changes in pollution and harvesting rights upon the market demand and supply functions for foreign exchange in the forward market operating through the private financial sector's demands for interbank deposits, just as we did in the spot market, because we have no a priori basis upon which to posit which country's response will be the stronger. Both the market demand and the market supply of foreign exchange in the forward market are also directly affected by the issuance of limited numbers of pollution and harvesting rights. In particular, the market demand for foreign exchange in the forward market includes the home non-financial business sector's demand for the foreign good, while the market supply of foreign exchange in the forward market includes the foreign non-financial business sector's demand for the home good. According to our earlier discussion, ceteris paribus, the greater the number of pollution or harvesting rights issued by the international agent, the smaller is the non-financial business sector's demand in each country for the good it imports from the other country; both the market demand and supply for foreign exchange fall in the forward market. We have no a priori reason to select either one of these two effects as dominating. Therefore, an increase in either the volume of pollution rights or the volume of harvesting rights for the renewable resource produces an indeterminate effect upon the excess demand in the forward market.

We may be able to say a bit more with respect to the effects of a change in the initial stocks of the non-renewable resources however, if we are again willing to assume the relative strengths of the price and quantity impacts. If the initial stock of the home country's non-renewable resource should decrease, the first responses include the home country announcing a higher price for its product (p_t increases) and increasing its demand for product of the foreign country (q^{*nd}_{t+1} rises). Assuming that this latter response dominates, and that the direct effect upon the market demand for foreign exchange in the forward market due to the rise in q^{*nd}_{t+1} dominates the effect upon the market supply of foreign exchange in the forward market via its effect upon the home financial sector's demand for interbank deposits, then the fall in $Q^{\wedge}_t$ creates an excess demand in the forward market, ($dx^f > 0$). Granting similar assumptions—as to both the relative strengths of the quantity and price effects generated by a fall in the initial stock of the foreign sector's initial stock of its non-renewable resource and the relative strengths of the direct effect upon market supply and the indirect effect upon market demand due to the change in the foreign financial sector's demand for interbank deposits—a fall in $Q^{\wedge *}_t$ creates an excess supply in the forward market, ($dx^f_t < 0$).

The F Plane

Linearize (7.9) and represent this equilibrium condition as a plane in (r^b_t, r^{b*}_t, $\varepsilon^{\wedge}_t$) space. Letting $ED^f = F^d_t - F^s_t$, the excess demand in the forward market, the linearized expression may be represented as:

$$(7.10)\quad \underset{+}{(\partial ED^f/\partial r^b_t)}dr^b_t + \underset{-}{(\partial ED^f/\partial r^{b*}_t)}dr^{b*}_t + \underset{+}{(\partial ED^f/\partial \varepsilon_t)}d\varepsilon_t$$

$$+\underset{-}{(\partial ED^f/\partial \varepsilon^{\wedge}_t)}d\varepsilon^{\wedge}_t + \underset{\pm}{(\partial ED^f/\partial x^f_t)}dx^f_t = 0$$

where dx^f_t denotes a change in any variable other than r^b_t, r^{b*}_t, ε_t, or $\varepsilon^{\wedge}_t$ that affects the excess demand for spot contracts. Then the F plane may be drawn as in Figure 7.4.

Figure 7.4 **The F Plane**

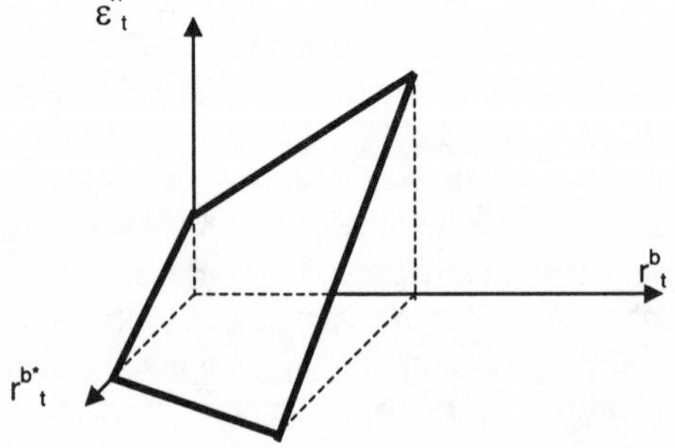

SF Locus

Refer to the intersection of the S plane with the F plane as the SF locus, as shown in Figure 7.5. This locus satisfies both (7.6) and (7.10) simultaneously.

Figure 7.5 **The SF Locus**

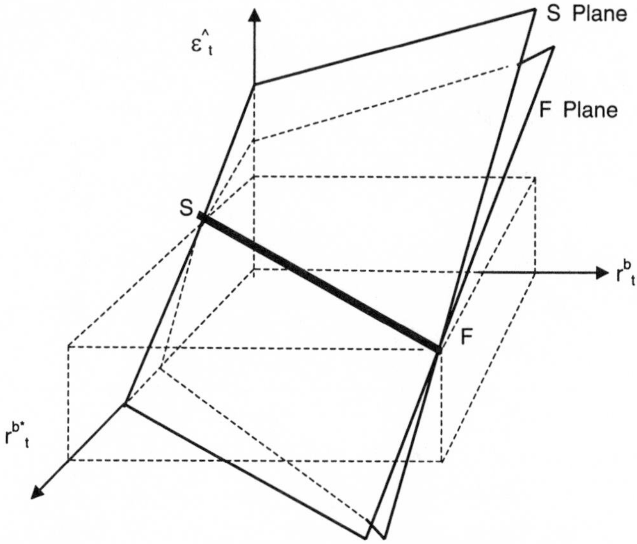

Projections of the SF Locus upon the $(r^b_t, \hat{\varepsilon}_t)$ and $(r^{b*}_t, \hat{\varepsilon}_t)$ Planes

The slope of the projection of the SF locus upon the $(r^b_t, \hat{\varepsilon}_t)$ plane is given by:

$$(7.11)\quad d\hat{\varepsilon}_t / dr^b_t = -[(\partial ED^f/\partial r^b_t)(\partial ED^s/\partial r^{b*}_t) - (\partial ED^f/\partial r^{b*}_t)(\partial ED^s/\partial r^b_t)] / [(\partial ED^f/\partial \hat{\varepsilon}_t)(\partial ED^s/\partial r^{b*}_t) - (\partial ED^f/\partial r^{b*}_t)(\partial ED^s/\partial \hat{\varepsilon}_t)].$$

The slope of the projection of the SF locus upon the $(r^{b*}_t, \hat{\varepsilon}_t)$ plane is given by:

$$(7.12)\quad d\hat{\varepsilon}_t / dr^{b*}_t = -[(\partial ED^f/\partial r^{b*}_t)(\partial ED^s/\partial r^b_t) - (\partial ED^f/\partial r^b_t)(\partial ED^s/\partial r^{b*}_t)] / [(\partial ED^f/\partial \hat{\varepsilon}_t)(\partial ED^s/\partial r^b_t) - (\partial ED^f/\partial r^b_t)(\partial ED^s/\partial \hat{\varepsilon}_t)].$$

Assuming that the change in the excess demand for foreign exchange in the forward market in response to a change in the forward rate dominates the other responses in the denominators of (7.11) and (7.12), these denominators are negative. However, assuming (i) the value of the foreign bonds held by the home country's private financial sector is comparable to the value of the home country bonds held by the foreign private financial sector, (ii) the response in the home private financial sector to a change in the rate of return on foreign bonds is comparable to the response in the foreign private financial sector to a change in the rate of return on home bonds, and (iii) the interest elasticity of the home non-financial business sector's demand for the good it imports is comparable to the interest elasticity of the foreign non-financial business sector's demand for the good it imports, then the numerators in (7.11) and (7.12) are both close to zero. For simplicity, we arbitrarily set them equal to zero. Consequently, the projections of the SF locus upon the $(r^b_t, \hat{\varepsilon}_t)$ and $(r^{b*}_t, \hat{\varepsilon}_t)$ planes are represented by horizontal lines in our analysis. See Figure 7.6.

Figure 7.6 **Projections of the SF Locus upon the $(r^b_t, \hat{\varepsilon}_t)$ and $(r^{b*}_t, \hat{\varepsilon}_t)$ Planes**

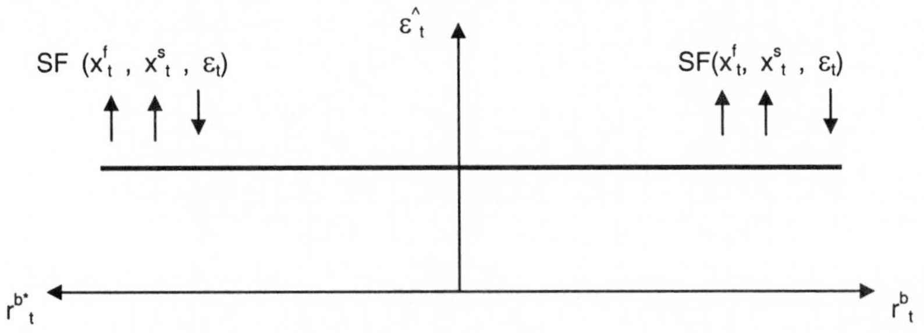

(Vertical) Shifts in the Projection of the SF Locus

The (vertical) shift in the projection of SF upon the $(r^b_t, \hat{\varepsilon}_t)$ plane in response to a change in the spot rate is given by:

$$(7.13)\ d\hat{\varepsilon}_t / d\varepsilon_t = -[(\partial ED^f/\partial\varepsilon_t)(\partial ED^s/\partial r^{b*}_t) - (\partial ED^f/\partial r^{b*}_t)(\partial ED^s/\partial\varepsilon_t)]$$

$$/[(\partial ED^f/\partial\hat{\varepsilon}_t)(\partial ED^s/\partial r^{b*}_t) - (\partial ED^f/\partial r^{b*}_t)(\partial ED^s/\partial\hat{\varepsilon}_t)] < 0.$$

Our assumption that the denominator of (7.11) is negative implies that the denominator of (7.13) is also taken to be negative. If we assume as well that the effect upon the excess demand in the spot market due to a change in the spot rate dominates the other terms in the numerator of (7.13), then the signed numerator in (7.13) is positive, so that expression (7.13) is negative. Ceteris paribus, an increase in the spot rate shifts the SF locus in the right-hand panel of Figure 7.6 downward, resulting in a lower forward rate. An equal response is found with respect to the effect on an increase in the spot rate upon the projection of the SF locus upon the $(r^{b*}_t, \hat{\varepsilon}_t)$ plane.

The shift in the projection of the SF locus upon the $(r^b_t, \hat{\varepsilon}_t)$ plane relative to the $\hat{\varepsilon}_t$ axis in response to any variable other than r^b_t, r^{b*}_t, ε_t, or $\hat{\varepsilon}_t$ that affects the excess demand in the spot market, but leaves the excess demand in the forward market unchanged, is given by:

$$(7.14)\ d\hat{\varepsilon}_t / dx^s_t = [(\partial ED^f/\partial r^{b*}_t)(\partial ED^s/\partial x^s_t)] / [(\partial ED^f/\partial \hat{\varepsilon}_t)(\partial ED^s/\partial r^{b*}_t) - (\partial ED^f/\partial r^{b*}_t)(\partial ED^s/\partial \hat{\varepsilon}_t)] > 0.$$

A change in any variable that increases the excess demand for foreign exchange in the spot market, but which leaves the excess demand for foreign exchange in the forward market unchanged, must cause the foreign bond rate to fall, ceteris paribus, if the excess demand in the spot market is to be eliminated.

As the foreign bond rate falls, an excess demand is created in the forward market necessitating a rise in the forward rate (holding the spot rate constant). Therefore, given our assumption as to the strength of the response in the excess demand in the forward market to a change the forward rate relative to the other responses appearing in the denominator of (7.14), the projection of the SF locus in the $(r^b_t, \hat{\varepsilon}_t)$ plane shifts upward as an excess demand is created in the spot market.

The shift in the projection of the SF locus upon the $(r^{b*}_t, \hat{\varepsilon}_t)$ plane relative to the $\hat{\varepsilon}_t$ axis in response to any variable other than r^b_t, r^{b*}_t, ε_t, or $\hat{\varepsilon}_t$ that affects the excess demand in the spot market, but leaves the excess demand in the forward market unchanged, is given by:

$$(7.15)\ d\hat{\varepsilon}_t / dx^s_t = [(\partial ED^f/\partial r^b_t)(\partial ED^s/\partial x^s_t)] / [(\partial ED^f/\partial \hat{\varepsilon}_t)(\partial ED^s/\partial r^b_t) - (\partial ED^f/\partial r^b_t)(\partial ED^s/\partial \hat{\varepsilon}_t)] > 0.$$

A change in any variable that increases the excess demand for foreign exchange in the spot market, but which leaves the excess demand unchanged in the forward market, must cause the foreign bond rate to fall, ceteris paribus, if the excess demand in the spot market is to be eliminated. As the foreign bond rate falls, an excess demand is created in the forward market necessitating a rise in the forward rate (holding the spot rate constant). Therefore, given our assumptions, the projection of the SF locus in the $(r^{b*}_t, \hat{\varepsilon}_t)$ plane also shifts upward as an excess demand is created in the spot market.

The (vertical) shift in the projection of SF upon the $(r^b_t, \hat{\varepsilon}_t)$ plane in response to a change in a variable other than r^b_t, r^{b*}_t, ε_t, or $\hat{\varepsilon}_t$ that affects the excess demand in the forward market, but leaves the excess demand in the spot market unchanged, is given by:

$$(7.16)\ d\hat{\varepsilon}_t / dx^f_t = -[(\partial ED^s/\partial r^{b*}_t)(\partial ED^f/\partial x^f_t)] / [(\partial ED^f/\partial \hat{\varepsilon}_t)(\partial ED^s/\partial r^{b*}_t) - (\partial ED^f/\partial r^{b*}_t)(\partial ED^s/\partial \hat{\varepsilon}_t)] > 0.$$

Again, given our assumptions, both the numerator and denominator in (7.16) are negative. The SF locus shifts upward in the (r^b_t, $\hat{\varepsilon}_t$) plane as an excess demand is created in the forward market by a variable other than r^b_t, r^{b*}_t, ε_t, or $\hat{\varepsilon}_t$. An equal response is found with respect to the projection of the SF locus upon the (r^{b*}_t, $\hat{\varepsilon}_t$) plane.

As indicated in our discussion above, an increase in the amount of pollution rights or harvesting rights issued by the international agent produces an indeterminate net effect upon both the excess demand for foreign exchange in the spot market and the excess demand for foreign exchange in the forward market. For simplicity, we assume therefore that an increase in either the level of pollution rights or harvesting rights exerts no direct influence upon the excess demands in either market. On the other hand, a decrease in amount of the non-renewable resource held by the home non-financial business sector at the beginning of the period, $\hat{Q}_t$, creates an excess demand for foreign exchange in both the spot and forward markets ($dx^s_t > 0$, $dx^f_t > 0$) while a decrease in the initial stock of the foreign country's non-renewable resource, $\hat{Q}^*_t$, creates an excess supply in both markets ($dx^s_t < 0$, $dx^f_t < 0$). Therefore a decrease in $\hat{Q}_t$ shifts the SF locus upward in both panels of Figure 7.6, while a decrease in $\hat{Q}^*_t$ produces the opposite result.

CHAPTER EIGHT

Non-Interest-Bearing Money and General Equilibrium in the Financial Markets

Introduction

In the present chapter we continue our discussion of the financial markets contained in our global economy model by combining the demands and supplies of non-interest-bearing assets into a competitive market for those non-interest-bearing assets denominated in the home country's unit of account and a separate competitive market for those non-interest-bearing assets denominated in the foreign country's unit of account. We then combine these equilibrium conditions and find, for a given spot rate, the locus of combinations of the forward rate and the bond rates on home and foreign bonds that produce equilibrium in both markets for non-interest-bearing assets simultaneously. Then we consider how changes in the spot rate and environmental factors affect the position of this locus.

Markets for Non-Interest-Bearing Money

The interest-bearing checkable deposits issued in each country bear a fixed value in terms of the corresponding country's unit of account; the interest-bearing bonds issued in each country bear a price that fluctuates in terms of the corresponding unit of account. Besides checkable deposits and bonds, there exists in each country non-interest-bearing money whose value is fixed relative to the country's unit of account. In the present model, this money consists of (coin and) currency and interbank deposits; neither currency nor interbank deposits pay interest to their holder and their value is fixed in terms of the unit of account of the country in which the issuing central bank, or—in the case of interbank deposits—the issuing private financial sector, is located.

Home Country (Non-Interest-Bearing) Money

In this section, we develop the market for the home country's non-interest-bearing money, consisting of the interbank deposits issued by the home private financial sector which are held by the foreign private financial sector and the (coin and) currency issued by the home central bank. We begin by deriving the market demand for the non-interest-bearing money of the home country and then derive the market supply for that money.

Market Demand for Home Country (Non-Interest-Bearing) Money

The market demand for the home country's non-interest-bearing money consists of the home country's household sector's end-of-period demand for home country currency plus the foreign private financial sector's demand for inter-bank deposits issued by the home private financial sector. Both of these items are denominated in the home country's unit of account. We begin with the demand function for home country currency derived in Chapter 5.

Demand for Home Country Currency. In this model, prior to the determination of current interest rates on checkable deposits, the reduced-form end-of-period market demand for the home country's currency corresponded to the home household sector's end-of-period demand, given by (5.47), repeated here as (8.1):

$$(8.1)\ Cu^{d}_{t+1} = Cu^{d}_{t+1}(\underset{+}{D_t}, \underset{+}{Cu_t}, \underset{-}{r^{d}_t}, \underset{+}{Q^{\wedge}_t}, \underset{+}{\phi\cdot \bar{P}}, \underset{+}{G(S_t, \bar{P}) - \Omega}).$$

However, now that the interest rate on the home country's checkable deposits has been established in Chapter 6, the new reduced form equation for the end-of-period demand for home country currency may be obtained by substituting the right-hand side of (6.2) for r^{d}_{t} into (8.1) to yield:

$$(8.2)\ Cu^{d}_{t+1} = Cu^{d}_{t+1}(\underset{+}{D_t}, \underset{+}{Cu_t}, \underset{+}{Q^{\wedge}_t}, \underset{+}{\phi\cdot \bar{P}}, \underset{+}{G(S_t, \bar{P}) - \Omega}, \underset{-}{\rho_t}).$$

Demand for Interbank Deposits Issued by the Home Private Financial Sector. The foreign private financial sector's end-of-period demand for (non-interest-earning) interbank deposits corresponds to (4.82), expressed here in terms of the home country's unit of account as (8.3), where we have inserted the reduced-form equations for p_t and q^{n*d}_{t+1} with respect to the environment variables of interest in this study.

$$(8.3)\ \Re^{d}_{t+1} = \varepsilon_t[\Re^{d}_{t+1}/\varepsilon_t(\underset{-}{\varepsilon^{\wedge}_t}, \underset{+}{\varepsilon_t}, \underset{-}{\rho^{*}_t}, p_t(\underset{-}{Q^{\wedge}_t}, \underset{-}{\phi\cdot \bar{P}}, \underset{-}{G(S_t, \bar{P}) - \Omega}),$$

$$q^{n*d}_{t+1}(\underset{-}{Q^{\wedge *}_t}, \underset{-}{\phi\cdot \bar{P}}, \underset{-}{G(S_t, \bar{P}) - \Omega}, \underset{+}{r^{b*}_t}, \underset{+}{\varepsilon^{\wedge}_t}))].$$

The forward exchange rate exerts two conflicting effects upon the foreign private financial sector's end-of-period demand for deposits due from the home country's private financial sector. First, the higher the forward rate, the less valuable these deposits next period in terms of the foreign country's unit of account; this induces the foreign private financial sector to reduce its demand for these deposits. However, the higher the forward rate, ceteris paribus, the less expensive home country goods become for the foreign non-financial business sector. As a result, a higher forward rate encourages the foreign non-financial business sector to increase its demand for home country goods (for payment and delivery next period). The foreign private financial sector holds interbank deposits at the home private financial sector in order to service the import spending by the foreign non-financial business sector in this model. Therefore, the foreign private financial sector will tend to increase its demand for interbank deposits due from the home country's private financial sector in response to the foreign non-financial business sector's increased orders for home country goods. Assuming that the primary purpose for holding interbank deposits is to service the import spending by its customers, the second effect dominates so that (8.3) may be written as:

$$(8.4)\ \Re^d_{t+1} = \varepsilon_t[\Re^d_{t+1}/\varepsilon_t(\underset{+}{\varepsilon_t}, \underset{-}{\rho^*_t}, \underset{-}{Q^{\wedge}_t}, \underset{-}{Q^{\wedge *}_t}, \underset{-}{\phi\cdot \bar{P}}, \underset{-}{G(S_t, \bar{P})-\Omega}, \underset{+}{r^{b*}_t}, \underset{+}{\varepsilon^{\wedge}_t})].$$

Market Demand for Home Country (Non-Interest-Bearing) Money. Summing (8.2) and (8.4), we obtain the following market demand for the home country's non-interest-bearing money:

$$(8.5)\ M^d_{t+1} = Cu^d_{t+1}(\underset{+}{D_t}, \underset{+}{Cu_t}, \underset{+}{Q^{\wedge}_t}, \underset{+}{\phi\cdot \bar{P}}, \underset{+}{G(S_t, \bar{P})-\Omega}, \underset{-}{\rho_t})$$

$$+\varepsilon_t[\Re^d_{t+1}/\varepsilon_t(\underset{+}{\varepsilon_t}, \underset{-}{\rho^*_t}, \underset{-}{Q^{\wedge}_t}, \underset{-}{Q^{\wedge *}_t}, \underset{-}{\phi\cdot \bar{P}}, \underset{-}{G(S_t, \bar{P})-\Omega}, \underset{+}{r^{b*}_t}, \underset{+}{\varepsilon^{\wedge}_t})]$$

$$= M^d_{t+1}(\underset{+}{D_t}, \underset{+}{Cu_t}, \underset{+}{\varepsilon^{\wedge}_t}, \underset{+}{\varepsilon_t}, \underset{-}{\rho_t}, \underset{-}{\rho^*_t}, \underset{+}{Q^{\wedge}_t}, \underset{-}{Q^{\wedge *}_t}, \underset{+}{\phi\cdot \bar{P}}, \underset{+}{G(S_t, \bar{P})-\Omega}, \underset{+}{r^{b*}_t}).$$

Ceteris paribus, the **smaller** the initial stock of the non-renewable resource held by the home country's non-financial business sector the lower the current output of the home country. This causes current disposable income in the home country to fall, thereby reducing the home household sector's end-of-period demand for currency. At the same time, the smaller the initial stock of this resource, the greater the product price that the home non-financial business sector announces during the current period for its product. While this produces an indeterminate effect upon the amount of the home good the foreign non-financial business sector orders this period, the higher product price, ceteris paribus, causes the value of the foreign non-financial business sector's demand for domestic goods to rise, inducing the foreign private financial sector to increase the volume of interbank deposits it holds at the home private financial sector by the end of the current period. However, we treat this effect as secondary to the effect upon the home household sector's demand for home currency.

By similar reasoning, an increase in either the volume of pollution rights or harvesting rights issued by the international agent induces greater current production in the home country and an increase in its disposable income. This causes the home household sector to increase its end-of-period demand for currency. On the other hand, an increase in either the volume of pollution or harvesting rights induces the home non-financial business sector to lower the product price it announces. It also causes the foreign non-financial business sector to reduce the quantity of the home goods it demands as it substitutes either its own non-renewable resource or the global renewable resource for the factor it purchases from the home country. These latter responses reduce the foreign private financial business sector's demand for interbank deposits held at the home private financial sector. However, assuming that the effect upon the home household sector's demand for currency dominates, the market demand for the home country's non-interest-bearing money increases with the volume of either pollution or harvesting rights.

The **smaller** the initial stock of the foreign non-renewable resource, the more the foreign non-financial business sector will plan to use the factor it imports from the home country in next period's production. This increase in the sector's demand for the good it imports from the home country correspondingly increases the marginal product of interbank deposits the foreign private financial sector holds at the home private financial sector. Thus, the smaller the stock of the foreign non-renewable resource, ceteris paribus, the greater the market demand for the home country's non-interest-bearing money.

Market Supply of Home Country (Non-Interest-Bearing) Money

In the present model, the market supply of home-country money refers to (i) the volume of home country currency that would be outstanding by the end of the current period consistent with the plans of the home central bank and the home private financial sector plus, (ii) the home private financial sector's ex ante end-of-period supply of interbank deposits denominated in the home country's unit of account.

Supply of Home Country Currency. The volume of the home country's monetary base that would be outstanding at the end of the period consistent with the plans of both the home central bank and the home private financial sector is equal to the volume of the home unborrowed monetary base consistent with the plans of the home central bank, UMB^s_{t+1}, plus the volume of advances the home private financial sector plans to have outstanding by the end of the current period, $A^d_{t+1}(\bullet)$. Subtracting from this sum the amount of high-powered money the home private financial sector plans to hold at the end of the period either as required reserves or excess reserves, $\hat{r}D^s_{t+1}(\bullet) + X^d_{t+1}(\bullet)$, equals the amount of home country currency that would be outstanding at the end of the period consistent with the plans of both the home central bank and the home private financial sector. We refer to this net amount as the end-of-period (ex ante) market supply of home currency, Cu^s_{t+1}. Therefore,

$$(8.6)\quad Cu^s_{t+1} = UMB^s_{t+1} + A^d_{t+1}(\underset{+}{r^b_t}, \underset{+}{r^{b*}_t}, \underset{+}{f^+_t}, \underset{+}{r^d_t}, \underset{-}{\rho_t}, \underset{-1}{NW^f_t}) - \hat{r}D^s_{t+1}(\underset{-}{r^d_t}, \underset{+}{\rho_t}) - X^d_{t+1}(\underset{-}{r^d_t}, \underset{-}{\rho_t})$$

where the last three terms are given in (4.71), (4.72) and (4.69) above, respectively. However, the current interest rate on home checkable deposits is now given by (6.2). Substituting the right-hand side of (6.2) into (8.6):

$$(8.7)\quad Cu^s_{t+1} = UMB^s_{t+1} + A^d_{t+1}(\underset{+}{r^b_t}, \underset{+}{r^{b*}_t}, \underset{+}{f^+_t}, \underset{-}{\rho_t}, \underset{-1}{NW^f_t}, \underset{-}{D_t}, \underset{-}{Cu_t}, \underset{-}{\hat{Q}_t}, \underset{-}{\phi\cdot \bar{P}}, \underset{-}{G(S_t, \bar{P})-\Omega})$$

$$-\hat{r}D^s_{t+1}(\underset{+}{D_t}, \underset{+}{Cu_t}, \underset{+}{\hat{Q}_t}, \underset{+}{\phi\cdot \bar{P}}, \underset{+}{G(S_t, \bar{P})-\Omega}, \underset{-}{\rho_t})$$

$$-X^d_{t+1}(\underset{+}{D_t}, \underset{+}{Cu_t}, \underset{+}{\hat{Q}_t}, \underset{+}{\phi\cdot \bar{P}}, \underset{+}{G(S_t, \bar{P})-\Omega}, \underset{-}{\rho_t})$$

where we have assumed that the direct effects of a change in the discount rate upon A^d_{t+1}, D^s_{t+1}, and X^d_{t+1} dominate those operating through r^d_t. From expression (8.7), the ex ante supply of home country currency for the end of the current period is given by:

$$(8.8)\quad Cu^s_{t+1} = Cu^s_{t+1}(\underset{+1}{UMB^s_{t+1}}, \underset{+}{r^b_t}, \underset{+}{r^{b*}_t}, \underset{+}{f^+_t}, \underset{-}{\rho_t}, \underset{-1}{NW^f_t}, \underset{-}{D_t}, \underset{-}{Cu_t}, \underset{-}{\hat{Q}_t}, \underset{-}{\phi\cdot \bar{P}}, \underset{-}{G(S_t, \bar{P})-\Omega}).$$

Supply of Home Country Interbank Deposits. The home private financial sector's ex ante end-of-period supply of interbank deposits denominated in the home country's unit of account is given by (4.74), repeated here as (8.9):

$$(8.9)\qquad \mathfrak{R}^{fs}_{t+1} = \mathfrak{R}^{fs}_{t+1}(\underset{+}{\rho_t}).$$

Supply of Home Country Non-Interest-Bearing Money. From (8.8) and (8.9), the ex ante end-of-period volume of non-interest-bearing money denominated in the home country's unit of account consistent with the plans of the home country's central bank and private financial sector is given by:

$$(8.10)\ M^s_{t+1} = Cu^s_{t+1}(UMB^s_{t+1}, r^b_t, r^{b*}_t, f^+_t, \rho_t, NW^f_t, D_t, Cu_t, Q^{\wedge}_t, \phi \cdot \bar{P}, G(S_t, \bar{P}) - \Omega)$$
+1 + + + - -1 - - - - -

$$+\Re^{fs}_{t+1}(\rho_t)$$
+

$$= M^s_{t+1}(UMB^s_{t+1}, r^b_t, r^{b*}_t, f^+_t, \rho_t, NW^f_t, D_t, Cu_t, Q^{\wedge}_t, \phi \cdot \bar{P}, G(S_t, \bar{P}) - \Omega)$$
+1 + + + - -1 - - - - -

where we assume that the effect of a change in the discount rate upon the ex ante supply of checkable deposits via the home private financial sector's demand for advances dominates the other effects of a change in the discount rate.

Home (Non-Interest-Bearing) Money Market Equilibrium

Equilibrium prevails in the market for home non-interest-bearing money when the end-of-period demand for that money equals the end-of-period supply of home (non-interest-bearing) money:

$$(8.11)\ M^s_{t+1}(UMB^s_{t+1}, r^b_t, r^{b*}_t, f^+_t, \rho_t, NW^f_t, D_t, Cu_t, Q^{\wedge}_t, \phi\ \bar{P}, G(S_t, \bar{P}) - \Omega)$$
+1 + + + - -1 - - - - -

$$= M^d_{t+1}(D_t, Cu_t, \varepsilon^{\wedge}_t, \varepsilon_t, \rho_t, \rho^*_t, Q^{\wedge}_t, Q^{\wedge *}_t, \phi\ \bar{P}, G(S_t, \bar{P}) - \Omega, r^{b*}_t).$$
+ + + + - - + - + + +

See Figure 8.1. While an increase in either the current forward rate or an increase in the current rate on foreign bonds shifts both the market demand and supply functions for the home country's non-interest-bearing money outward, we assume that the effects operating through the money supply function dominate, since they reflect the most direct effects upon the financial markets resulting from these changes.

Figure 8.1 **Equilibrium in the Home Non-Interest-Bearing Money Market**

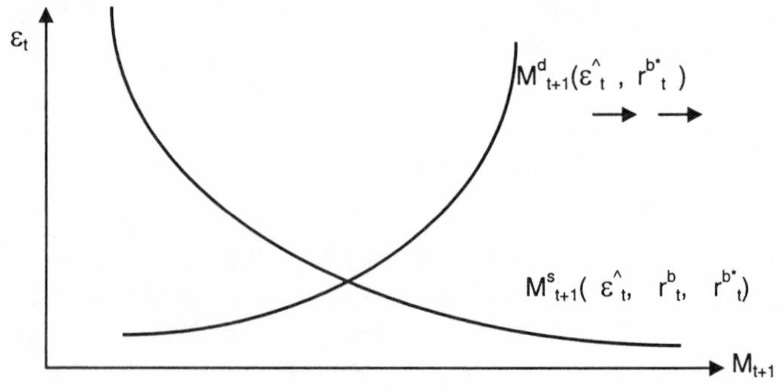

The M Plane

Linearizing (8.11), we represent the home money equilibrium condition by a plane in ($r^b{}_t$, $r^{b*}{}_t$, $\hat{\varepsilon}_t$) space, which we denote as the "M plane," see Figure 8.2.

Figure 8.2 **The M Plane**

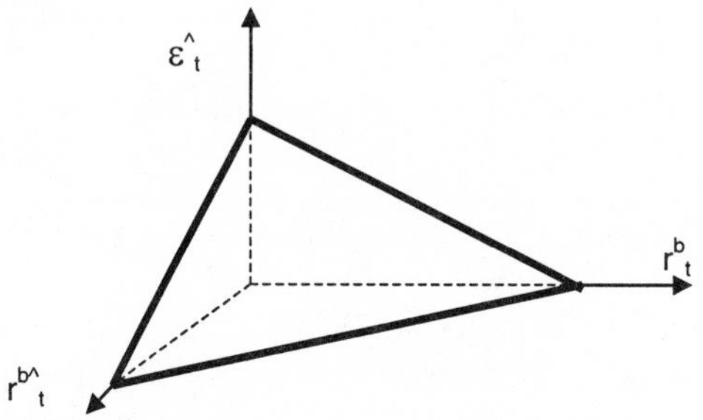

The expression for the M plane is given by:

$$(8.12)\ \underset{+}{(\partial ES^m/\partial r^b{}_t)}dr^b{}_t + \underset{+}{(\partial ES^m/\partial r^{b*}{}_t)}dr^{b*}{}_t + \underset{-}{(\partial ES^m/\partial \varepsilon_t)}d\varepsilon_t$$

$$+ \underset{+}{(\partial ES^m/\partial \hat{\varepsilon}_t)}d\hat{\varepsilon}_t + \underset{\pm}{(\partial ES^m/\partial x^m{}_t)}dx^m{}_t = 0$$

where $x^m{}_t$ denotes all variables other than $r^b{}_t$, $r^{b*}{}_t$, ε_t, or $\hat{\varepsilon}_t$ that affect the excess supply of home (non-interest-bearing) money.

Foreign Country (Non-Interest-Bearing) Money

In this section, we develop the market for the foreign country's non-interest-bearing money, consisting of the interbank deposits issued by the foreign private financial sector which are held by the home private financial sector and the (coin and) currency issued by the foreign central bank. We begin by deriving the market demand for the non-interest-bearing money of the foreign country and then derive the market supply for that money.

Market Demand for Foreign Country (Non-Interest-Bearing) Money

The foreign household sector's end-of-period demand for foreign currency was presented in (5.57). This demand plus the home private banking sector's end-of-period demand for interbank deposits denominated in the foreign country's unit of account, expression (4.73), together constitute the market demand for foreign money. We express it here in terms of the home country's unit of account.

$$(8.13)\ \varepsilon_t M^{*d}_{t+1} = \varepsilon_t Cu^{*d}_{t+1}(\underset{+}{D^*_t},\ \underset{+}{Cu^*_t},\ \underset{+}{Q^{\wedge *}_t},\ \underset{+}{\phi\ \bar{P}},\ \underset{+}{G(S_t,\ \bar{P})-\Omega},\ \underset{-}{\rho^*_t})$$

$$+\ \varepsilon_t \Re^{*d}_{t+1}(\underset{-}{\varepsilon^\wedge_t},\ \underset{-}{\varepsilon_t},\ \underset{-}{\rho_t},\ \underset{-}{Q^{\wedge *}_t},\ \underset{-}{Q^\wedge_t},\ \underset{-}{\phi\ \bar{P}},\ \underset{-}{G(S_t,\ \bar{P})-\Omega},\ \underset{+}{r^b_t})$$

$$= \varepsilon_t \cdot M^{*d}_{t+1}(\underset{+}{D^*_t},\ \underset{+}{Cu^*_t},\ \underset{-}{\varepsilon^\wedge_t},\ \underset{-}{\varepsilon_t},\ \underset{-}{\rho_t},\ \underset{-}{\rho^*_t},\ \underset{-}{Q^\wedge_t},\ \underset{+}{Q^{\wedge *}_t},\ \underset{+}{\phi\ \bar{P}},\ \underset{+}{G(S_t,\ \bar{P})-\Omega},\ \underset{+}{r^b_t}).$$

Market Supply of Foreign Country (Non-Interest-Bearing) Money

In the present model, the market supply of foreign country money refers to (i) the volume of foreign country currency that would be outstanding by the end of the current period consistent with the plans of the foreign central bank and the foreign private financial sector plus, (ii) the foreign private financial sector's ex ante end-of-period supply of interbank deposits denominated in the foreign country's unit of account.

Supply of Foreign Country Currency. In a manner analogous to that associated with the derivation of the home country's end-of-period supply of currency, we may express the end-of-period supply of foreign currency, expressed in terms of the home country's unit of account by:

$$(8.14)\ \varepsilon_t Cu^{s*}_{t+1} =$$

$$\varepsilon_t \cdot Cus^*_{t+1}(\underset{+1}{UMB^{s*}_{t+1}},\ \underset{+}{r^b_t},\ \underset{+}{r^{b*}_t},\ \underset{-}{f^+_t},\ \underset{-}{\rho^*_t},\ \underset{-1}{NW^{f*}_t},\ \underset{-}{D^*_t},\ \underset{-}{Cu^*_t},\ \underset{-}{Q^{\wedge *}_t},\ \underset{-}{\phi \cdot \bar{P}},\ \underset{-}{G(S_t,\ \bar{P})-\Omega}).$$

Supply of Foreign Country Interbank Deposits. The foreign private financial sector's ex ante supply of interbank deposits is shown by (4.83), repeated here, in terms of the home country's unit of account as (8.15):

$$(8.15)\ \varepsilon_t \Re^{*f*s}_{t+1} = \varepsilon_t \Re^{*f*s}_{t+1}(\underset{+}{\rho^*_t}).$$

Market Supply of Foreign Country (Non-Interest-Bearing) Money. Therefore, the end-of-period market supply of non-interest-bearing money denominated in the foreign country's unit of account (and valued here in terms of the home country's unit of account) is given by:

$$(8.16)\ \varepsilon_t \cdot M^{*s}_{t+1} = \varepsilon_t \cdot Cu^{s*}_{t+1}(\bullet) + \varepsilon_t \cdot \Re^{*f*s}_{t+1}(\bullet)$$

$$= \varepsilon_t \cdot M^{*s}_{t+1}(\underset{+1}{UMB^{s*}_{t+1}}, \underset{+}{r^b_t}, \underset{+}{r^{b*}_t}, \underset{-}{f^{+}_t}, \underset{-}{\rho^*_t}, \underset{-1}{NW^{f*}_t}, \underset{-}{D^*_t}, \underset{-}{Cu^*_t}, \underset{-}{Q^{\wedge *}_t}, \underset{-}{\phi \cdot \bar{P}}, \underset{-}{G(S_t, \bar{P}) - \Omega}).$$

Foreign (Non-Interest-Bearing) Money Market Equilibrium

Equilibrium prevails in the market for foreign money when the end-of-period demand for that money equals the ex ante end-of-period supply of foreign money:

$$(8.17)\ \varepsilon_t \cdot M^{*s}_{t+1}(\underset{+1}{UMB^{s*}_{t+1}}, \underset{+}{r^b_t}, \underset{+}{r^{b*}_t}, \underset{-}{f^{+}_t}, \underset{-}{\rho^*_t}, \underset{-1}{NW^{f*}_t}, \underset{-}{D^*_t}, \underset{-}{Cu^*_t}, \underset{-}{Q^{\wedge *}_t}, \underset{-}{\phi \cdot \bar{P}}, \underset{-}{G(S_t, \bar{P}) - \Omega})$$

$$= \varepsilon_t \cdot M^{*d}_{t+1}(\underset{+}{D^*_t}, \underset{+}{Cu^*_t}, \underset{-}{\hat{\varepsilon}_t}, \underset{-}{\varepsilon_t}, \underset{-}{\rho_t}, \underset{-}{\rho^*_t}, \underset{-}{\hat{Q}_t}, \underset{+}{Q^{\wedge *}_t}, \underset{+}{\phi\ \bar{P}}, \underset{+}{G(S_t, \bar{P}) - \Omega}, \underset{+}{r^b_t}).$$

See Figure 8.3. While an increase in the current forward rate reduces both the market demand and supply of foreign non-interest-bearing money, we assume that the effect upon market supply dominates. Similarly, we assume that the effect of an increase in the home bond rate upon the market supply of foreign non-interest-bearing money dominates the effect upon the market demand for this asset.

Figure 8.3 **Equilibrium in the Foreign Money Market**

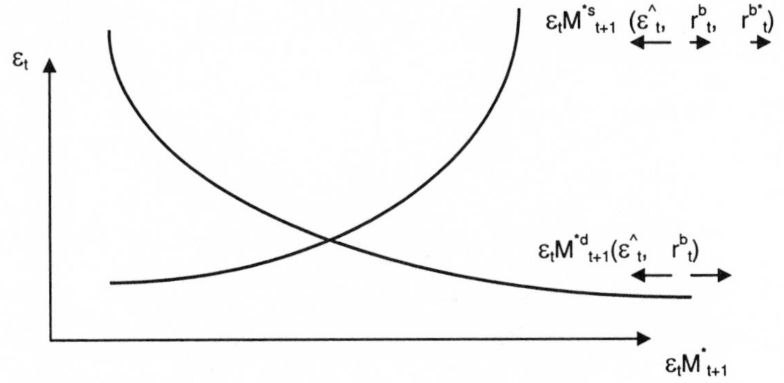

The M Plane*

Linearizing (8.17) yields (8.18):

$$(8.18)\quad \underset{+}{(\partial ES^{m*}/\partial r^{b}_{t})dr^{b}_{t}} + \underset{+}{(\partial ES^{m*}/\partial r^{b*}_{t})dr^{b*}_{t}} + \underset{+}{(\partial ES^{m*}/\partial \varepsilon_{t})d\varepsilon_{t}}$$

$$+ \underset{-}{(\partial ES^{m*}/\partial \hat{\varepsilon}_{t})d\hat{\varepsilon}_{t}} + \underset{\pm}{(\partial ES^{m*}/\partial x^{m*}_{t})dx^{m*}_{t}} = 0$$

where x^{m*}_{t} denotes all variables other than r^{b}_{t}, r^{b*}_{t}, ε_{t}, or $\hat{\varepsilon}_{t}$ that affect the excess supply of foreign non-interest-bearing money. We represent the foreign non-interest-bearing money equilibrium condition by a plane in (r^{b}_{t}, r^{b*}_{t}, $\hat{\varepsilon}_{t}$) space, which we denote as the "M* plane"; see Figure 8.4.

Figure 8.4 **The M* Plane**

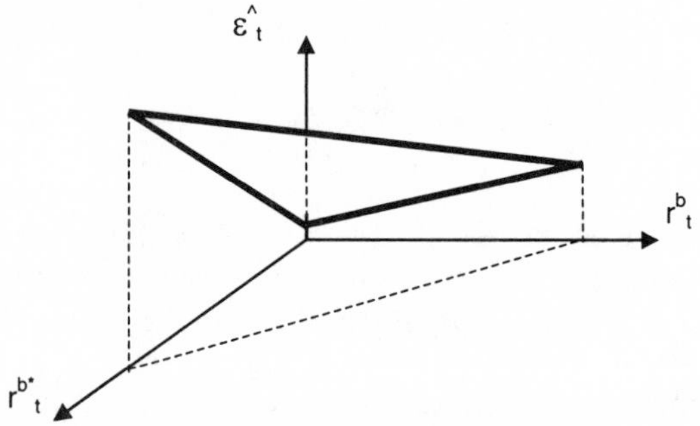

The MM Locus*

Refer to the intersection of the M plane with the M* plane as the MM* locus, as shown in Figure 8.5. This locus satisfies both condition (8.12) and condition (8.18) simultaneously.

Figure 8.5 **The MM* Locus**

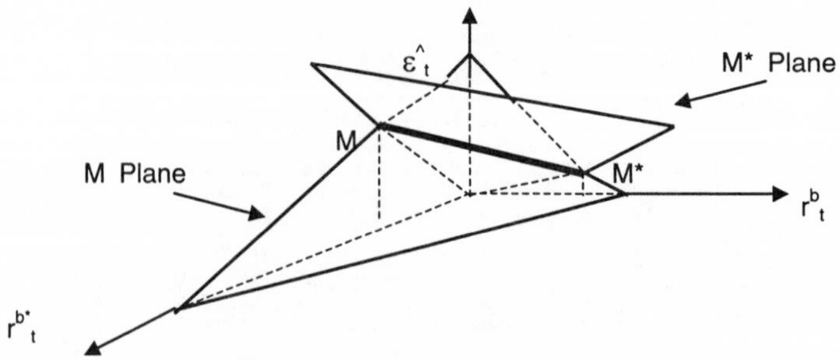

Projections of the MM Locus upon the (r^b_t, $\hat{\varepsilon}_t$) and (r^{b*}_t, $\hat{\varepsilon}_t$) Planes*

The slope of the projection of the MM* locus upon the (r^b_t, $\hat{\varepsilon}_t$) plane is given by:

$$(8.19)\ d\hat{\varepsilon}_t / dr^b_t = -[(\partial ES^{m*}/\partial r^b_t)(\partial ES^m/\partial r^{b*}_t) - (\partial ES^{m*}/\partial r^{b*}_t)(\partial ES^m/\partial r^b_t)]$$

$$/[(\partial ES^{m*}/\partial \hat{\varepsilon}_t)(\partial ES^m/\partial r^{b*}_t) - (\partial ES^{m*}/\partial r^{b*}_t)(\partial ES^m/\partial \hat{\varepsilon}_t)].$$

We assume that a unit change in the home bond rate produces (i) a greater response in the home private financial sector's demand for home country bonds than it does in the foreign private financial sector's demand for home country bonds and (ii) a greater wealth effect upon the home private financial sector's initial holdings of home bonds than upon the initial stock of home bonds held by the foreign private financial sector. Under these circumstances, the absolute value of $\partial ES^m/\partial r^b_t$ exceeds that of $\partial ES^{m*}/\partial r^b_t$. In addition, we assume that a unit change in the foreign bond rate produces (i) a greater response in the foreign private financial sector's demand for foreign bonds than it does with respect to the home private financial sector's demand for those bonds and (ii) a greater wealth effect upon foreign private financial sector's initial holdings of foreign bonds than upon the initial stock of foreign bonds held by the home private financial sector. Then the absolute value of $\partial ES^{m*}/\partial r^{b*}_t$ exceeds that of $\partial ES^m/\partial r^{b*}_t$. Granting these assumptions, the signed numerator in (8.19) is positive.

Since the denominator in that expression is negative, the slope of the projection of the MM* locus upon the (r^b_t, $\hat{\varepsilon}_t$) plane is negative. See Figure 8.6. The slope of the projection of the MM* locus upon the (r^{b*}_t, $\hat{\varepsilon}_t$) plane is given by expression (8.20).

Figure 8.6 **Projections of the MM* Locus upon the (r^b_t, $\hat{\varepsilon}_t$) and (r^{b*}_t, $\hat{\varepsilon}_t$) Planes**

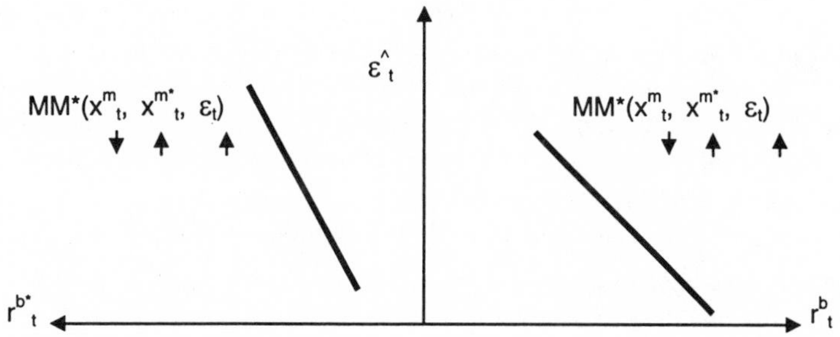

$$(8.20)\ d\hat{\varepsilon}_t / dr^{b*}_t = -[(\partial ES^{m*}/\partial r^{b*}_t)(\partial ES^m/\partial r^b_t) - (\partial ES^{m*}/\partial r^b_t)(\partial ES^m/\partial r^{b*}_t)]$$

$$/[(\partial ES^{m*}/\partial \hat{\varepsilon}_t)(\partial ES^m/\partial r^b_t) - (\partial ES^{m*}/\partial r^b_t)(\partial ES^m/\partial \hat{\varepsilon}_t)].$$

Granting the same assumptions as immediately above, the signed numerator in (8.20) is negative. Since the denominator in (8.20) is negative, the slope of the projection of the MM* locus upon the (r^{b*}_t, $\hat{\varepsilon}_t$) plane is positive.

(Vertical) Shifts in the Projection of the MM Locus upon the (r^b_t, $\hat{\varepsilon}_t$) Plane*

The (vertical) shift in the projection of the MM* locus upon the (r^b_t, $\hat{\varepsilon}_t$) plane in response to a change in the spot rate is given by:

$$(8.21)\ d\hat{\varepsilon}_t / d\varepsilon_t = -[(\partial ES^{m*}/\partial \varepsilon_t)(\partial ES^m/\partial r^{b*}_t) - (\partial ES^{m*}/\partial r^{b*}_t)(\partial ES^m/\partial \varepsilon_t)]$$

$$/[(\partial ES^{m*}/\partial \hat{\varepsilon}_t)(\partial ES^m/\partial r^{b*}_t) - (\partial ES^{m*}/\partial r^{b*}_t)(\partial ES^m/\partial \hat{\varepsilon}_t)].$$

Both the signed numerator and the denominator in (8.21) are negative; an increase in the spot rate shifts the projection of the MM* locus upon the (r^b_t, $\hat{\varepsilon}_t$) plane upward.

The vertical shift in the projection of the MM* locus upon the (r^b_t, $\hat{\varepsilon}_t$) plane in response to a change in any variable other than r^b_t, r^{b*}_t, ε_t, or $\hat{\varepsilon}_t$ that affects the excess supply of home currency is shown by (8.22):

$$(8.22)\ d\hat{\varepsilon}_t / dx^m_t = [(\partial ES^{m*}/\partial r^{b*}_t)(\partial ES^m/\partial x^m_t)]$$

$$/[(\partial ES^{m*}/\partial \hat{\varepsilon}_t)(\partial ES^m/\partial r^{b*}_t) - (\partial ES^{m*}/\partial r^{b*}_t)(\partial ES^m/\partial \hat{\varepsilon}_t)].$$

The numerator in (8.22) is positive, but the denominator is negative; ceteris paribus, an increase in the excess supply of home currency requires that the forward rate fall to restore equilibrium in that market. An increase in either the volume of pollution or harvesting rights issued by the international agent or an increase in the home country's initial stock of its non-renewable resource causes the home country's GNP and current disposable income to rise, producing, ceteris paribus, an increase in the home household sector's end-of-period demand for home currency, thereby creating an excess demand in that market ($dx^m_t < 0$) and shifting the MM* locus upward in the (r^b_t, $\hat{\varepsilon}_t$) plane.

The vertical shift in the projection of the MM* locus upon the (r^b_t, $\hat{\varepsilon}_t$) plane in response to a change in any variable other than r^b_t, r^{b*}_t, ε_t, or $\hat{\varepsilon}_t$ that affects the excess supply of foreign currency is shown by (8.23):

(8.23) $d\hat{\varepsilon}_t / dx^{m*}_t = -[(\partial ES^m/\partial r^{b*}_t)(\partial ES^{m*}/\partial x^{m*}_t)]$

$$/[(\partial ES^{m*}/\partial \hat{\varepsilon}_t)(\partial ES^m/\partial r^{b*}_t) - (\partial ES^{m*}/\partial r^{b*}_t)(\partial ES^m/\partial \hat{\varepsilon}_t)].$$

Both the signed numerator and denominator in (8.23) are negative; ceteris paribus, an increase in the excess supply of foreign currency requires that the forward exchange rate increase to eliminate the excess supply—the MM* locus shifts upward in the $(r^b_t, \hat{\varepsilon}_t)$ plane. An increase in either the volume of pollution or harvesting rights issued by the international agent or an increase in the foreign country's initial stock of its non-renewable resource causes the foreign country's GNP and current disposable income to rise, producing, ceteris paribus, an increase in the foreign household sector's end-of-period demand for foreign currency, thereby creating an excess demand in that market ($dx^{m*} < 0$) and shifting the MM* locus downward in the $(r^b_t, \hat{\varepsilon}_t)$ plane. Therefore, given that the effect of an increase in pollution or harvesting rights upon the MM* locus operating through the home country's disposable income is opposite to that operating through the foreign country's disposable income, the net direct effect of an increase in these rights upon the position of the projection of the MM* locus in the $(r^b_t, \hat{\varepsilon}_t)$ plane appears to be indeterminate. However, given our assumptions that the own interest rate effects dominate the cross interest rate effects (the absolute value of $\partial ES^m/\partial r^b_t$ exceeds that of $\partial ES^{m*}/\partial r^b_t$ and the absolute value of $\partial ES^{m*}/\partial r^{b*}_t$ exceeds that of $\partial ES^m/\partial r^{b*}_t$), then the net effect of an increase in these rights is to shift the projection of the MM* locus in the $(r^b_t, \hat{\varepsilon}_t)$ plane upward.

An increase in $\hat{Q}_t$ shifts the projection of the MM* locus in the $(r^b_t, \hat{\varepsilon}_t)$ plane upward, while an increase in $\hat{Q}^*_t$ shifts it downward.

(Vertical) Shifts in the Projection of the MM Locus upon the $(r^{b*}_t, \hat{\varepsilon}_t)$ Plane*

The (vertical) shift in the projection of the MM* locus upon the $(r^{b*}_t, \hat{\varepsilon}_t)$ plane in response to a change in the spot rate is given by:

(8.24) $d\hat{\varepsilon}_t / d\varepsilon_t = -[(\partial ES^{m*}/\partial \varepsilon_t)(\partial ES^m/\partial r^b_t) - (\partial ES^{m*}/\partial r^b_t)(\partial ES^m/\partial \varepsilon_t)]$

$$/[(\partial ES^{m*}/\partial \hat{\varepsilon}_t)(\partial ES^m/\partial r^b_t) - (\partial ES^{m*}/\partial r^b_t)(\partial ES^m/\partial \hat{\varepsilon}_t)].$$

Both the signed numerator and the denominator in (8.24) are negative; an increase in the spot rate shifts the projection of the MM* locus upon the $(r^{b*}_t, \hat{\varepsilon}_t)$ plane upward.

The vertical shift in the projection of the MM* locus upon the $(r^{b*}_t, \hat{\varepsilon}_t)$ plane in response to a change in any variable other than r^b_t, r^{b*}_t, ε_t, or $\hat{\varepsilon}_t$ that affects the excess supply of home currency is shown by (8.25):

$$(8.25)\ d\hat{\varepsilon}_t / dx^m_t = [(\partial ES^{m*}/\partial r^b_t)(\partial ES^m/\partial x^m_t)] / [(\partial ES^{m*}/\partial \hat{\varepsilon}_t)(\partial ES^m/\partial r^b_t) - (\partial ES^{m*}/\partial r^b_t)(\partial ES^m/\partial \hat{\varepsilon}_t)].$$

The numerator in (8.25) is positive, but the denominator is negative; ceteris paribus, an increase in the excess supply of home non-interest-bearing money requires that the forward rate fall to restore equilibrium in that market. Therefore, ceteris paribus, an increase in pollution or harvesting rights or an increase in the home country's initial stock of the non-renewable resource causes the projection of the MM* locus upon the (r^{b*}_t, $\hat{\varepsilon}_t$) plane to shift upward (via $dx^m < 0$).

The vertical shift in the projection of the MM* locus upon the (r^{b*}_t, $\hat{\varepsilon}_t$) plane in response to a change in any variable other than r^b_t, r^{b*}_t, ε_t, or $\hat{\varepsilon}_t$ that affects the excess supply of foreign non-interest-bearing money is shown by (8.26):

$$(8.26)\ d\hat{\varepsilon}_t / dx^{m*}_t = -[(\partial ES^m/\partial r^b_t)(\partial ES^{m*}/\partial x^{m*}_t)] / [(\partial ES^{m*}/\partial \hat{\varepsilon}_t)(\partial ES^m/\partial r^b_t) - (\partial ES^{m*}/\partial r^b_t)(\partial ES^m/\partial \hat{\varepsilon}_t)].$$

Both the signed numerator and denominator in (8.26) are negative; ceteris paribus, an increase in the excess supply of foreign non-interest-bearing money requires that the forward exchange rate increase to eliminate the excess supply—the MM* locus shifts upward in the (r^{b*}_t, $\hat{\varepsilon}_t$) plane. Therefore, ceteris paribus, an increase in pollution or harvesting rights or an increase in the foreign country's initial stock of the non-renewable resource causes the projection of the MM* locus upon the (r^{b*}_t, $\hat{\varepsilon}_t$) plane to shift downward (via $dx^{m*}_t < 0$).

Since an increase in pollution or harvesting rights operating through the excess demand for home country money causes the projection of the MM* locus upon the (r^{b*}_t, $\hat{\varepsilon}_t$) plane to shift upward while an increase in pollution or harvesting rights operating through the excess demand for foreign country money causes the projection of the MM* locus upon the (r^{b*}_t, $\hat{\varepsilon}_t$) plane to shift downward, the net effect is indeterminate on the surface. However, given our earlier assumptions that the absolute value of $\partial ES^m/\partial r^b_t$ exceeds that of $\partial ES^{m*}/\partial r^b_t$ and the absolute value of $\partial ES^{m*}/\partial r^{b*}_t$ exceeds that of $\partial ES^m/\partial r^{b*}_t$, then the net effect of an increase in these rights is to shift the projection of the MM* locus in the (r^{b*}_t, $\hat{\varepsilon}_t$) plane downward.

General Equilibrium in the Financial Markets

After the home government sector has announced next-period's production of public goods and next period's taxes, after the home non-financial business sector has decided current-period production of privately-produced goods and announced current wages and product prices, after the home discount rate has been announced by the home central bank, and after the current-period level of pollution and the current-period level of extraction of the shared renewable resource have been announced by the international agent, the following budget or cash flow restrictions face the home country's government, non-financial business, household, private financial, and central banking sectors, respectively:

$$(8.27)\quad \rho_{t-1}A_t + B^c_t + \varepsilon_t B^{*c}_t = \Pi^c_t$$

$$(8.28)\quad (UMB^s_{t+1} - UMB_t) = p^b_t(B^{cd}_{t+1} - B^c_t) + \varepsilon_t p^{b*}_t (B^{*cd}_{t+1} - B^{*c}_t)$$

$$(8.29)\quad B^f_t + \varepsilon^\wedge_{t-1} B^{*f}_t - W_{t-1}h^f_t N^f_t - \rho_{t-1}A_t - r^d_{t-1}D_t = \Pi^f_t$$

$$(8.30)\quad \varepsilon^\wedge_{t-1}[p^{b*f}_t B^{*f}_t + \Re^*_t] + \varepsilon_t(p^{b*}_t - p^{b*f}_t)B^{*f}_t + X_t - A_t - (1-r^\wedge)(D_t + \Re_t) - r^\wedge \varepsilon_t \Re^*_t$$

$$= (p^b_t B^{fd}_{t+1} - p^b_t B^f_t) + \varepsilon_t p^{b*}_t B^{*fd}_{t+1} + X^d_{t+1} - A^d_{t+1} - (1-r^\wedge)(D^s_{t+1} + \Re^{fs}_{t+1} - \varepsilon_t \Re^{*d}_{t+1})$$

$$(8.31)\quad p^b_t(B^{gs}_{t+1} - B^g_t) = W_{t-1}h^g_t N^g_t + p_t(K^{gd}_{t+1} - K^g_t) + B^g_t - T_t - \Pi^c_t - p^x_t R^x_t - p^p_t\ \bar{P}^{pd}$$

$$(8.32)\quad p_t q_t - W_{t-1}h^n_t N^n_t - \varepsilon^\wedge_{t-1} p^*_{t-1} q^{*n}_t - B^n_t - p^x_t R^x_t - p^p_t\ \bar{P}^{pd} = \Pi^n_t$$

$$(8.33)\quad p^b_t(B^{ns}_{t+1} - B^n_t) = p_t[q_t - c^d_t - (K^{gd}_{t+1} - K^g_t)] - p_{t-1}q^{n*}_t$$

$$(8.34)\quad W_{t-1}(h^n_t N^n_t + h^g_t N^g_t + h^f_t N^f_t) + \Pi^n_t + \Pi^f_t + r^d_{t-1}D_t - T_t$$

$$= p_t c^d_t + (D^d_{t+1} - D_t) + (Cu^d_{t+1} - Cu_t).$$

As we sum across these equations, we eliminate T_t, Π^c_t, Π^f_t, Π^n_t, $\rho_{t-1}A_t$, $p_t \cdot q_t$, $p_t \cdot c^d_t$, $W_{t-1} \cdot h^f_t \cdot N^f_t$, $W_{t-1} \cdot h^g_t \cdot N^g_t$, $W_{t-1} \cdot h^n_t \cdot N^n_t$, $r^d_{t-1} \cdot D_t$, $p_t(K^{gd}_{t+1} - K^g_t)$, $p^x_t R^x_t + p^p_t\ \bar{P}^{pd}$, and D_t, yielding:

$$(8.35)\quad B^c_t + \varepsilon_t B^{*c}_t + (UMB^s_{t+1} - UMB_t) + B^f_t + \varepsilon^\wedge_{t-1} B^{*f}_t$$

$$+ \varepsilon^\wedge_{t-1}[p^{b*f}_t B^{*f}_t + \Re^*_t] + \varepsilon_t(p^{b*}_t - p^{b*f}_t)B^{*f}_t + p^b_t(B^{ns}_{t+1} - B^n_t)$$

$$+ X_t - A_t + r^\wedge D_t - (1-r^\wedge)\Re_t - r^\wedge \varepsilon_t \Re^*_t - \varepsilon^\wedge_{t-1} p^*_{t-1} q^{*n}_t - B^n_t + p^b_t(B^{gs}_{t+1} - B^g_t)$$

$$= p^b_t(B^{cd}_{t+1} - B^c_t) + \varepsilon_t p^{b*}_t (B^{*cd}_{t+1} - B^{*c}_t) + (p^b_t B^{fd}_{t+1} - p^b_t B^f_t) + \varepsilon_t p^{b*}_t B^{*fd}_{t+1} + X^d_{t+1}$$

$$- A^d_{t+1} - (1-r^\wedge)(D^s_{t+1} + \Re^{fs}_{t+1} - \varepsilon_t \Re^{*d}_{t+1}) + B^g_t - p_{t-1}q^{n*}_t. + D^d_{t+1} + (Cu^d_{t+1} - Cu_t).$$

Next, since the unborrowed monetary base, UMB_t, is defined as the sum of coin and currency in circulation, Cu_t, plus the unborrowed reserves of the private financial sector, where unborrowed reserves are defined as required reserves,

$\hat{r}(D_t + \mathfrak{R}_t - \varepsilon_t \mathfrak{R}^*_t)$, plus excess reserves, X_t, less advances, A_t, expression (8.35) reduces to:

$$(8.36)\quad (B^c_t + B^f_t - B^n_t - B^g_t) + p^b_t(B^c_t + B^f_t - B^n_t - B^g_t) + \varepsilon_t B^{*c}_t + UMB^s_{t+1} + \hat{\varepsilon}_{t-1} B^{*f}_t$$

$$+ \hat{\varepsilon}_{t-1}[p^{b*f}_t B^{*f}_t + \mathfrak{R}^*_t] + \varepsilon_t(p^{b*}_t - p^{b*f}_t)B^{*f}_t - \mathfrak{R}_t - \hat{\varepsilon}_{t-1} p^*_{t-1} q^{*n}_t + p^b_t B^{gs}_{t+1} + p^b_t B^{ns}_{t+1}$$

$$= p^b_t B^{cd}_{t+1} + \varepsilon_t p^{b*}_t (B^{*cd}_{t+1} - B^{*c}_t) + p^b_t B^{fd}_{t+1} + \varepsilon_t p^{b*}_t B^{*fd}_{t+1} + X^d_{t+1}$$

$$- A^d_{t+1} - (1-\hat{r})(D^s_{t+1} + \mathfrak{R}^{fs}_{t+1} - \varepsilon_t \mathfrak{R}^{*d}_{t+1}) - p_{t-1} q^{n*}_t + D^d_{t+1} + Cu^d_{t+1}.$$

Next, since the interest paid by the home non-financial business and government sectors on home country bonds, $B^n_t + B^g_t$, necessarily equals the sum of the interest income received on home country bonds by the home and foreign central banks, $B^c_t + B^{c*}_t$, plus the home and foreign private financial institutions, $B^f_t + B^{f*}_t$, and since the market value of the home country bonds outstanding at the beginning of the period, $p^b_t(B^n_t + B^g_t)$, necessarily equals the market value of those bonds held by the home and foreign central banks, $p^b_t(B^c_t + B^{c*}_t)$, plus the market value of those bonds held by the home and foreign private financial sectors, $p^b_t(B^f_t + B^{f*}_t)$, expression (8.36) may be written as:

$$(8.37)\quad -(B^{c*}_t + B^{f*}_t) - p^b_t(B^{c*}_t + B^{f*}_t) + \varepsilon_t B^{*c}_t + UMB^s_{t+1} + \hat{\varepsilon}_{t-1} B^{*f}_t$$

$$+ \hat{\varepsilon}_{t-1}[p^{b*f}_t B^{*f}_t + \mathfrak{R}^*_t] + \varepsilon_t(p^{b*}_t - p^{b*f}_t)B^{*f}_t - \mathfrak{R}_t - \hat{\varepsilon}_{t-1} p^*_{t-1} q^{*n}_t + p^b_t B^{gs}_{t+1} + p^b_t B^{ns}_{t+1}$$

$$= p^b_t B^{cd}_{t+1} + \varepsilon_t p^{b*}_t (B^{*cd}_{t+1} - B^{*c}_t) + p^b_t B^{fd}_{t+1} + \varepsilon_t p^{b*}_t B^{*fd}_{t+1} + X^d_{t+1}$$

$$- A^d_{t+1} - (1-\hat{r})(D^s_{t+1} + \mathfrak{R}^{fs}_{t+1} - \varepsilon_t \mathfrak{R}^{*d}_{t+1}) - p_{t-1} q^{n*}_t + D^d_{t+1} + Cu^d_{t+1}.$$

By the same token, the ex ante end-of-period market supply of home country bonds, $p^b_t B^s_{t+1}$, is represented by $p^b_t B^{gs}_{t+1} + p^b_t B^{ns}_{t+1}$, while the end-of-period market demand for home country bonds, $p^b_t B^d_{t+1}$, is defined as the sum of the end-of-period demands for home country bonds by the home and foreign central banks and the home and foreign private financial sectors, $p^b_t B^{cd}_{t+1} + p^b_t B^{fd}_{t+1} + p^b_t B^{c*d}_{t+1} + p^b_t B^{f*d}_{t+1}$. Therefore, (8.37) may be written as:

$$(8.38)\quad Cu^s_{t+1} - (B^{c*}_t + B^{f*}_t) - p^b_t(B^{c*}_t + B^{f*}_t) + \varepsilon_t B^{*c}_t + \hat{\varepsilon}_{t-1} B^{*f}_t + \hat{\varepsilon}_{t-1}[p^{b*f}_t B^{*f}_t + \mathfrak{R}^*_t]$$

$$+ \varepsilon_t(p^{b*}_t - p^{b*f}_t)B^{*f}_t - \mathfrak{R}_t - \hat{\varepsilon}_{t-1} p^*_{t-1} q^{*n}_t + p^b_t B^s_{t+1}$$

$$= p^b_t B^d_{t+1} - p^b_t B^{c*d}_{t+1} - p^b_t B^{f*d}_{t+1} + \varepsilon_t p^{b*}_t (B^{*cd}_{t+1} - B^{*c}_t) + \varepsilon_t p^{b*}_t B^{*fd}_{t+1}$$

$$- (D^s_{t+1} + \mathfrak{R}^{fs}_{t+1} - \varepsilon_t \mathfrak{R}^{*d}_{t+1}) - p_{t-1} q^{n*}_t + D^d_{t+1} + Cu^d_{t+1}$$

where Cu^{s}_{t+1} denotes the volume of home country currency in circulation at the end of the period consistent with the plans of both the home country's central bank and the home country's private financial sector and is equal to $UMB^{s}_{t+1} - \hat{r}(D^{s}_{t+1} + \mathfrak{R}^{fs}_{t+1} - \varepsilon_t \mathfrak{R}^{*d}_{t+1}) - X^{d}_{t+1} + A^{d}_{t+1}$. Next, from (7.1) we may replace $\varepsilon_t p^{b*}_{t} B^{*fd}_{t+1} + \varepsilon_t p^{b*}_{t} B^{*c}_{t} + \beta^{*c} + \varepsilon_t \mathfrak{R}^{*d}_{t+1} + [\mathfrak{R}^{fs}_{t+1} - \mathfrak{R}^{f}_{t}] + p^{b}_{t} B^{f*}_{t} + (1+p^{b}_{t}) B^{c*}_{t}$ with $S^{d}_{t} + p^{bf*} B^{f*}_{t}$. Also, from (7.2), we may replace $-p^{b}_{t} B^{f*d}_{t+1} - p^{b}_{t} B^{c*}_{t} - \varepsilon_t \beta^{c*}_{t} - \varepsilon_t (p^{b*}_{t} - p^{b*f}_{t}) B^{*f}_{t} - \varepsilon_t (1+p^{b*}_{t}) B^{*c}_{t}$ with the amount $-S^{s}_{t} + \mathfrak{R}^{d}_{t+1}$. Then (8.38) becomes:

$$(8.39)\ [(\mathfrak{R}^{fs}_{t+1} + Cu^{s}_{t+1}) - (\mathfrak{R}^{d}_{t+1} + Cu^{d}_{t+1})] + (D^{s}_{t+1} - D^{d}_{t+1}) + p^{b}_{t}(B^{s}_{t+1} - B^{d}_{t+1})$$

$$= (S^{d}_{t} - S^{s}_{t}) + p^{bf*}_{t} B^{f*}_{t} + B^{f*}_{t} + \mathfrak{R}_t + \hat{\varepsilon}_{t-1} p^{*}_{t-1} q^{*n}_{t} - p_{t-1} q^{n*}_{t} - \hat{\varepsilon}_{t-1} B^{*f}_{t}$$

$$- \hat{\varepsilon}_{t-1} [p^{b*f}_{t} B^{*f}_{t} + \mathfrak{R}^{*}_{t}].$$

Then, from (7.5) and (7.6), (8.39) becomes:

$$(8.40)\ [(\mathfrak{R}^{fs}_{t+1} + Cu^{s}_{t+1}) - (\mathfrak{R}^{d}_{t+1} + Cu^{d}_{t+1})] + (D^{s}_{t+1} - D^{d}_{t+1}) + p^{b}_{t}(B^{s}_{t+1} - B^{d}_{t+1})$$

$$= (S^{d}_{t} - S^{s}_{t}) + (F^{d}_{t-1} - F^{s}_{t-1}).$$

Analogously, by summing across the current-period budget constraints facing the foreign country's sectors, expressed in terms of the home country's unit of account, we obtain the following restriction among the excess supplies in the financial markets:

$$(8.41)\ \varepsilon_t [p^{b*}_{t}(B^{*s}_{t+1} - B^{*d}_{t+1}) + (D^{*s}_{t+1} - D^{*d}_{t+1}) + (Cu^{*s}_{t+1} - Cu^{*d}_{t+1}) + (F^{s}_{t-1} - F^{d}_{t-1})/\hat{\varepsilon}_{t-1}]$$

$$+ (S^{d}_{t} - S^{s}_{t}) = 0.$$

Since the markets for checkable deposits in both countries clear before the other financial markets in this model (i.e., according to the recursive nature of our model, the interest rates on home and foreign checkable deposits influence current bond rates and exchange rates, but are not influenced by current activity in those markets), if we assume that the forward market cleared last period and that both markets for checkable deposits clear in the current period, then restrictions (8.40) and (8.41) become, respectively:

$$(8.42)\ p^{b}_{t}(B^{s}_{t+1} - B^{d}_{t+1}) + (S^{s}_{t} - S^{d}_{t}) + (M^{s}_{t+1} - M^{d}_{t+1}) = 0$$

$$(8.43)\ \ \varepsilon_t [p^{b*}_{t}(B^{*s}_{t+1} - B^{*d}_{t+1}) + (M^{*s}_{t+1} - M^{*d}_{t+1})] + (S^{d}_{t} - S^{s}_{t}) = 0.$$

From (8.42), if we solve simultaneously for equilibrium in the home bond market and the spot market, the market for the home country's non-interest-bearing money also achieves equilibrium at that solution. From (8.43), if we solve simultaneously for equilibrium in the foreign bond market and the spot market, the market for the foreign country's non-interest-bearing money also reaches equilibrium at that solution. Therefore, if we achieve equilibrium in both the home and foreign bond markets and in the current spot market, both the home and foreign money markets also achieve equilibrium. See Figure 8.7.

Since current contracts struck in the forward market for foreign exchange are not financed or realized until next period, the excess demand in the forward market during the current period is linearly independent of the excess demands in the remaining financial markets. But, since the excess demands for spot contracts, forward contracts, home country bonds and foreign country bonds all depend jointly upon the home and foreign bond rates and the spot and forward exchange rates, we must solve these equilibrium conditions jointly for the home and foreign bond rates and the spot and forward exchange rates.

Figure 8.7 **Simultaneous Solution for r^b_t, r^{b*}_t, ε_t, and $\hat{\varepsilon}_t$**

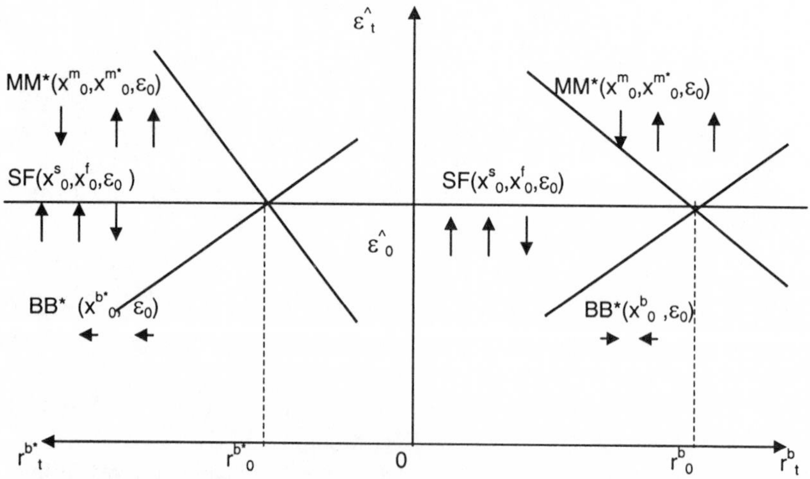

According to Figure 8.7, a joint solution occurs in a given plane at the intersection of the BB* and SF projections, ***provided*** both the spot rate and the other bond rate implicit on both projections are consistent not only with each other, but also with the bond rate revealed by the intersection of the BB* and SF projections in the other plane at the relevant spot rate.

CHAPTER NINE

Macroeconomic Impacts of Environmental Policies

Introduction

In the present chapter we conduct three conceptual experiments involving a change in an environmental policy variable. In the first case, we consider the effects upon the global economy of an increase in the volume of pollution or harvesting rights issued by the international agent. In the second, we consider the effects of a reduction in the initial stock of the home country's non-renewable resource. In the third, we consider the effects of a reduction in the foreign country's initial stock of its non-renewable resource. We close this analysis with a brief consideration of the critical role of markets for pollution and harvesting rights in revealing the anticipated benefits from current efforts to devote real resources during the current period to develop technologies that either reduce emissions associated with the extraction and use of the non-renewable resource or reduce the amount of pollution in the biosphere.

Increase in the Volume of Pollution or Harvesting Rights Issued

As we discussed earlier, an increase in either the volume of pollution rights issued by the international agent or an increase in the volume of harvesting rights for the renewable resource issued by that agent, increases the amount the non-financial business sectors in both countries produce during the current period and lowers the product prices they announce. If the volume of pollution rights increases, both non-financial business sectors will substitute their non-renewable resource for the other inputs they use in current production. If the international agent increases the volume of harvesting rights for the renewable resource, both non-financial business sectors will substitute that resource for their other inputs, including their non-renewable resource. In both cases, both these sectors will tend to reduce their current use of the labor input.

Since both non-financial business sectors produce more during the current period, gross domestic product and disposable income increase in both countries. The increases in disposable income cause current consumption to increase in both countries as well, but the increase is less than the rise in the value of production. As a result, an excess supply of bonds is created in both countries, shifting the BB* projections outward in both panels of Figure 9.1 and thereby pushing interest rates on both home and foreign bonds higher.

In both countries, the increase in disposable income increases the market demand for checkable deposits, producing a lower interest rate on checkable deposits in both countries. Together the rise in disposable income and the fall in the interest rate on checkable deposits produces an excess demand for non-interest-bearing money in both countries ($dx^m_t < 0$ and $dx^{m*}_t < 0$). The resulting shift of the MM* projection in the (r^b_t, $\hat{\varepsilon}_t$) plane is found by comparing the numerators in (8.20) and (8.21), since their denominators are the same. We assume that no cross-country differences exist with respect to the initial change in excess demand for currency (measured in the home country's unit of account), so that $\partial ES^{m*}/\partial x^{m*}_t \approx \partial ES^m/\partial x^m_t$; we also assume that the excess demand for money in the home country is less responsive to a change in the foreign bond rate than is the excess demand for money in the foreign country with respect to that rate. Under these conditions, even though an excess demand is created in both money markets as a result of the issue of extra pollution or harvesting rights, the projection of the MM* locus shifts upward in the (r^b_t, $\hat{\varepsilon}_t$) plane.

Figure 9.1 **Shifts in BB* and MM* Loci Due to an Increase in Pollution or Harvesting Rights**

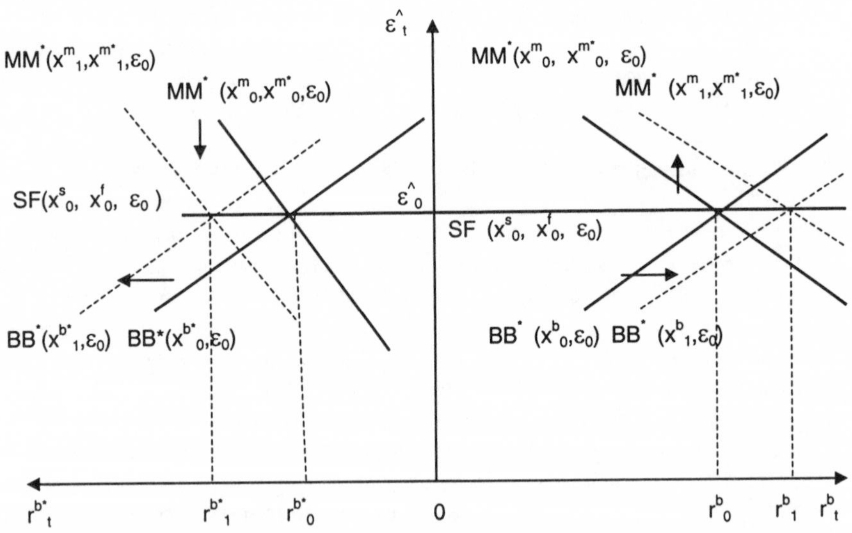

The resulting shift of the MM* projection in the (r^{b*}_t, $\hat{\varepsilon}_t$) plane is found by comparing the numerators in (8.23) and (8.24), since their denominators are the same. We assume, again, that no cross-country differences exist with respect to the initial change in excess demand for money (measured in the home country's unit of account), so that $\partial ES^{m*}/\partial x^{m*}_t \approx \partial ES^m/\partial x^m_t$; we also assume that the excess demand for money in the home country is more responsive to a change in the home bond rate than is the excess demand for money in the foreign country with respect to that rate. Under these conditions, even though an excess demand is created in both money markets as a result of the issue of extra pollution or harvesting rights, the projection of the MM* locus shifts downward in the $(r^{b*}_t, \varepsilon\hat{}_t)$ plane.

As a result of an issue of more pollution rights, both countries will tend to substitute their own non-renewable resource for the factor they import from the other. As a result of an issue of more harvesting rights for the shared renewable resource, each country will tend to substitute that resource for the input it imports from the other. These similar responses by both countries produce opposing forces upon the excess demand for foreign exchange in the forward market. The SF locus may shift up or down. If we assume that the responses do not differ across countries, the SF locus remains unchanged. In this case, bond rates rise in both countries, but no major change occurs in either the spot or forward exchange rates. In general, however, the net effects upon the spot and forward rates remain indeterminate, with bond rates rising in both countries. Because bond rates rise in both countries, real capital formation is lower than otherwise in both countries.

Reduction in Initial Stock of Home Country's Non-Renewable Resource

The smaller the home country's initial stock of its non-renewable resource at the beginning of the current period, Q^, the less output the home non-financial business sector produces during the current period. Given the negative slope of its forecast of the current demand curve for its product, the home non-financial business sector also raises current product price as it reduces output. However, because the sector produces in the elastic portion of its forecasted product demand curve, then to the extent that the forecasted demand curve closely approximates the actual demand curve, the value of GDP falls. The reduction in GDP produces a corresponding reduction in current disposable income. The smaller current disposable income reduces the end-of-period market demand for checkable deposits in the home country, causing the interest rates on home checkable deposits to rise.

Assuming that the rise in interest rates on home checkable deposits produces a relatively small effect upon the home household sector's demand for privately-produced home country goods, then the amount of aggregate demand for these goods also diminishes. But, because the marginal propensity to consume in the home country is less than one, the reduction in the quantity demanded is less than the reduction in the home country's GDP. This creates an excess demand in the home bond market as real investment by the private firms falls (since production falls more than aggregate demand decreases, firms experience an unanticipated reduction in inventories). The excess demand created in the home bond market shifts the projection of the BB* locus in the $(r^b_t, \varepsilon\hat{}_t)$ plane to the left, but produces no immediate shift in the projection of the BB* locus in the $(r^{b*}_{t}, \varepsilon^{\wedge}_{t})$ plane. See Figure 9.2.

Figure 9.2 **Initial Shifts in BB*, SF and MM* Due to a Fall in Q^**

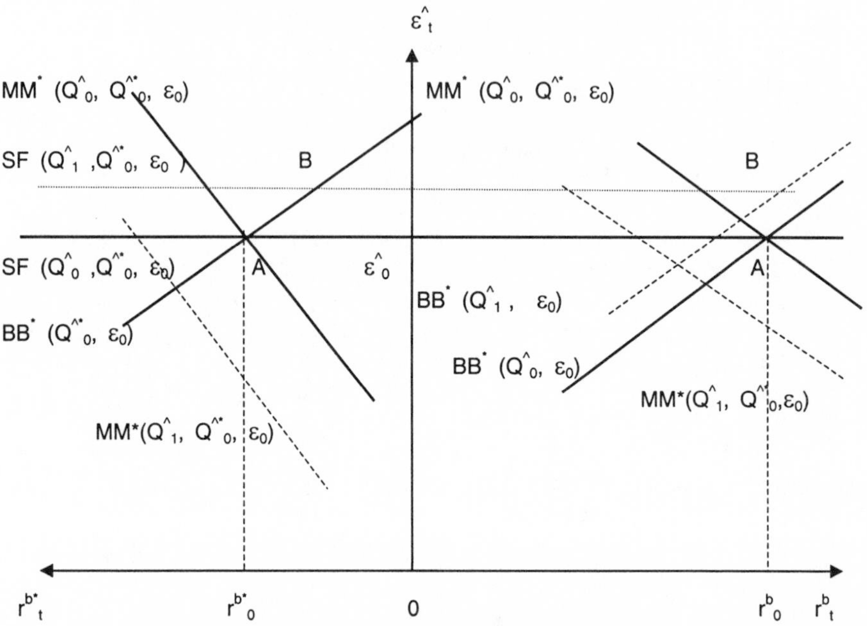

Ceteris paribus, a decrease in the initial stock of the home non-financial business sector's non-renewable resource causes it to order more this period of the good it imports from the other country, since it will plan to substitute that good for the non-renewable resource in next period's production, even though it also reduces the amount it plans to produce next period. Its increased orders for the foreign goods creates an excess demand for foreign exchange. Ceteris paribus, this excess demand causes the projection of the SF locus to shift upward in both the $(r^{b}_{t}, \varepsilon^{\wedge}_{t})$ and $(r^{b*}_{t}, \varepsilon^{\wedge}_{t})$ planes.

Neither the spot nor forward foreign exchange markets are directly affected by the current changes in disposable income or interest rates on checkable deposits in the home country. As home disposable income falls and interest rates rise on home checkable deposits, the end-of-period market demand for home money falls, creating an excess supply of home non-interest-bearing money. Also, as the home non-financial business sector increases its import demand, the home private financial sector increases its desired end-of-period balances of interbank deposits due from the foreign banks; an excess demand is created in the market for non-interest-bearing foreign money. Therefore, the projection of the MM* locus shifts downward in both planes.

Holding the spot rate constant, temporarily, the aforementioned initial shifts in the BB*, SF, and MM* projections cause the new BB* and SF projections to intersect (see point B in both panels of Figure 9.2) above the new MM* projection in both planes. (In each plane, the MM* projection need not pass through the BB* and SF intersection, if, at this point, the implicit bond rate, i.e., the bond rate not measured explicitly in that plane, on either (or both of) the BB* or SF projection(s) is inconsistent with the value of that bond rate revealed by the BB* and SF intersection in the other plane.) In Figure 9.2, since the new MM* projection now passes below the new intersection of the BB* and SF projections in both planes, the spot rate must adjust, if general equilibrium is to be restored in the financial markets.

If the spot rate were to fall, a new general equilibrium could not be achieved, since the MM* projection would then move even farther away from the intersection of BB* and SF. What happens instead is that the rising forward exchange rate associated with the initial shift in SF induces the home private financial sector to increase its end-of-period demand for foreign bonds and causes the foreign private financial sector to reduce its end-of-period demand for home bonds; both actions create an excess demand for foreign exchange in the spot market. As the spot rate rises, in both planes, the SF projection shifts downward, the MM* projection shifts upward and the BB* projection shifts leftward. This enables a new general equilibrium to be restored in the financial markets. See point C in both planes drawn in Figure 9.3.

If we assume that the initial excess demand created in the forward market by the home non-financial business sector as it increased its orders for the foreign country's good dominates that market, then the forward rate at the new general equilibrium position, point C, will exceed its original value (in both planes, the SF projection associated with the new general equilibrium will lie above its original position). Assuming that the original excess demand created in the home bond market dominates the home bond rate, that rate diminishes. If we ignore transactions costs, we know that covered interest parity must hold. That is, r^b_t must (approximately) equal $r^{b*}_t + \varepsilon^{\wedge}_t/\varepsilon_t$. Since r^b_t falls in response to the initial excess demand created in the home bond market, so must $r^{b*}_t + \varepsilon^{\wedge}_t/\varepsilon_t$.

If the tendency for the forward exchange rate to rise created by the initial excess demand in that market (stemming from the fall in the initial stock of the non-renewable resource) dominates the less direct effects upon the spot and forward exchange rates, then the ratio of the forward rate to the spot rate rises, which creates an excess demand for foreign bonds, pushing the foreign bond rate downward as well. Granted these assumptions, the net effect of a reduction in the home country's initial stock of its non-renewable resource is to push current world interest rates lower as well as to reduce the value of the home country's unit of account in both the spot and forward markets (as measured here, both exchange rates rise in value).

Figure 9.3 **Secondary Shifts in BB*, SF and MM* due to a Rise in ε After a Fall in Q^**

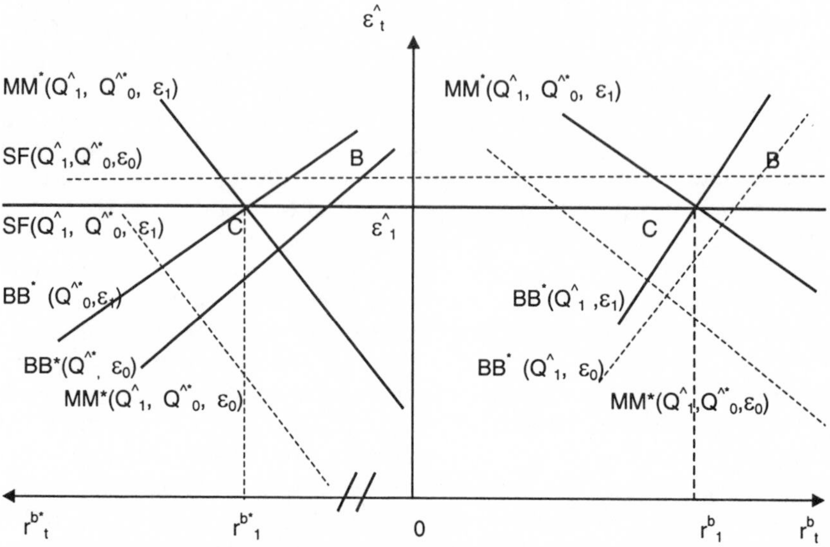

As we have seen, a reduction in the initial stock of the non-renewable resource held by the home non-financial business sector causes that sector to reduce current output and to attempt to substitute labor, physical capital and the imported factor for the non-renewable resource in next period's production, which the sector plans will be smaller than it would have been if the initial stock of its non-renewable resource had not fallen. The resulting excess demands created in the home bond market and in the forward market for foreign exchange push home bond rates lower and forward exchange rates higher, further affecting the sector's end-of-period demands for factors. In particular, the falling home bond rate and the rising forward rate both tend to cause the sector to use even more physical capital in next period's production, the latter effect arising because on the margin the sector will substitute physical capital for the imported factor as the forward exchange rate rises.

The foreign non-financial business sector's end-of-period demand for physical capital will tend to increase, since it now becomes cheaper for that sector to borrow the funds necessary to finance that real investment. Although the rise in the forward exchange rate tends to increase the foreign non-financial business sector's current orders for the good produced in the home country, that demand will tend to fall as a result of the higher price the home non-financial business sector has announced for its product; if this latter effect dominates, the foreign sector reduces its demand for home country goods. Furthermore, the increase in the home country's demand for the foreign good, ceteris paribus, increases the foreign non-financial business sector's forecasted demand for its product next period. This would tend to cause the sector to plan to produce more next period and to charge a higher product price than otherwise. Therefore, as a result of the reduction of the initial stock of the home country's non-renewable resource, production will tend to shift from the home country to the foreign country, the home country will raise product price in the current period because of the increase in its production costs, and the foreign country will tend to raise product price next period because of the increased demand for its product. The home country's non-financial business sector will tend to substitute physical capital, labor, and the foreign country's good for its own non-renewable resource in future production. The foreign non-financial business sector will tend to substitute physical capital for the factor it buys from the home country in its own future production.

Reduction in Initial Stock of Foreign Country's Non-Renewable Resource

The smaller the foreign country's initial stock of its non-renewable resource at the beginning of the current period, $Q^{\wedge *}$, the less output the foreign non-financial business sector produces during the current period. This sector also raises current product price as it reduces output. However, because the sector produces in the elastic portion of its forecasted product demand curve, then to the extent that the forecasted demand curve closely approximates the actual demand curve, the value of GDP* falls. The reduction in GDP* produces a corresponding reduction in current disposable income. The smaller current disposable income reduces the end-of-period market demand for checkable deposits in the foreign country, causing the interest rates on foreign checkable deposits to rise.

Assuming that the rise in interest rates on foreign checkable deposits produces a relatively small effect upon the foreign household sector's demand for privately-produced foreign country goods, then the aggregate demand for these goods also diminishes. But, because the marginal propensity to consume in the foreign country is less than one, the reduction in aggregate demand is less than the reduction in the foreign country's GDP. This creates an excess demand in the foreign bond market as real investment by the private firms falls (since production falls more than aggregate demand decreases, firms in the foreign country experience an unanticipated reduction in inventories). The excess demand created in the foreign bond market shifts the projection of the BB* locus in the $(r^{b*}_t, \varepsilon^{\wedge}_t)$ plane to the right, but produces no immediate shift in the projection of the BB* locus in the $(r^b_t, \varepsilon^{\wedge}_t)$ plane. See Figure 9.4.

Ceteris paribus, a decrease in the initial stock of the foreign non-financial business sector's non-renewable resource causes it to order more this period of the good it imports from the home country, since it will plan to substitute that good for the non-renewable resource in next period's production, even though it also reduces the amount it plans to produce next period. Its increased orders for the home country good creates an excess supply of foreign exchange. Ceteris paribus, this excess supply causes the projection of the SF locus to shift downward in both the $(r^b_t, \hat{\varepsilon}_t)$ and $(r^{b*}_t, \hat{\varepsilon}_t)$ planes. Neither the spot nor forward foreign exchange markets are directly affected by the current changes in disposable income or interest rates on checkable deposits in the foreign country.

As foreign disposable income falls and interest rates rise on foreign checkable deposits, the end-of-period market demand for foreign non-interest-bearing money falls, creating an excess supply of foreign money. Therefore, the projection of the MM* locus shifts upward in both planes. See Figure 9.4.

Figure 9.4 **Initial Shifts in BB*, SF and MM* Due to a Fall in $Q^{\wedge *}$**

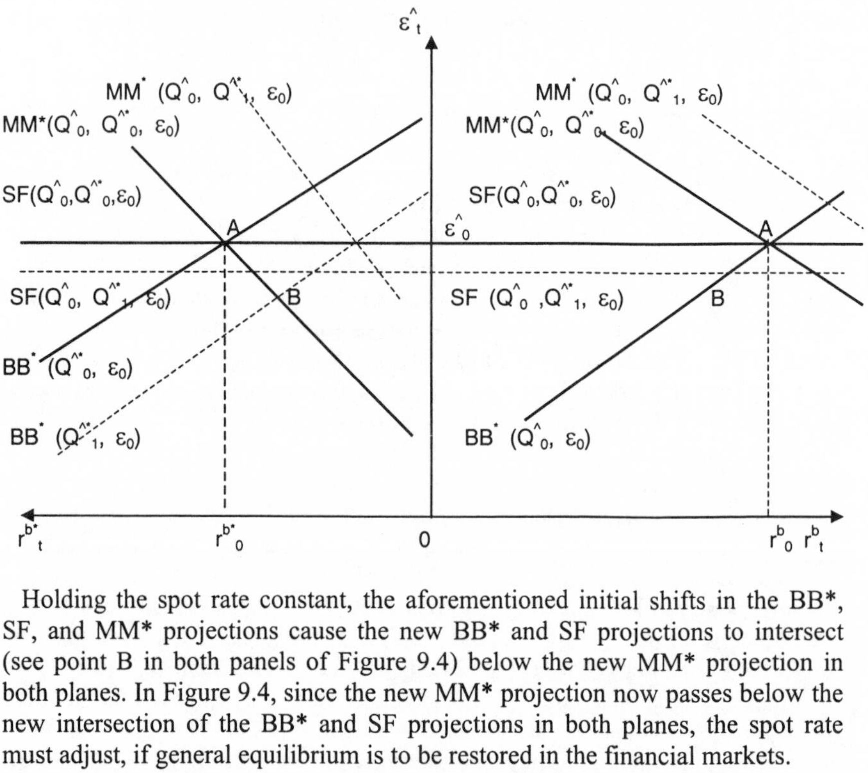

Holding the spot rate constant, the aforementioned initial shifts in the BB*, SF, and MM* projections cause the new BB* and SF projections to intersect (see point B in both panels of Figure 9.4) below the new MM* projection in both planes. In Figure 9.4, since the new MM* projection now passes below the new intersection of the BB* and SF projections in both planes, the spot rate must adjust, if general equilibrium is to be restored in the financial markets.

If the spot rate were to rise, a new general equilibrium could not be achieved, since the MM* projection would then move even farther from the intersection of BB* and SF. What happens instead is that the falling forward exchange rate associated with the initial shift in SF induces the foreign private financial sector to increase its end-of-period demand for home bonds and causes the home private financial sector to reduce its end-of-period demand for foreign bonds; both actions create an excess supply of foreign exchange in the spot market. As the spot rate falls, in both planes shown in Figure 9.5, the SF projection shifts upward, the MM* projection shifts downward, and the BB* projection shifts to the

Figure 9.5 **Secondary Shifts in BB*, SF and MM* Due to a Fall in ε After a Fall in Q^***

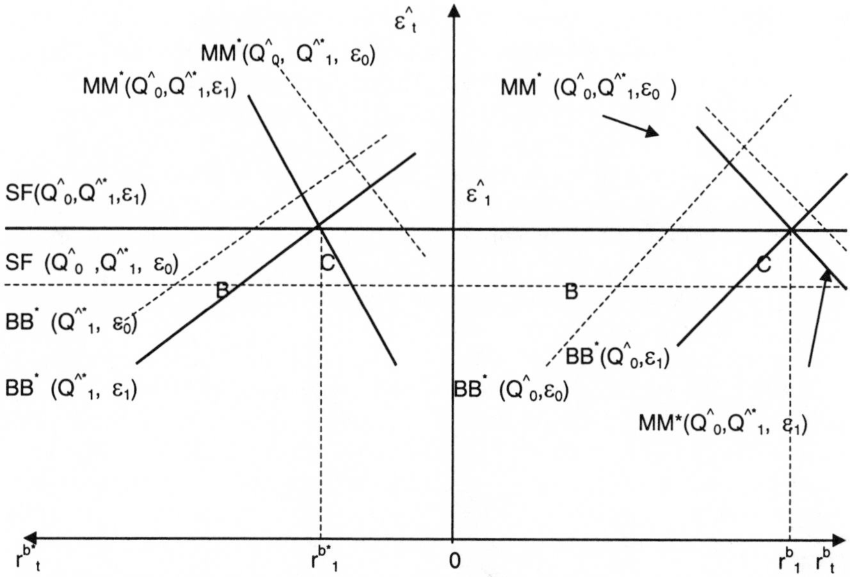

right. This enables a new general equilibrium to be restored in the financial markets. See point C in both planes drawn in Figure 9.5.

If we assume that the initial excess supply created in the forward market by the foreign non-financial business sector as it increased its orders for the home country's good dominates that market, then the forward rate at the new general equilibrium position, point C, will be less than its original value (in both planes, the SF projection associated with the new general equilibrium will lie below its original position). Assuming that the original excess demand created in the foreign bond market dominates the foreign bond rate, that rate diminishes.

If we ignore transactions costs, we know that covered interest parity must hold. That is, r^{b*}_t must (approximately) equal $r^b_t - \hat{\varepsilon}_t/\varepsilon_t$. Since r^{b*}_t falls in response to the initial excess demand created in the foreign bond market, so must $r^b_t - \hat{\varepsilon}_t/\varepsilon_t$. If the tendency for the forward exchange rate to fall created by the initial excess supply in that market, stemming from the fall in the initial stock of the non-renewable resource, dominates the less direct effects upon the spot and forward exchange rates, then the ratio of the forward rate to the spot rate falls, which creates an excess demand for home bonds, pushing the home bond rate downward as well. Granted these assumptions, the net effect of a reduction in the foreign country's initial stock of its non-renewable resource is to push current world interest rates lower as well as to raise the value of the home country's unit of account in both the spot and forward markets, with the ratio of the forward rate to the spot rate falling.

As we have seen, a reduction in the initial stock of the non-renewable resource held by the foreign non-financial business sector causes that sector to reduce current output and to attempt to substitute labor, physical capital and the imported factor for the non-renewable resource in next period's production, which the sector plans will be smaller than it would have been if the initial stock of its non-renewable resource had not fallen. The resulting excess demand created in the foreign bond market and the resulting excess supply created in the forward market for foreign exchange push foreign bond rates lower and forward exchange rates lower, further affecting the sector's end-of-period demands for factors. In particular, the falling foreign bond rate and the falling forward exchange rate both tend to cause the foreign non-financial business sector to use even more physical capital in next period's production, the latter arising because the sector will tend to substitute physical capital for the imported factor as the forward exchange rate falls.

The home non-financial business sector's end-of-period demand for physical capital will also tend to increase, since it now becomes cheaper for that sector to borrow the funds necessary to finance that real investment in the home bond market. The fall in the forward exchange rate tends to increase the home non-financial business sector's current orders for the good produced in the foreign country. However, the foreign sector will tend to announce a higher price for its product in the current period. If the latter effect dominates, the home non-financial business sector will tend to use less of the foreign good in next period's production. Furthermore, the increase in the foreign country's demand for the home good, ceteris paribus, increases the home non-financial business sector's forecasted demand for its product next period. This would tend to cause the sector to plan to produce more next period and to charge a higher product price than otherwise. Therefore, as a result of the reduction of the initial stock of the foreign country's non-renewable resource, production will tend to shift from the foreign country to the home country, the foreign country will raise product price in the current period because of the increase in its production costs, and the home country will tend to raise product price next period because of the increased demand for its product. The foreign country will tend to substitute physical capital, labor, and the home country's good for its non-renewable resource in future production. The home non-financial business sector will tend to substitute physical capital for the factor it buys from the foreign country in its own future production.

Role of Market for Pollution Rights in Pollution Control Technology

In the introduction, we mentioned that in order for technology to rescue the world economy from certain environmental constraints, the return to technology in pollution abatement and in reducing emissions would need to be made explicit. In the present section we show how these returns to technology are revealed explicitly in our global economy model through market prices for pollution emission rights.

We now modify the model of the non-financial business sector that we developed in Chapter 3 by permitting the sector to divert some current-period labor hours away from current production of the private product and away from current pollution abatement and toward the development of technologies that will either reduce next period the amount of pollution emitted by the extraction and use of a unit of the nation's non-renewable resource or will increase next period the productivity of labor in pollution abatement.

For that purpose, let

$h^{\kappa}_{t}N^{n}_{t}$ = number of hours of labor during the current period devoted to reducing the emissions associated with a unit of non-renewable resources next period.

$h^{\mu}_{t}N^{n}_{t}$ = the number of labor hours during the current period devoted to increasing the ability of a unit of future labor effort to clean up pollution.

$\kappa^{e}(h^{\kappa}_{t}N^{n}_{t})$ = the anticipated amount of pollution emitted next period per unit of the non-renewable resource extracted and used next period, where $\kappa^{e}(\bullet)$ is a decreasing function of the number of labor hours the sector devotes to developing this technology during the current period.

$\theta^{e}(h^{\mu e}_{t}N^{n}_{t})$ = the anticipated productivity of a unit of next period's labor in pollution abatement, where $\theta^{e}(\bullet)$ is viewed as positively related to the number of current labor hours devoted to developing this technology.

Given these modifications, the number of hours the non-financial business sector currently devotes to pollution abatement is given by $h^{n}N^{n}_{t} - h^{\kappa}_{t}N^{n}_{t} - h^{\mu e}_{t}N^{n}_{t} - h^{q}_{t}N^{n}_{t}$. To accommodate the above modifications the objective function (3.18) specified in Chapter 3 then becomes:

$$
\begin{aligned}
(9.1)\quad \Pi^{n}_{t} + \Pi^{ne}_{t+1}/(1 + r^{d}_{t}) = \bar{R}\{\ \bar{q}(h^{q}_{t}N^{n}_{t}, q^{*n}_{t}, K^{n}_{t}, R^{x}_{t}, \hat{q}_{t})\\
-[(1+p^{bn}_{t+1})/p^{bn}_{t}(1 + r^{d}_{t})]\cdot[(K^{nde}_{t+1} - K^{n}_{t}) - Q_{t}], \alpha\}\\
-W_{t-1}h^{n}_{t}N^{n}_{t} - \hat{\varepsilon}_{t-1}p^{*}_{t-1}q^{*n}_{t} - B^{n}_{t} - p^{x}_{t}R^{x}_{t}\\
-p^{p}_{t}[\kappa\,\hat{q}_{t} - \mu(h^{n}N^{n}_{t} - h^{\kappa}_{t}N^{n}_{t} - h^{\mu e}_{t}N^{n}_{t} - h^{q}_{t}N^{n}_{t})]\\
+\{\ R^{e}[q^{ne}(hN^{nde}_{t+1}, q^{*ne}_{t+1}, K^{nde}_{t+1}, R^{xdn}_{t+1}, \hat{Q}_{t} - \hat{q}_{t}) + K^{nde}_{t+1}, \beta]\\
-h\cdot \bar{C}(N^{nde}_{t+1}, \gamma) - \hat{\varepsilon}^{n}_{t}p^{*n}_{t}q^{*ne}_{t+1} - p^{xe}_{t+1}R^{xdn}_{t+1} - (1 + p^{bn}_{t+1})B^{n}_{t}\\
-p^{pe}_{t+1}\{\kappa^{e}(h^{\kappa}_{t}N^{n}_{t})(\hat{Q}_{t} - \hat{q}_{t}) - \mu^{e}[\theta(h^{\mu e}_{t}N^{n}_{t})(hN^{nde}_{t+1} - hN^{qde}_{t+1})]\}\}/(1 + r^{dn}_{t}).
\end{aligned}
$$

Partially differentiating this new objective function with respect to current labor effort, h^{κ}_{t}, devoted to developing technology to reduce emissions for each unit of the non-renewable resource extracted and used during the current period, we obtain condition (9.2):

$$(9.2)\ -p^{p}_{t}\mu'N^{n}_{t} - [p^{pe}_{t+1}\kappa^{e'}N^{n}_{t}(\hat{Q}_{t} - \hat{q}_{t})]/(1 + r^{dn}_{t}) = 0.$$

According to this condition, the sector should continue to devote labor resources during the current period to developing technology to reduce the amount of pollution created by the extraction and use of a unit of the non-renewable resource until the present value of the anticipated market value of the anticipated marginal reduction in pollution equals the current opportunity cost of the labor time devoted to developing that technology, which may be viewed as the market value of the pollution that this labor time could be eliminating during the current period. (Condition (3.19) ensures that this opportunity cost also equals the marginal wage expense associated with the extra labor effort.) It is important to note that according to condition (9.2) if the sector does not reckon with an anticipated market price for pollution rights in the future, the sector has no incentive in this model for investing in the technology. The very existence of a market for pollution rights induces the sector to consider devoting real resources, labor in our case, to developing new technology.

Partially differentiating (9.1) with respect to current labor effort, h^{μ}_{t}, devoted to developing technology for removing pollution from the biosphere yields a similar condition, namely (9.3):

$$(9.3)\ -p^{p}_{t}\mu'N^{n}_{t} + [p^{pe}_{t+1}\mu^{e'}\theta'N^{n}_{t}](hN^{nde}_{t+1} - hN^{qde}_{t+1})/(1 + r^{dn}_{t}) = 0.$$

This first-order condition indicates that, within the context of the present model, if there were no explicit market for pollution rights, the projected future benefit of reduced future pollution would not be reckoned with and firms would have no incentive to invest today in technology to improve productivity in pollution abatement.

In the present setting, the potential benefit to the non-financial business sectors in both countries in terms of reductions in anticipated expenditures on future pollution rights motivate them to contemplate a current-period effort to develop new technologies either to reduce pollution emissions or to increase the productivity of pollution abatement efforts. They will undertake these technological efforts as long as the present value of the anticipated savings is at least as great as the current expense associated with this effort. In the present model, the current explicit expense is represented by the nominal wage, because labor is viewed as the only factor used in developing new technologies.

An added benefit from the technological developments stimulated by the anticipated prices for pollution rights resulting from the existence of an explicit market for those rights, is that should the technological developments succeed in reducing pollution in the future, they will enable the renewable resource to grow at a faster rate than otherwise, exerting downward pressure on the market price associated with harvesting this resource. Therefore, the existence of explicit markets for pollution and harvesting rights provides a vehicle that promotes technological advances which will not only reduce pollution, but also increase the ability of the global economy, on the margin, to substitute the renewable resource for the non-renewable resources as the latter become depleted.

Conclusion

Our purpose in this study has been to offer a comprehensive theoretical macroeconomic model that incorporates the basic issues concerning the relationships between the open global economy and the closed global ecosystem. In particular we have attempted to develop a dynamic macroeconomic model of the world economy in which the global economy operates as a subsystem of a larger ecosystem containing finite amounts of non-renewable resources and exhibiting a limited ability to absorb waste. We have assumed the existence of an international agent charged with protecting the "global commons" who issues a limited number of tradable rights both to pollute and to extract the global renewable resource, with neither country permitted to draw down its non-renewable resource below a prescribed maintainable level. We have also presented a national income accounting framework consistent with this model that deducts payments for pollution and harvesting rights for the renewable resource as well as reductions in inventories of non-renewable resources from the measure of a country's national product. We have traced the effects of changes in pollution and harvesting rights and reductions in the initial stocks of non-renewable resources upon the global economy. These changes affect not only the current levels of production and the current allocations of resources, but also current prices, wages, interest rates and exchange rates, all of which affect future production and resource allocation world-wide. Within the context of our model, if a country experiences a reduction in a non-renewable resource, for instance, production tends to shift away from that country. Product prices tend to rise not only in that country—due to the increase in the marginal cost of current production—but also elsewhere. Furthermore, producers world-wide tend to increase their use of physical capital and labor, on the margin, in the production process, urged by concomitant changes in interest rates and exchange rates. Therefore, as the non-renewable resource dwindles in one country, market forces tend to cause a shift to other resources and to production processes that do not rely upon that resource. Ceteris paribus, this process also stimulates efforts to develop technologies that make this transition possible.

Glossary

A_t = the level of advances the home central bank has granted its private financial sector by the beginning of the current period.

A^*_t = the level of advances the foreign central bank has granted its private financial sector by the beginning of the current period.

B^c_t = the number of home country bonds held by the home central bank at the beginning of the current period.

B^{cd}_{t+1} = the number of home country bonds the home central bank plans to hold by the end of the current period.

B^{c*}_t = the number of home country bonds held by the foreign central bank at the beginning of the current period.

B^f_t = the number of home country bonds the home private financial sector holds at the beginning of the current period.

B^{fd}_{t+1} = the number of home country bonds the home private financial sector plans to hold by the end of the current period.

B^{f*}_t = the number of home country bonds the foreign private financial sector holds at the beginning of the current period.

B^{f*d}_{t+1} = the number of home country bonds the foreign private financial sector plans to hold by the end of the current period.

B^g_t = the (predetermined) number of home country bonds the home government sector has outstanding at the beginning of the current period.

B^{gse}_{t+1} = the number of home country bonds the home government sector plans at the beginning of the current period (before current product prices, wages and interest rates are established) to have outstanding by the end of the current period. The government will be free during the current period to alter its end-of-period supply of home country bonds as these prices and interest rates become known.

B^n_t = the number of bonds (issued in the home country's bond market) the home country's non-financial business sector has outstanding at the beginning of the current period.

B^{nse}_{t+1} = the number of home country bonds the home non-financial business sector plans at the beginning of the current period (as it announces its current product price and the wage rate and decides current production, but before current interest rates and exchange rates are established) to have outstanding by the end of the current period. The sector will be free during the current period to alter its end-of-period supply of home country bonds as these interest rates and exchange rates become known.

B^{*c}_{t} = the number of foreign bonds held by the home central bank at the beginning of the current period.

B^{*cd}_{t+1} = the number of foreign bonds the home central bank plans to hold by the end of the current period.

B^{c*d}_{t+1} = the number of home country bonds the foreign central bank plans to hold by the end of the current period.

B^{*c*}_{t} = the number of foreign bonds held by the foreign central bank at the beginning of the current period.

B^{*c*d}_{t+1} = the number of foreign bonds the foreign central bank plans to hold by the end of the current period.

B^{*f}_{t} = the number of foreign country bonds the home private financial sector holds at the beginning of the current period.

B^{*fd}_{t+1} = the number of foreign country bonds the home private financial sector plans to hold by the end of the current period.

B^{*f*}_{t} = the number of foreign country bonds the foreign private financial sector holds at the beginning of the current period.

B^{*f*d}_{t+1} = the number of foreign country bonds the foreign private financial sector plans to hold by the end of the current period.

c^{d}_{t} = the home household sector's current period demand for goods produced by the home non-financial business sector.

c^{he}_{t} = the home household sector's notional demand at the beginning of the current period for privately-produced home country goods during the current period, before the sector learns current period prices, wages, or interest rates.

c^{he}_{t+1} = the home household sector's notional demand at the beginning of the current period for privately-produced home-country goods next period, before the sector learns current-period prices, wages, or interest rates.

c^{*d}_{t} = the foreign household sector's current period demand for goods produced by the foreign non-financial business sector.

Cu_t = the amount of (coin and) currency denominated in the home country's unit of account held by the home country's households at the beginning of the current period.

Cu^{d}_{t+1} = the home household sector's end-of-period demand for home country (coin and) currency.

Cu^{he}_{t+1} = the home household sector's notional demand at the beginning of the current period for currency issued by the home central bank (denominated in the home country's unit of account) to be held by the end of the current period.

Cu^{*}_{t} = the amount of (coin and) currency denominated in the foreign country's unit of account held by the foreign country's households at the beginning of the current period.

Cu^{*d}_{t+1} = the foreign household sector's end-of-period demand for foreign country (coin and) currency.

D_t = the volume of checkable deposits (valued in the home country's unit of account) that the home private financial sector has outstanding at the beginning of the current period.

D^{d}_{t+1} = the home household sector's end-of-period demand for checkable deposits at the home private financial sector.

D^{he}_{t+1} = the home household sector's notional demand at the beginning of the current period for checkable deposits issued by the home private financial sector (denominated in the home country's unit of account) to be held by the end of the current period.

D^{s}_{t+1} = the volume of checkable deposits outstanding at the end of the current period at the home private financial sector consistent with the plans of that sector (i.e., the home private financial sector's ex ante end period supply of checkable deposits).

D^*_t = the volume of checkable deposits (valued in the foreign country's unit of account) that the foreign private financial sector has outstanding at the beginning of the current period.

D^{*d}_{t+1} = the foreign household sector's end-of-period demand for checkable deposits at the foreign private financial sector.

D^{*s}_{t+1} = the volume of checkable deposits outstanding at the end of the current period at the foreign private financial sector consistent with the plans of that sector (i.e., the foreign private financial sector's ex ante end period supply of checkable deposits).

f^+_t = the ratio of the current forward exchange rate to the current spot exchange rate ($f^+_t = \varepsilon^{\wedge}_t/\varepsilon_t$).

g_t = the number of public goods and services to be produced by the home government sector during the current period.

g_{t+1} = the number of public goods and services to be produced by the home government sector next period

$G(S_t, \bar{P})$ = the natural amount of growth in the renewable resource, where $G(\bullet)$ is positively related to S_t, but negatively related to $\bar{P}$, the target level of pollution.

h = the "standard" average number of hours, which every sector expects this period that its employees will work next period.

$h^f_t N^f_t$ = the number of hours the home private financial sector uses its current employees.

$h^{f*}_t N^{f*}_t$ = the number of hours the foreign private financial sector uses its current employees.

h^g_t = the average number of hours the home government sector decides to use its employees during the current period.

$h^h_t N_t$ = the total number of hours the home country's household sector anticipates at the beginning of the current period that it will work during the current period for all three of its employers.

h^n_t = the overall average number of hours the home country's non-financial business sector uses its current employees.

$h^n{}_t N^n{}_t - h^q{}_t N^n{}_t$ = the amount of labor the home country's non-financial business sector devotes to pollution abatement during the current period.

$h^q{}_t$ = the average number of hours the home country's non-financial business sector uses their current employees during the current period for the purpose of producing private goods.

$\bar{h}$ = the total number of hours in the current period.

$h^{\wedge}$ = the total number of hours in the next period.

$K^g{}_t$ = the (predetermined) amount of physical capital held by the home government sector at the beginning of the current period.

$K^{gde}{}_{t+1}$ = the amount of physical capital the home government sector expects at the beginning of the current period (before it learns current product prices, wage rates or interest rates) that it will hold by the beginning of next period. The government will be free during the current period to alter its demand for physical capital for next period as current product prices, wage rates and interest rates become established.

$K^n{}_t$ = the home country's non-financial business sector's stock of physical capital at the beginning of the current period.

$K^{nde}{}_{t+1}$ = the amount of physical capital the home non-financial business sector expects at the beginning of the current period (as it announces its current product price and the wage rate and decides current production, but before it learns current interest rates or exchange rates) that it will hold by the beginning of next period. The sector will be free during the current period to alter its demand for physical capital for the beginning of next period as current interest rates and exchange rates become established.

MB_t = the amount of the home country's monetary base outstanding at the beginning of the current period ($MB_t = Cu_t + R_t$).

$MB^*{}_t$ = the amount of the foreign country's monetary base outstanding at the beginning of the current period ($MB^*{}_t = Cu^*{}_t + R^*{}_t$).

N = the total adult population in the home country.

$N^{fd}{}_{t+1}$ = the home private financial sector's end of current period demand for employees.

N^{f*d}_{t+1} = the foreign private financial sector's end of current period demand for employees.

N^{g}_{t} = the (predetermined) number of workers employed by the home government sector at the beginning of the current period.

N^{gde}_{t+1} = the number of workers the home government expects at the beginning of the current period (before it learns current product prices, wage rates, interest rates or exchange rates) that it will employ by the beginning of next period. The government will be free during the current period to alter its demand for workers for next period as current product prices, wage rates and interest rates become established.

N^{he}_{t+1} = the number of people the home household sector would like to have working by the end of the current period before the sector learns current wages, product prices and interest rates; i.e., the sector's notional supply of labor at the beginning of the current period for next period.

N^{n}_{t} = the number of people employed by the home country's non-financial business sector at the beginning of the current period.

N^{nde}_{t+1} = the number of people the home non-financial business sector expects at the beginning of the current period (as it announces its current product price and the wage rate and decides current production, but before it learns current interest rates or exchange rates) that it will employ by the beginning of next period. The sector will be free during the current period to alter its demand for workers for the beginning of next period as current interest rates and exchange rates become established.

N^{s}_{t+1} = the home households' ex ante supply of labor to the home labor market.

N^{*s}_{t+1} = the foreign households' ex ante supply of labor to the foreign labor market.

p_t = the price (in terms of the home country's unit of account) announced by the home country's non-financial business sector at the beginning of the current period for the goods it sells during the current period.

p^{b}_{t} = the current period price of home country bonds, denominated in the home country's unit of account.

p^{bg}_t = the current period price of home country bonds anticipated by the home government sector at the beginning of the current period before current product prices, wages and interest rates are established.

p^{bn}_t = the current period average price of home country bonds (in terms of the home country's unit of account) that the home non-financial business sector anticipates at the beginning of the current period before this price is determined.

p^{b*}_t = the current period price of foreign country bonds, denominated in the foreign country's unit of account.

p^{g}_t = the current period price of privately-produced home country goods anticipated by the home government sector at the beginning of the current period, before that price is announced by the home private non-financial business sector.

p^{g}_{t+1} = the average price of privately-produced home country goods which the home country's government sector anticipates at the beginning of the current period will prevail next period.

p^{h}_t = the current-period price of privately-produced goods in the home country (expressed in terms of the home country's unit or account) anticipated by the home household sector at the beginning of the current period.

p^{he}_{t+1} = the price of home country goods (expressed in units of the home country's unit of account) that the home household sector anticipates at the beginning of the current period will prevail next period (before the sector learns current wages, product prices and interest rates).

p^{n}_{t+1} = the product price (in terms of the home country's unit of account) which the home non-financial business sector plans at the beginning of the current period to announce next period.

p^{p}_t = the current equilibrium price of pollution rights (expressed in terms of the home country's currency).

$\bar{P}^{pd}_t$ = the amount of pollution rights the home country's non-financial business sector demands during the current period.

$\bar{P}^{p*d}_t$ = the amount of pollution rights the foreign country's non-financial business sector demands during the current period.

$\bar{P}^{pdg}_t$ = the amount of pollution rights the home government anticipates its non-financial business sector will buy during the current period.

$\bar{p}^{pdg}_{t+1}$ = the amount of pollution rights the home government sector anticipates at the beginning of the current period that its private non-financial business sector will buy next period.

$\bar{p}^{pdn}_{t+1} = \kappa^e (\hat{Q}_t - \hat{q}_t) - \mu^e (hN^{nde}_{t+1} - hN^{qde}_{t+1})$ = the amount of pollution rights the home non-financial business sector anticipates at the beginning of the current period that it will buy next period.

$\bar{p}^{p*dg*}_t$ = the amount of pollution rights the foreign government anticipates its non-financial business sector will buy during the current period.

p^{pg}_t = the current period price (expressed in terms of the home country's unit of account) of the right to emit a unit of pollution anticipated by the home government sector at the beginning of the current period before that price is determined.

p^{pg}_{t+1} = the price (expressed in terms of the home country's unit of account) of the right to emit a unit of pollution which the home government sector anticipates at the beginning of the current period will prevail next period.

p^{pg*}_t = the current period price (expressed in terms of the home country's unit of account) of the right to emit a unit of pollution anticipated by the foreign government sector at the beginning of the current period.

p^{pn}_{t+1} = the price (expressed in terms of the home country's unit of account) of the right to emit a unit of pollution which the home non-financial business sector anticipates at the beginning of the current period will prevail next period.

p^x_t = the current market price of extraction rights for the renewable resource (expressed in units of the home country's currency).

p^{xg}_t = the current period price (expressed in terms of the home country's unit of account) of a unit of extraction rights for the renewable resource anticipated by the home government sector at the beginning of the period before that price is established.

p^{xg}_{t+1} = the price (expressed in terms of the home country's unit of account) of a unit of extraction rights which the home government sector anticipates at the beginning of the current period will prevail next period.

p^{xg*}_t = the current period price (expressed in terms of the home country's unit of account) of a unit of extraction rights for the renewable resource anticipated by the foreign government sector.

p^{xn}_{t+1} = the price (expressed in terms of the home country's unit of account) of a unit of extraction rights which the home non-financial business sector anticipates at the beginning of the current period will prevail next period.

p^{*}_{t-1} = the price (in terms of the foreign unit of account) of the foreign (intermediate) good ordered by the home country's non-financial business sector last period and which the sector agreed to pay upon delivery of the foreign good this period.

$p^{*\,n}_{t}$ = the price (in terms of the foreign unit of account) of the foreign (intermediate) good that the home non-financial business sector anticipates that the foreign business sector will announce this period.

q_t = the number of goods produced by the home country's non-financial business sector during the current period.

Q_t = the home non-financial business sector's inventory of unsold goods at the beginning of the current period. The sector presumably sets product price during the current period at a level that it plans will yield no unsold inventory by the end of the period.

q^{ne}_{t+1} = the number of goods the home non-financial business sector plans in the current period to produce next period.

$q^{\wedge}_{t}$ = the amount of its non-renewable resource the home country's non-financial business sector extracts and uses during the current period.

$Q^{\wedge}_{t}$ = the amount of the non-renewable resource that the home non-financial business sector has available at the beginning of the current period.

$q^{\wedge d}_{t}$ = the amount of the home country's non-renewable resource that the home country's non-financial business sector desires to extract and use during the current period.

$q^{\wedge * d}_{t}$ = the amount of the foreign country's non-renewable resource that the foreign country's non-financial business sector desires to extract and use during the current period.

q^{*n}_{t} = the number of intermediate goods the home country's non-financial business sector decided last period to import during the current period; i.e., its order placed last period for delivery and use this period.

q^{*ne}_{t+1} = the number of intermediate goods the home country's non-financial business sector plans at the beginning of the current period (as it announces its current product price and the wage rate and decides current production, but before it learns current interest rates or exchange rates) to buy from the foreign country next period. The sector will be free during the current period to alter its demand (orders) for the intermediate good during the current period as interest rates and the exchange rate become known. The orders the sector places by the end of the current period will be delivered and paid for next period.

R_t = the volume of reserves held by the home private financial sector at the beginning of the current period (consisting of vault cash denominated in the home country's unit of account plus deposits denominated in the home country's unit of account held by the home private financial sector at the home central bank).

r^d_{t-1} = the interest rate on checkable deposits issued by the home country's private financial sector announced by that sector last period and payable during the current period on each unit of those checkable deposits outstanding at the beginning of the current period.

r^d_t = the current period interest rate on checkable deposits issued by the home private financial sector.

r^{de}_t = the interest rate the home household sector anticipates at the beginning of the current period (before it learns current wages, product prices and interest rates) will prevail during the current period on checkable deposits issued by the home private financial sector. (The interest rate established during the current period will be paid next period on each unit of checkable deposits held at the beginning of next period.)

r^{d*}_t = the current period interest rate on checkable deposits issued by the foreign private financial sector.

R^x_t = the amount of the renewable resource the home country's non-financial business sector extracts and uses during the current period.

R^{xd}_t = the amount of the shared renewable resource that the home country's non-financial business sector demands for extraction and use this period.

R^{x*d}_t = the amount of the shared renewable resource that the foreign country's non-financial business sector demands for extraction and use this period.

R^{xdg}_t = the amount of the renewable resource the home government sector anticipates its non-financial business sector will extract during the current period.

R^{xdg}_{t+1} = the amount of the renewable resource the home government sector anticipates at the beginning of the current period that its private non-financial business sector will extract next period.

R^{xdn}_{t+1} = the amount of the world's renewable resource that the home country's non-financial business sector anticipates this period that it will extract and use next period. The sector will be free next period to demand a different amount in light of changing market conditions.

R^{x*dg*}_t = the amount of the renewable resource the foreign government sector anticipates its non-financial business sector will extract during the current period.

R^*_t = the volume of reserves held by the foreign private financial sector at the beginning of the current period (consisting of vault cash denominated in the foreign country's unit of account plus deposits denominated in the foreign country's unit of account held by the foreign private financial sector at the foreign central bank).

S_t = the beginning-of-period world stock of the renewable resource.

S^{ne}_{t+1} = the amount that the home non-financial business sector anticipates this period that it will save next period.

T_t = the (predetermined) tax revenue the home country's government sector collects during the current period.

T_{t+1} = the level of taxes to be collected by the home government sector next period.

UMB_t = the stock of the home country's unborrowed monetary base outstanding at the beginning of the current period ($UMB_t = MB_t - A_t$).

UMB^s_{t+1} = the volume of the home country's unborrowed monetary base at the end of the current period consistent with the plans of the home country's central bank.

UMB^*_t = the stock of the foreign country's unborrowed monetary base outstanding at the beginning of the current period ($UMB^*_t = MB^*_t - A^*_t$).

UMB^{*s}_{t+1} = the volume of the foreign country's unborrowed monetary base at the end of the current period consistent with the plans of the foreign country's central bank.

W_{t-1} = the money wage rate announced last period by the home country's private non-financial business sector. This wage rate is paid during the current period to all workers employed during the current period in the home country.

W_t = the wage rate (in the home unit of account) that the home non-financial business sector announces at the beginning of the current period. All people employed by the beginning of next period by a sector in the home country will receive that wage rate next period.

W^g_t = the money wage rate the home government sector anticipates its non-financial business sector will announce this period. The wage rate set by that sector will be paid next period to all workers employed next period in the home country.

W^h_t = the wage rate (in the home unit of account) that the home household sector anticipates at the beginning of the current period the home non-financial business sector will announce in the current period and that will be paid next period to everyone employed by the end of the current period in the home country.

X_t = the volume of excess reserves (valued in terms of the home country's unit of account) held by the home private financial sector at the beginning of the current period.

X^d_{t+1} = the home private financial sector's end-of-period demand for excess reserves (valued in terms of the home country's unit of account).

X^*_t = the volume of excess reserves (valued in terms of the foreign country's unit of account) held by the foreign private financial sector at the beginning of the current period.

X^{*d}_{t+1} = the foreign private financial sector's end-of-period demand for excess reserves (valued in terms of the foreign country's unit of account).

$\bar{Y}^h_t$ = the home household sector's beginning-of-current-period estimate of its current disposable income ($= W_{t-1}h^h_tN_t + \Pi^{nh}_t + \Pi^{fh}_t + r^d_{t-1}D_t - T_t$).

β^c = the home central bank's planned purchase of home country bonds during the current period, a policy parameter.

β^{c*} = the foreign central bank's planned purchase of home country bonds (valued in terms of the foreign country's unit of account) during the current period, a policy parameter.

β^{*c} = the home central bank's planned purchase of foreign country bonds (valued in terms of the home country's unit of account) during the current period, a policy parameter.

β^{*c*} = the foreign central bank's planned purchase of foreign country bonds (valued in terms of the foreign country's unit of account) during the current period, a policy parameter.

Γ = the vector of parameters other than g_{t+1} and current revenue from the sale of pollution and extraction rights that influence the level of taxes the government must collect next period. An increase in Γ represents a parametric change, such as an increase in current wage rates, that results, ceteris paribus, in an increase in next period's taxes.

Γ^* = the vector of parameters, other than the level of next period's production of public goods and the current revenue from the sale of pollution and extraction rights, affecting next period's taxes.

ε_t = the current period price (value) of the foreign country's unit of account in terms of the home country's unit of account.

ε^f_{t+1} = the spot rate that the home private financial sector expects will prevail next period.

ε^{g*}_t = the current spot value of the foreign country's unit of account in terms of the home country's unit of account anticipated by the foreign country's government sector before that spot rate is established.

$\varepsilon^{\wedge}_{t-1}$ = last period's forward exchange rate; the value of the foreign country's unit of account in terms of the home country's unit of account contracted last period for exchanges during the current period involving items denominated in different units of account.

$\varepsilon^{\wedge}_t$ = the current forward exchange rate (i.e., the value of the foreign country's unit of account in terms of the home country's unit of account in current contracts calling for the exchange next period of assets denominated in different units of account).

$\varepsilon^{\wedge n}_{t}$ = the current-period forward exchange rate that the home non-financial business sector anticipates at the beginning of the current period (as it announces its current product price and the wage and as it decides current production, but before it learns current interest rates or exchange rates) will prevail during the current period.

κ = the amount of pollution created per unit of the home country's non-renewable resources extracted during the current period.

κ^{*} = the amount of pollution created per unit of the foreign country's non-renewable resources extracted during the current period.

μ = the level of pollution abatement by the home country's non-financial business sector.

μ^{*} = the level of pollution abatement by the foreign country's non-financial business sector.

Π^{c}_{t} = the (predetermined) revenue the home central bank collects and distributes to the home government sector during the current period.

Π^{cg}_{t+1} = the revenue that the home country's government sector anticipates this period that it will receive from the home central bank next period.

Π^{c*}_{t} = current period income of the foreign central bank, all of which is assumed to be distributed to the foreign country's government sector during the current period.

Π^{fh}_{t} = the dividends the home country's household sector anticipates at the beginning of the current period that it will receive from the home private financial sector during the current period.

Π^{h}_{t+1} = the total dividends the home household sector anticipates at the beginning of the current period that it will receive next period from the home non-financial business and home private financial sectors (denominated in the home country's unit of account).

Π^{n}_{t} = the dividends that the home country's non-financial business sector announces at the beginning of the current period that it will distribute to its shareholders (i.e., to the home household sector) during the current period.

Π^{ne}_{t+1} = the dividends that the home non-financial business sector plans this period to distribute next period.

Π^{nh}_t = the dividends the home country's household sector anticipates at the beginning of the current period that it will receive from the home non-financial business sector during the current period.

ρ_{t-1} = the discount rate set by the home central bank last period.

ρ^*_{t-1} = the discount rate set by the foreign central bank last period.

τ = the home household sector's transactions time next period.

$\overline{\tau}$ = current-period transactions time for the home country's household sector.

$\phi \cdot \overline{P}$ = the amount of pollution the biosphere can assimilate at the target level of pollution, where $\phi \leq 1$. The international body issues pollution rights during the current period equal to $\phi \cdot \overline{P}$.

Ω = the international agent's target increase in the stock of the renewable resource.

Bibliography

E.B. Barbier, "Alternative Approaches to Economic–Environmental Interactions," *Ecological Economics* 2 (April 1990): 7–26.

M. Common and C. Perrings, "Towards an Ecological Economics of Sustainability," *Ecological Economics* 6 (July 1992): 7–34.

H.E. Daly, "Allocation, Distribution, and Scale: Towards an Economics That Is Efficient, Just, and Sustainable," *Ecological Economics* 6 (December 1992): 185–193.

N.R. Goodwin, "Introduction—Global Commons: Site of Peril, Source of Hope," published in *World Development* 19 (January 1991): 1–15.

J.P. Neary and S. Wijnbergen, eds., *Natural Resources and the Macroeconomy*, Cambridge, MA: MIT Press, 1986.

J. Pezzey, *Economic Analysis of Sustainable Growth and Sustainable Development*, Working Paper 15, World Bank, Washington, D.C., 1989.

Salah El Serafy, "The Environment as Capital," published in *Toward Improved Accounting for the Environment*, ed. Ernst Lutz (Washington, D.C.: The World Bank, 1993), 17–21.

S. El Serafy and E. Lutz, "Environmental and Resource Accounting: An Overview," published in *Environmental Accounting for Sustainable Development*, eds. Yusif J. Ahmad, Salah El Serafy, and Ernst Lutz (Washington, D.C.: The World Bank, 1989), 1–7.

H. Whitmore, *World Economy Macroeconomics*, Armonk, NY: M.E. Sharpe, Inc., 1997.

Index

About the Author

Harland Wm. Whitmore, Jr. graduated from Lawrence College (Appleton, WI) in 1961 with a B.A. degree in mathematics. He then earned both the M.B.A. and Ph.D degrees (economics) at Michigan State University. He is currently a professor of economics at the University of Cincinnati's McMicken College of Arts and Sciences. Professor Whitmore has published articles in monetary and macroeconomic theory as well as two other books in macroeconomic theory. The present manuscript represents an extension of his *World Economy Macroeconomics*, published by M.E. Sharpe, Inc. in 1997.